SHAKESPEARE, COMPUTERS, AND THE MYSTERY OF AUTHORSHIP

Hugh Craig, Arthur F. Kinney, and their collaborators confront the main unsolved mysteries in Shakespeare's canon through computer analysis of Shakespeare's and other writers' styles. In some cases their analysis confirms the current scholarly consensus, bringing long-standing questions to something like a final resolution. In other areas the book provides more surprising conclusions: that Shakespeare wrote the 1602 Additions to *The Spanish Tragedy*, for example, and that Marlowe, along with Shakespeare, was a collaborator on *Henry VI, Parts 1 and 2*. The methods used are more wholeheartedly statistical, and computationally more intensive, than any that have yet been applied to Shakespeare studies. The book also reveals how word-patterns help create a characteristic personal style. In tackling traditional problems with the aid of the processing power of the computer harnessed through computer science, and drawing upon large amounts of data, the book is an exemplar of the new domain of digital humanities.

HUGH CRAIG is Professor of English at the University of Newcastle, Australia, where he also directs the Centre for Literary and Linguistic Computing. He has published books on Sir John Harington and Ben Jonson, and articles on English Renaissance literature and on computational stylistics.

ARTHUR F. KINNEY is Thomas W. Copeland Professor of Literary History at the University of Massachusetts at Amherst, and Director of the Massachusetts Center for Renaissance Studies. His most recent books are *Shakespeare's Webs* (2004), *Challenging Humanism: Essays in Honor of Dominic Baker-Smith* (2005), and *Shakespeare and Cognition* (2006).

SHAKESPEARE, COMPUTERS, AND THE MYSTERY OF AUTHORSHIP

HUGH CRAIG AND ARTHUR F. KINNEY

CAMBRIDGE
UNIVERSITY PRESS

CAMBRIDGE UNIVERSITY PRESS

Cambridge, New York, Melbourne, Madrid, Cape Town, Singapore, São Paulo, Delhi

Cambridge University Press
The Edinburgh Building, Cambridge CB2 8RU, UK

Published in the United States of America by Cambridge University Press, New York

www.cambridge.org
Information on this title: www.cambridge.org/9780521516235

First published 2009

Printed in the United Kingdom at the University Press, Cambridge

A catalogue record for this publication is available from the British Library

Library of Congress Cataloguing in Publication data
Craig, D. H., 1952–
Shakespeare, computers, and the mystery of authorship / Hugh Craig,
Arthur F. Kinney.
p. cm.
Includes bibliographical references and index.
ISBN 978-0-521-51623-5 (hardback)   1. Shakespeare, William, 1564–1616–Spurious and
doubtful works.   2. Shakespeare, William, 1564–1616–Authorship.   3. Shakespeare, William,
1564–1616–Literary style.   4. Authorship, Disputed.   5. Language and languages–Style–
Statistical methods.   I. Kinney, Arthur F., 1933–
II. Title.
PR2875.C73 2009
822.3′3–dc22   2009020687

ISBN 978-0-521-51623-5 hardback

Contents

Figures

Tables

Contributors

HUGH CRAIG is Professor of English at the University of Newcastle, Australia, where he also directs the Centre for Literary and Linguistic Computing. He has published books on Sir John Harington and Ben Jonson, and articles on English Renaissance literature and on computational stylistics.

ARTHUR F. KINNEY is Thomas W. Copeland Professor of Literary History at the University of Massachusetts at Amherst, and Director of the Massachusetts Center for Renaissance Studies. His most recent books are *Shakespeare's Webs* (2004), *Challenging Humanism: Essays in Honor of Dominic Baker-Smith* (2005), and *Shakespeare and Cognition* (2006).

PHILIP PALMER is a doctoral student at the University of Massachusetts at Amherst, and Curator of the Massachusetts Center for Renaissance Studies. His research interests include representations of remote space in Renaissance drama and poetry, travel literature, pamphlet culture, and manuscript studies.

TIMOTHY IRISH WATT is a doctoral candidate at the University of Massachusetts at Amherst, where he has been the Walter T. Chmielewski Fellow for *English Literary Renaissance*.

Preface and acknowledgments

This project began in 2001 when one of the editors, Arthur Kinney, spent a period as a research visitor at the University of Newcastle in New South Wales, where the other editor, Hugh Craig, works. A collaborative project was hatched. It was to combine Kinney's knowledge of Shakespeare with Craig's familiarity with numbers, and thus pioneer a Shakespearean computational stylistics. Kinney would supply the questions and Craig would furnish numerical results. In what they jointly wrote they would keep in mind an audience that had no interest in arcane statistics or in interminable tables of figures. Authorship would be the core of the enterprise. Coworkers were recruited from Kinney's Massachusetts Center for Renaissance Studies in Amherst, as was a programmer and research assistant from Craig's Centre for Literary and Linguistic Computing in Newcastle, so it has been an American–Australian and a Center–Centre collaboration.

Computational stylistics stems from the work of John Burrows, beginning in the 1980s. He was convinced that the smallest elements of literary language (down to very common grammatical words such as *and* and *but*) had things of stylistic interest buried in them, and he sought to bring latent patterns in their use to light, through multivariate statistical procedures analysing the word-count information from large tracts of machine-readable text. The new method revealed a patterning that pervaded all levels of language and could be measured. Readers, however perceptive they may be, have only one lifetime to read in, and remember what they read selectively and imperfectly. The computer, on the other hand, is brutally simple in its relationship to the text, but it has superhuman powers of memory, and can deal with what it knows with unthinkable rapidity (and always in a predictable and repeatable way). With its help, Burrows' computational stylistics offers new views of literary landscapes. In its most obvious application, where experts disagree on the authorship of a text and there is no external evidence to help, computational stylistics can offer an objective arbitration. It can also work in a more exploratory way, by looking for unexpected patterns and quirks in the dataset itself, rather than testing a hypothesis. In the book we have examples of both approaches.

One might expect a stubborn contradiction between language, and other artistic means, and computation. One of the purposes of the book is to show that there is in fact a considerable sympathy between them. Early Modern plays were written to be seen or read, not subjected to tabulation and statistical analysis, but the plays do work by frequency and distribution as well as by the impact of the individual word, speech, and scene. This means that computational work (we believe) opens a new gateway to complexity and nuance in language, rather than running roughshod over them.

Beyond the immediate questions of Shakespeare authorship the work in the book is meant as a contribution to the larger question of stylistic individuality. Computational stylistics offers abundant evidence that writers leave subtle and persistent traces of a distinctive style through all levels of their syntax and lexis. This brings to the fore a central paradox of language. Speakers and writers share the words they use in a given language. They could not communicate otherwise. Yet from that common set speakers and writers make individual selections that persist across all their uses of the language. They create a personal and identifiable style from within the common language. Computational analysis reveals the richness of this variation within the dialogue of Shakespeare and his contemporaries. It persists even when dramatists strive to create their own fictional linguistic individualities in characters. Hal, Falstaff, and Hotspur do have their own languages, but underlying them all is a Shakespearean idiom, which means they are all distinct from Jonson, Marlowe, or Middleton characters. This idiom is so powerful and persistent that even the computer can detect it. We can even turn this around and say that it wasn't until the computer came along that we could properly appreciate some aspects of this miraculous secret working of language in these very familiar plays and characters.

We believe the book is more wholeheartedly statistical, and computationally more intensive, than any previous Shakespeare study. It embraces statistical principles such as testing samples with known classifications before trying the measures on doubtful cases. Where possible we have used multiple separate tests for a given problem. We hope we have incorporated a fully fledged, built-in scepticism about the reliability of the results. Extensive work has already been done in the area of quantitative study of Shakespearean authorship, by scholars from the literary world like

MacDonald P. Jackson, Gary Taylor, and Brian Vickers, and by researchers from the computer-science and statistics side like Ward E. Y. Elliott, Thomas Merriam, M. W. A. Smith, and Robert J. Valenza. We have tried to unite the literary and statistical sides through our collaboration, and to build on previous work to give the most holistic computational modelling of style so far. We aim to resolve a number of questions in the Shakespeare canon, so that the business of interpretation, which is so often stymied by uncertainty of authorship, can proceed. Vickers' book *Shakespeare, Co-Author* (2002) has already done this for the division of five collaborative plays among their various authors; we hope to bring a similar level of confidence to the question of the Shakespearean authorship of *Edward III*; *Arden of Faversham*; the Additions to *The Spanish Tragedy*; the Hand-D Addition to *Sir Thomas More*; *Edmond Ironside*; the Folio *King Lear*; and *Henry VI, Parts 1 and 2*.

Readers will want to know how many texts we have included, to judge the basis on which we generalize about authors and trends, and will be curious about the nature of the texts that underlie the whole enterprise. We use early printed versions as copy-texts, to minimize the effects of modern editing and to open up the corpus to two or more editions where these differ significantly. Each text is tied therefore to a single early witness. Consequently spellings are Early Modern and highly variable. We standardize selected function words to modern usage. For the rest, a process has been developed within the software we use for word-counting to group variant spellings as teams, collecting the different forms of the same word under a single head word, which can then form the basis for counting. Thus instances of 'folly', 'follie', and 'folie' are all counted under the head word *folly*. The corpus we have assembled for the book consists of 165 Early Modern English plays, around 3.25 million words of dialogue in all (they are listed in Appendix A of this book). Of these, 138 are from a more narrowly defined 'Shakespearean' period, which one might define as 1580–1619 (the four decades in which Shakespeare is presumed to have been active). Some of these plays are of mixed or disputed authorship, and are the subject of investigation, so cannot form a set of standards for the core purpose of the study, the defining of Shakespearean authorship. For this we need single-author, well-attributed plays to serve as exemplars of Shakespeare's style and those of his contemporaries. There are 112 such plays within the 138 in our corpus. The *Annals of English Drama* (1964 edition) lists 174 surviving well-attributed single-author plays from this period. The corpus thus contains 112 out of 174 – just under two-thirds – of all the available usable plays for attribution purposes. It includes complete sets of the surviving Shakespeare, Marlowe, Jonson, Middleton, and Webster plays: complete, at least, according to a conservative standard of what is 'well-attributed' for each writer. We have four or more plays by seven other playwrights: Lyly, Greene, Peele, Dekker, Heywood, Ford, and Fletcher; and three each by Robert Wilson, Chapman, and Shirley.

As to methods and procedures, our aim in the chapters that follow has been to explain the steps we took to get from these texts to the results with enough detail so that anyone wishing to replicate the findings is able to do so. The patterns we have uncovered should be robust enough to survive the variations that will arise from using different texts and software, provided the same basic procedures are followed. (The question of whether we have made the right judgments in choosing among the possible procedures, and in setting the various parameters, is quite another matter.)

Warren Stevenson's *Shakespeare's Additions to Thomas Kyd's* The Spanish Tragedy (Lewiston, NY: Edwin Mellen, 2008) came to our attention after this book was in production. We regret not being able to make use of Stevenson's amplified case for Shakespeare's authorship of the Additions here. We quote extensively from Stevenson's 1968 article on the topic, which presents a briefer version of his evidence, below.

The project was made possible by funding from the National Endowment for the Humanities and the Australian Research Council, for which we are grateful. Sarah Stanton at Cambridge University Press has done everything one could ask of a commissioning editor, asking searching questions of us at a formative stage and then championing the project when it ran into controversy. We have also had the assistance of a great many expert and generous co-workers, and we would like to thank all of them. Graham Christian, Youngjin Chung, Kimberly C. Elliott, Kevin Petersen, and Anne-Marie Strohman were all involved in the early stages of the project, and have contributed to it in numerous ways. R. Whipp developed the software for the Intelligent Archive, which has been the 'two-handed engine' making light work of the word-counting lying behind the quantitative studies. Alexis Antonia and Ruth Lunney have prepared play texts for the project. Penny de Sylva of Oxford University Press arranged for us to use the electronic *Oxford English Dictionary* as a source for the variant spellings incorporated in the Intelligent Archive. John Burrows, Andrew Craig, David Craig, Henry Craig, Mark Gauntlett, David Hoover, John Jowett, and Ruth Lunney have all read chapters and saved us from many errors. We would also like to acknowledge the generosity of Mac Jackson, Tom Merriam, and Brian Vickers in letting us see unpublished results and sending hard-to-find publications in authorial attribution. We also owe a debt to the three anonymous readers for Cambridge University Press, who gave us a greatly improved sense of what an audience for a book like this might expect and much detailed guidance besides. It only remains to say that the errors that remain are entirely the responsibility of the four authors of this volume.

CHAPTER I

Introduction

Hugh Craig and Arthur F. Kinney

One of the earliest champions of language in Shakespeare's time was Thomas Wilson. In *The Arte of Rhetorique* (1553) he declares that

Suche force hath the tongue, and such is the power of eloquence and reason, that most men are forced euen to yelde in that, whiche most standeth against their will. And therfore the Poetes do feyne that Hercules being a man of greate wisdome, had all men lincked together by the eares in a chaine, to draw them and leade them euen as he lusted. For his witte was so greate, his tongue so eloquente, & his experience suche, that no one man was able to withstand his reason, but euerye one was rather driuen to do that whiche he woulde, and to wil that whiche he did, agreeing to his aduise both in word & worke, in all that euer they were able.

Neither can I see that menne coulde haue bene broughte by anye other meanes to lyue together in felowshyppe of life, to mayntayne Cities, to deale trulye, and willyngelye to obeye one another, if menne at the firste hadde not by Art and eloquence perswaded that, which they ful oft found out by reason. (sigs. A3v–A4r)

At the time such ideas were not especially original – the works of Aristotle and Cicero in the Tudor grammar schools had made them commonplace – but Wilson's ambition and vision are nevertheless unusual. His manual, however – establishing the art of language in ways all the skilled dramatists of Shakespeare's day would observe – is grounded in a philosophy of mind that is sophisticated even by today's insights. Despite Wilson's high aims – they would reach well into the realm of poetry and drama – his counsel was up to the task. '[E]uery Orator', he teaches his readers,

should earnestly laboure to file his tongue, that his woordes maie slide with ease, and that in his deliueraunce, he maie haue suche grace, as the sound of a lute, or any suche instrument doeth geue. Then his sentences must be well framed, and his wordes aptly vsed, throughout the whole discourse of his Oracion. (sig. a2r)

Such ideas are restated nearly three decades later in the more famous *Defence of Poetry* of Sir Philip Sidney. Sidney begins his essay by noting that the word poet comes from the Greek word ποιειν, 'which is, to make', adding, 'we Englishmen have met with the Greeks in calling him a maker: which name, how high and incomparable a title it is, I had rather were known by marking the scope of other sciences than by any partial allegation'.[1] But the force of poetry for Sidney leads, as it does for Wilson, not only to agreement and pleasure, but to a kind of emotional sharing, even a kind of rapture. The poet, Sidney says,

> beginneth not with obscure definitions, which must blur the margin with inter-pretations, and load the memory with doubtfulness; but he cometh to you with words set in delightful proportion, either accompanied with, or prepared for, the well enchanting skill of music; and with a tale forsooth he cometh unto you, with a tale which holdeth children from play, and old men from the chimney corner. (p. 92)

We have not substantially bettered these concepts in the twenty-first century, but we have deepened our knowledge of just how such poetic language comes to be; psychology, linguistics, physics, and neuroscience have all come into confluence, showing us how the human brain works – not just ours, but those of Shakespeare and his contemporaries. They have shown us the processes by which we acquire, process, and interpret know-ledge; how the human brain processes language; and, most significantly and most amazing of all, how each person's processing of language is indi-vidually distinct. Word deployment is individual to a high degree; and understanding this permits us, for the first time, to address and answer, at least provisionally, some basic questions about the lives and works of Shakespeare and his contemporaries. As Harold Love comments, a per-sonal idiolect individualizes the sociolect.[2]

'Every mental process', such as that of creating poetry, and drama, Edward O. Wilson contended in *Consilience: The Unity of Knowledge* in 1998, 'has a physical grounding and is consistent with the natural sciences'.[3] John Carey expands on this premise in *What Good Are the Arts?* (2005):

> [There] are innate operations in the sensory system and the brain. They are laid down by the joint operation of two kinds of evolution, genetic and cultural. Genes prescribe certain regularities of sense-perception or mental development, and culture helps determine which of the prescribing genes survive and multi-ply. There are primary epigenetic rules and secondary ones. The primary ones

---

[1] Sir Philip Sidney, *A Defence of Poetry*, in *Miscellaneous Prose of Sir Philip Sidney*, ed. K. Duncan-Jones and J. van Dorsten (Oxford: Clarendon Press, 1973), p. 77.
[2] H. Love, *Attributing Authorship: An Introduction* (Cambridge: Cambridge University Press, 2002), p. 222.
[3] Quoted in J. Carey, *What Good Are the Arts?* (London: Faber and Faber, 2005), p. 65.

determine the way our senses apprehend the world – the way, for example, our sight splits the wavelengths of visible light into the distinct units that we call the colour spectrum. The secondary epigenetic rules relate to our thinking and behaviour. They include the neural mechanisms of language ... (p. 66)

Although our culture has changed considerably since Shakespeare wrote, our brains have not, as Carey's first sense of epigenetic operations indicates. Our process of cognition, then, is transhistorical, and in applying its operations to the sort of mental processing that is revealed in Shakespeare's language, neuroscience has taught us how to determine, through his individual handling of language, how we (even today) can determine new influences on, and accomplishments of, Shakespeare's plays. For language is not just 'a cultural artifact', as Steven Pinker wrote in *The Language Instinct* (1994), but 'a distinct piece of the biological makeup of our brains',[4] although the complicated process of cognition and subsequent representation of thought is not a conscious process. 'The workings of language', Pinker adds, 'are as far from our awareness as the rationale for egg laying is from the fly's'.[5] We can understand more precisely how language works and poetry is formed – and with it, always, the accessible individual voice – by first understanding the dynamics of the brain. Recent cognitive scientists have studied the brain by dividing it into its components: the thalamus, the hippocampus, and the cortical gyri. Each section is made up of complex networks of cells that relate, in countless possible combinations and networks, to one another, leading to patterns that, once constituted by individually processing data from the external world, will provide those tell-tale individual tics that set each person apart, even when that person undergoes the same experience as another at the same moment (seeing a movie with someone else, for instance). The basic working element of the brain is the neuron, an electrically charged type of body cell that can receive and transmit electrochemical impulses; and by long extensions of its cell bodies, neurons form connections with other neurons through synapses. In operation, neurons receive such impulses from literally thousands of other neurons – it is the huge number and their arrangements that will allow for the formation of individual responses. Some of these impulses (rather than others) will excite a particular neuron and cause it to 'fire' out its own reaction as an impulse to other neurons, while inhibiting and withholding other received impulses. As a consequence, each neuron provides a continuous analysis of the activity of large numbers of other neurons: they form, that is, their own links, never acting finally alone and

[4] S. Pinker, *The Language Instinct* (London: Penguin, 1994), p. 18.   [5] *Ibid.*, p. 21.

always forging combinations that may be strengthened through repeated activity. Even with a very small number of neurons, such as ten or twelve, the number of possible combinations is surprisingly great; but the whole situation is enhanced by the fact that the human brain contains at least ten billion of these tiny cells (and some neuroscientists have estimated as many as a hundred billion). Moreover, a neuron over time will form synapses with at least a thousand other neurons, so that in time there will be as many as a hundred trillion (100 000 000 000 000) in a human brain. Such a huge number is incomprehensible, but there is no question that such dynamic brain functions happen all the time and so quickly that we ourselves sense no pause between a sensation – hearing a line from Shakespeare, say – and responding to it; or, if Shakespeare, seeing a character (in the external world or in his mind's eye, his 'imagination') and verbally expressing it. But since Shakespeare processes the idea or the object in his own way, the expression will bear some stamp of individuality, too; and a scene or an act will become uniquely identifiable.

The brain's operation is unimaginably complex and sophisticated, though, so that we need a sufficient amount of evidence to essay the habits of a particular mind, just as the complexity of the DNA sample provides its own reassurances. The brain works through a densely cooperative and collaborative system, interconnecting its thousands of neurons instantaneously; yet at the same time, the billions of neurons are poised to admit new electrical charges and to form, or reform, their neural pathways that have established the brain's particularity over time. This allows for what we might see, for instance, in the change of Shakespeare's style that we would call, rather simply and superficially, his 'development'. His new experiences can always lead to new patterns, but they will always relate to older ones as well, since they are being processed by the same individually identifiable mind.

Pinker has written that

virtually every sentence that a person utters or understands is a brand-new combination of words, appearing for the first time in the history of the universe. Therefore a language cannot be a repertoire of responses; the brain must contain a recipe or program that can build an unlimited set of sentences out of a finite list of words. That program may be called a mental grammar. (p. 22)

'The way language works, then', he continues, 'is that each person's brain contains a lexicon of words and the concepts they stand for (a mental dictionary) and a set of rules that combine the words to convey relationships among concepts (a mental grammar)' (p. 85). In compiling data in the form of language, we need to pay attention to the lexicon (the number and pattern of common words – common to a culture, common to an individual writer), as well as rare or suddenly new words and patterns of words (pairs, for instance). To define and appreciate an individual's linguistic DNA, so to speak, we need to examine both his mental dictionary and his mental grammar.

The computer now allows us to establish the identifiable, distinguishing use of language of individual Renaissance English playwrights, Shakespeare foremost among them. The results we present in this book demonstrate the consistent style of a single author, showing how the linguistic uniqueness sets it apart from works by other playwrights. The visual displays of the data are helpful in another way, too; they show how parts of individual works by some authors can depart from the main set, inviting questions about the nature of this variation, by means of data that is concrete, specific, and rediscoverable.

Pinker's seminal study of language and language behaviour takes up this interest in special patterns – what he calls 'phrase structure' – that is 'the kind of stuff language is made of' (p. 103):

The discrete combinatorial system called 'grammar' makes human language infinite (there is no limit to the number of complex words or sentences in a language), digital (this infinity is achieved by rearranging discrete elements in particular orders and combinations, not by varying some signal along a continuum like the mercury in a thermometer), and compositional (each of the infinite combinations has a different meaning predictable from the meanings of its parts and the rules and principles arranging them). (p. 334)

Combinations of words, then, are another way in which brains, and persons, expose and identify themselves, usually unconsciously, whether or not they wish to do so. Once neuroscientists began unscrambling and understanding the areas and processes of the human brain, linguists have been enabled to determine, more or less scientifically, how language is formed, by understanding the neural processes and pathways that are responsible.

Pinker goes further, introducing proteins into the equation that brings the brain activity into alignment with the uniqueness of DNA:

The molecules that guide, connect, and preserve neurons are proteins. A protein is specified by a gene, and a gene is a sequence of bases in the DNA string found in a chromosome. A gene is turned on by 'transcription factors' and other regulatory molecules – gadgets that latch on to a sequence of bases somewhere on a DNA molecule and unzip a neighboring stretch, allowing that gene to be transcribed into RNA [ribonucleic acid, carrying DNA instructions for chemical synthesis to the cell], which is then translated into protein. Generally these regulatory factors are themselves proteins, so the process of building an organism is an intricate cascade of DNA making proteins, some of which interact with other DNA to make more proteins, and so on. Small differences in the timing or amount of some protein can have large effects on the organism being built. (p. 321)

The confluence of several areas of research, then, including physics and chemistry, leads to their own kind of 'consilience', by which individuality is established with a kind of insight and a sense of certainty heretofore unavailable.

If such advanced science is staggering in its determinations and its implications, its outcome, in some ways, is not unexpected at all. How many times, for example, have we said, 'This passage reminds me of X', or, 'This cannot be by X; it seems nothing at all like him'? Carey finds such visible distinctions between Shakespeare and Marlowe, for instance, by sensing that one uses metaphor, the other tends to employ images directly, rather than comparatively. His sense is corroborated by applying something like Pinker's mental dictionary and mental grammar (although he undoubtedly arrived at his observations by some other means). This is Carey:

It is often said that Shakespeare took up where Marlowe left off, and could not have written his plays without Marlowe's example. But Marlowe is actually a completely different kind of writer, much more wooden and solid and distinct than Shakespeare for all his flamboyance. Shakespeare's superior indistinctness can easily be seen if we compare the way Marlowe's Jew, Barabas, and Shakespeare's Jew, Shylock, talk about their wealth. Here is Barabas:

> Bags of fiery opals, sapphires, amethysts,
> Jacinth, hard topaz, grass-green emeralds,
> Beauteous rubies, sparkling diamonds ... [I.i.25–7]

And so on. Pretty good, you will say. Yes, it is. But it is not very indistinct, so the imagination has not much to do. You can easily picture bags of jewels. Of course, even Marlowe's lines are beyond the reach of visual arts like painting or photography. You cannot paint grass-green emeralds, except by some ponderous device like juxtaposing painted grass and painted emeralds, whereas language can merge the two in a flash. Painting cannot manage metaphor, which is the gateway to the subconscious, and that hugely limits it by comparison with literature. True, there is Surrealist painting, but it is static and deliberate, and quite unlike the flickering, inconsequential nature of thought. However, with all due credit to Marlowe's jewels, compare Shakespeare's Shylock when he hears that his daughter (who has run off with her lover, taking some of her father's gold and jewels with her) is living it up in Genoa and has exchanged a ring for a monkey.

> Thou torturest me Tubal, – it was my turquoise, I had it of Leah when I was a bachelor: I would not have given it for a wilderness of monkeys. [*The Merchant of Venice*, III.i.112]

Marlowe could never have written that. Quite apart from the human depth, the indistinctness is what stamps it as Shakespeare's. 'A wilderness of monkeys', the lightning phrase with which Shylock registers his wit, scorn and outrage, is unforgettable and unimaginable – or, rather, imaginable in an infinite number of ways. How do you imagine it? Are there trees and grass in the wilderness? Or just monkeys? Are they mixed monkeys, or all of one kind? With tails or without? Of what colour? What are they doing? Or are these questions too demanding? Is the impression you get much more fleeting, much less distinguishable from the mere blur of total indistinctness? At all events, compared to 'grass-green emeralds', 'a wilderness of monkeys' is a wilderness of possibilities. We are tempted to say that it is a 'vivid' phrase, and it is understandable that we should want to use that word about it. But 'vivid' is often used to describe clear-cut effects, such as a bright pattern or colour composition, and Shakespeare's phrase is not vivid in that way, rather the opposite. It manages to be at once vivid and nebulous. It is brilliantly and unfathomably indistinct, which is why the imagination is gripped by it and cannot leave it alone. (pp. 216–17)

Carey has an especially well-honed literary sensibility, and he can often observe what many readers would not. But to describe jewels by visually conveying their direct appearance and to let that imply wealth alongside using an incident, even a far-fetched incident, to measure wealth – one jewel misspent is a very different sense of wealth than accumulating it – is a distinction we can easily comprehend. Assembling long lists of examples of Shakespearean uses of language alongside Marlovian uses helps us to question comparisons, too, and guard against false analogies. But the labour-intensive task of compiling such data – not to mention the margin of error – makes such a comparison daunting, if not unlikely. Using a computer to gather the evidence to be analysed by the critic, and its utility and interpretation to be determined, the fundamental process of computational stylistics gives to literary criticism (and its associated concerns such as authorship, development, or influence) the means by which we may substantially advance our knowledge of Shakespeare, his works, and even (despite our cultural differences) his differentiated meanings.

We can look at such compilations of data another way. Ian Lancashire of the University of Toronto has used the computer to assemble the data by which he can compare the language and the language usage of Shakespeare and Chaucer.

I studied two passages from Shakespeare's works, *Hamlet* III.1 (the so-called 'nunnery scene'), and *Troilus and Cressida*, I.3.1–29 (Agamemnon's first speech), and two parts of Chaucer's *Canterbury Tales*, the General Prologue and the Manciple's prologue and tale, both in the context of the complete *Canterbury Tales*. The principal repeated vocabulary unit of both authors was the word-combination. In *The Canterbury Tales*, Chaucer used 12 000 word-forms but 22 000 repeating fixed phrases. Over two periods, 1589–94 and 1597–1604, Shakespeare's different fixed phrases at least doubled his word types. The vocabulary of both poets consisted, not of single words, but of little networks, a fact consistent with associative long-term memory. The sizes of these networks were well within what working memory could accommodate. The 464 phrasal repetends appearing in both Chaucer's General Prologue and the rest of his *Canterbury Tales* averaged 2.45 words. They fell into 177 networks. Repeating fixed phrases in Shakespeare's texts in both periods averaged 2.5 words. Chaucer's largest repeating combination in the General Prologue (853 lines) had nine words. Shakespeare's largest in *Hamlet* III.l, under 200 lines long, had five words. A second Shakespeare analysis, of Agamemnon's speech in *Troilus and Cressida*, I.3.1–29, found 107 phrasal repetends (repeating elsewhere in Shakespeare's works) in a passage that has only 159 different word-forms. Most combinations are two words in length, and the maximum has four. It is possible that the constraints of working memory affected the quantitative profile of the verbal networks employed by both men.[6]

Such a comparison in linguistic profiles for Lancashire can characterize an author, but, by the same token, it can also help to identify him. Repetends of word-combinations (what he called fixed phrases) are another key linguistic figure made visible through computational stylistics. Lancashire also reminds us that memory plays a major role in cognitive theory and practice. Stimuli processed by the brain that are similar or even repetitive strengthen the memory of them in the brain, but the hippocampus also retains unique memories until later stimuli merge or modify them, or finally displace them as they fade over time. Such data are another legacy that advanced science, especially in the anatomy of the brain, provides for a study of the humanities at the beginning of the twenty-first century.

Historically, most of the work of computational stylistics has gone into authorship studies. Language is a shared system – it must be, if we are to use it as our fundamental means of communication – but each person uses language in a special and individual way. Literary language is only an extreme form of this self-expression. Writers, in fact, often seek to use language in new ways to express their own sensibility, their own particular vision and interpretation. This is especially helpful, then, because the data will show those particularities and can establish individual profiles of literary writers more quickly. Furthermore, when a work is anonymous, such stylistic choices and practices will help to identify authors. It can therefore be no surprise that attribution studies have been especially prevalent in computational analyses over the past several decades. But such a concern

---

[6] I. Lancashire, 'Cognitive Stylistics and the Literary Imagination', in *A Companion to Digital Humanities*, ed. S. Schreibman, R. Siemens, and J. Unsworth (Oxford: Blackwell, 2004), pp. 397–414 (p. 408).

is not new. Modern attribution studies actually began in the Renaissance itself when texts were abundant enough to make such comparisons possible. In the fifteenth century Lorenzo Valla showed that the Donation of Constantine was a forgery through what were then new disciplines, developed by the humanists, of philology and history.[7] From then onwards, the loose collections of writing that survived of the Bible, Homer, and even playwrights like Shakespeare, were no longer accepted uncritically. Since then, much effort has gone into determining what is canonical and what, on the other hand, is apocryphal. External evidence, such as manuscripts, licensing records, and commercial sales, which could sometimes be used to fix authorship, could thus be used in conjunction with internal evidence of a writer's style.

There are difficulties, of course. An author can limit his style, vary it, imitate someone else to pose as that person, or write a parody so dependent on the original and so different from his own style that the actual authorship of the parody, rather than its target text, is more difficult to discern. Ben Jonson, for example, is now known to have deliberately redrafted his earlier writings to align them with later material so as to give a sense of unity and cohesion to his great folio of 1616.[8] (This was not the case with King James, whose own folio appeared in the same year.) The issue of imitation is an equally thorny one. Alexander Pope, writing in the early eighteenth century, thought that it was folly to try to attribute a work to an author on the grounds of style alone; Joseph Spence thought that Pope must have had in mind the ease with which writers could adopt styles.[9] Samuel Johnson, on the other hand, told Boswell that he thought that 'every man whatever has a peculiar style, which may be discovered by nice examination and comparison with others: but a man must write a great deal', he added, 'to make his style obviously discernible'.[10] In addition, style changes over time (as Jonson had observed): it is well known, for instance, that early Henry James and late Henry James sound quite different.[11] But what computational stylistics has shown is that, even so, tests of common words, rare words, and word pairings, especially when used in conjunction, can detect the similarities that continue to ride as

---

[7] Love, *Attributing Authorship*, pp. 18–19.

[8] The revision of one play in the Jonson Folio is studied in detail in H. Craig, ' "An Image of the Times": Ben Jonson's Revision of *Every Man in His Humour*', *English Studies*, 82 (2001), 14–33.

[9] Joseph Spence, *Observations, Anecdotes, and Characters of Books and Men*, ed. J. M. Osborn (Oxford: Clarendon Press, 1966), 2 vols., Vol. I, pp. 171–2.

[10] Love, *Attributing Authorship*, p. 7.

[11] For a computational-stylistics analysis of the change in James's style, see D. L. Hoover, 'Corpus Stylistics, Stylometry, and the Styles of Henry James', *Style*, 41 (2007), 160–89.

a foundation underneath such easily perceived changes. While even the most perceptive, informed, and experienced readers may be challenged to find the basic (and telling) consistencies, the benefit of computational stylistics is that it can, in fact, do so.

Computational stylistics, that is, can measure change in an author's body of work by balancing such changes against basic consistencies. Such studies can show how variation is 'nested' – how early and late James differ but are still more alike than, say, a contemporary such as Thomas Hardy. Shakespeare's characters, given different lexicons as a means of characterization, can also be detected as the work of the same author, since such a range of word choices and uses remains in a kind of 'envelope' of style that is demonstrably Shakespeare's. Such an 'envelope' still distinguishes Shakespeare from Jonson – or, for that matter, from Marlowe, Middleton, Webster, and Fletcher. Unexpectedly, the study of computational stylistics, and its practices, is perhaps best summarized by someone who is not known for his writing at all, but for his painting: George Braque's dictum was that 'One's style is one's inability to do otherwise.'[12] It is because of the genetic basis, as well as the cultural perceptions of each individual writer that together establish the cognitive processes, that computational stylistics can help us make new discoveries and verify or deny previous ones.

The methods allow us to put intuitions about the distinctiveness of an individual's style on an objective basis, and to estimate systematically the criss-crossing relations of authorial style and other commonalities. They may have some general value in contributing to an overall reassessment of authorship, in an era in literary studies when the individual agency of the author has been subject to intense scrutiny. Indeed, Andrew Bennett in *The Author* (2005), says that the 'crisis of authorship' (Bakhtin's term) has become central to critical debate and interpretation.[13] But now the stylistic dimension to authorship brings a new aspect to this discussion. Once such questions could be approached only through a sophisticated reader's impressions, and seemed to belong to connoisseurship rather than to literary studies proper. They could be overlooked, as they are in Bennett's book. The strength of the effects recorded in the graphs in our chapters changes the picture.

The first decision to make in any computational-stylistics study is what features to count. It is desirable that the features be unambiguous. (In doing the counting any two researchers should come to the same tallies, or

---

[12] Cited in H. Garner, 'I', in *The Best Australian Essays 2002*, ed. P. Craven (Melbourne: Black Inc., 2002), p. 152.
[13] A. Bennett, *The Author* (London: Routledge, 2005), p. 113.

as near as possible to this.) Words, the lowest level of sense unit in language, have been the most popular features for this reason. There are decisions to be made about old-spelling variations, lemmatizing words, standardizing spelling, disambiguating multiple senses, and so on, but once these are made and declared there should be as little room as possible for dispute.

Most of the existing studies in this field devise a specific test that can be shown to distinguish one author's work from others'. The test is then applied to the disputed case. The procedures used so far draw on a remarkable range of data: not only frequencies of individual words or collocations, but counts of abbreviations, contractions, expletives, spellings, metrical features, and figures of speech. The most respected practitioners, such as Ward E. Y. Elliott and Robert J. Valenza, Macdonald P. Jackson, Gary Taylor, and Brian Vickers, use a series of such tests to increase the reliability of their determinations. A single test can show that a work may be by a given author because it falls within the normal range of his or her work, and may allow the elimination of a second author, but one indicator will almost certainly not allow the full range of other possible authors to be excluded. There will be plays outside the Shakespeare canon that use his individual favourite words even more than he does, and others that use the words he uses sparingly even less than he does. A single measure, like the frequency of use of one word, is not enough, therefore, to group his plays across the board and away from all the others. So computational stylistics takes a further step by uniting the results of a series of tests to make a single new measure that can distinguish an author's work from most, if not all, comparable writers. In combination, as in the procedures illustrated in the graphs, these patterns of use do add up to an authorial signature. Combining tests means that we can also begin the work of describing and defining authorial styles by empirical means, rather than simply impressions, and classify them accordingly.

If counting involves broader patterns in style, then the best features for us to choose are those independent of local subject matter. For this reason, function words have been the commonest features counted in computational-stylistics studies, since they have syntactical functions rather than semantic ones. The web of interrelatedness between topic and kind of text alongside even the most neutral-seeming function words is remarkable, however. Pronouns, for instance, are among the strongest markers of genre (*me* is unusually common in Shakespeare comedy, as *we* and *they* are in Shakespeare's Roman plays[14]), and adverbs of place are most frequent in

---

[14] On the latter, see D. H. Craig, 'Plural Pronouns in Roman Plays by Shakespeare and Jonson', *Literary and Linguistic Computing*, 6 (1991), 180–6.

narrative. In a sense it is computational stylistics that has made possible for us the study of function-word frequencies (their sheer abundance defeated much counting until it could be done by machine), and has revealed to us that they are not inert, insignificant structural material, but in fact vary in concert with almost any differentiation of text one might think of, from authorial styles to national linguistic differences.

Beyond the single word are word-combinations. These are attractive because language itself, according to cognitive linguistics, works by word–image–concept–sound combinations rather than by individual words.[15] If, as Lancashire argues, language production is mainly instinctive, and uses associative memory, then short sections of language are spontaneously produced from an individual (and unique) linguistic unconscious, which is conditioned by genetic make-up, life experience, and language experience, as well as mood.[16] Markers based on combinations of words may give special access to this sort of authorial signature. What we need here are large corpora of comparable language by others, so that markers can be tested to see if they are truly characteristic and unusual. (Here there may be an escape from the traditional conundrum of parallel passages. How much of a resemblance between passages is wishful thinking, more the result of a shared culture or common sources, and how much is truly unusual?)

The heart of computational stylistics remains frequencies of common words. They are ubiquitous, abundant, and perform a wide range of syntactic functions. They can thus serve us as indicators of an unlimited range of stylistic effects, not as individual instances but as a pattern or tendency, especially in combinations. John Burrows provides an analogy with the threads of a woven rug: the principal point of interest is neither a single stitch, nor a single thread, but the overall effect.[17]

Burrows rightly points out that the old stylistics and the new have much in common. In forming estimates of style both draw on a quantity of local instances. The seemingly intuitive insights and discriminations of traditional literary analysis have in fact rested on accumulated observations in reading comparisons and contrasts in the details of language.[18] Computational stylistics does the same, but stores the accumulated instances as an accounting of features that are defined in advance.

[15] Lancashire, 'Cognitive Stylistics', p. 406.
[16] I. Lancashire, 'Empirically Determining Shakespeare's Idiolect', *Shakespeare Studies*, 25 (1997), 171–85 (pp. 178–80).
[17] J. Burrows, 'Textual Analysis', in *A Companion to Digital Humanities*, p. 324.
[18] *Ibid.*, p. 345.

Common words account for most of the bulk of a text (typically, the fifty commonest words together represent three-quarters of all words used), but they are barely noticed by a reader, and might seem essentially only a framework for the rarer words, which are the ones we are conscious of. Most of the common words are function words, which have a grammatical job, and belong to closed classes that are only rarely added to. Lexical words by contrast have independent meaning, and regularly go in and out of use. They are produced in different parts of the brain.[19] A play with twenty thousand words of dialogue in total will use between two and three thousand different words, many only once. These rarer words are also a resource for computational stylistics. In establishing an authorial style, we can look to words that are relatively uncommon in general, but nevertheless used more by one author than another. Cases where an author uses a word never used by his fellows are rare in the nature of language; words are shared, but there is no doubt that of all the language resources available to a writer, each makes a quite idiosyncratic selection. Using electronic text we can quickly identify them.

Rare words or relatively uncommon words provide a second string for authorship attribution. While perhaps not entirely independent of common words (since many of the same stylistic forces moderate the frequencies in both categories) they at least draw on the corpus in a different way. They give a different kind of insight into the relationship between texts.

Counting individual words, whether common ones or the rarer type, whatever their neighbours, whatever order they appear in, has been the bread and butter of computational stylistics and has yielded remarkable results. But words in actual use are in the context of others, and researchers have been turning to phrases and looser collocations as further material for analysis. We can use either fixed phrases (*high and low, a jewel in a dunghill*) or looser associations (*brave* within five words either side of *lion*). Is there a group of these that comes up frequently in one writer's work, and rarely in the corpus generally? If so, does it, or do some of its members, appear in the text we are testing? The interest of these items is not limited to attribution tests, since they reveal something of the writer's deeper predilections, even the neural pathways laid down in the language production areas of his/her brain.

Authorship will probably remain the focus of most work in computational stylistics. It is the area of literary studies where we seek a single definite answer, and makes a natural fit with quantitative methods. It takes

---

[19] Lancashire, 'Cognitive Stylistics', p. 403.

up the majority of the studies in our book. Yet there is no reason why the methods should not provide useful perspectives on other aspects. There are other categorical classifications where a specific answer is of interest. Is this work early or late? Is prose dialogue consistently different from speeches in verse? Do playwrights from different classes, with different education, or brought up in different places write differently? Beyond these are generalizations which, though often made on intuitive grounds, could only be tested with an empirical study: which playwrights are the most diverse stylistically across their various works? Which show the widest variation across their characters?

As the amount of electronic text available to us for this kind of work has grown, more of the method's potential is being realized. For practical purposes there is no limit to the size of corpus a computational-stylistic technique can accommodate. The more text of the right type and period we use, the sounder are the generalizations that can be made. Comparing Shakespeare's work systematically to those of half a dozen contemporaries is very useful. Being able to assess it against nearly all surviving literary texts from the period, as the Chadwyck-Healey database already makes possible, or against all printed books from the period, as the Early English Books Online project promises, will allow a truer estimate of its distinctive style.[20]

No amount of introduction to the methods can match a demonstration, especially in an area so new and perhaps so unfamiliar, and below we present a series of studies that show some of the possibilities for computational stylistics in Shakespearean attributions. This relatively new critical method promises to yield much in the years ahead.

---

[20] *Literature Online*, http://lion.chadwyck.co.uk (Cambridge: Chadwyck-Healey, 1996–). *Early English Books Online*, http://eebo.chadwyck.com/home.

CHAPTER 2

Methods

Hugh Craig and Arthur F. Kinney

In almost anything we read there are phrases that seem to resonate with an authorial voice. Over longer stretches of writing all sorts of small signals confirm that we are in touch with a recognizable originating consciousness, even if we realize that this imagined source is our own conjecture, created from the indirect but familiar indications in what we read or hear. Without thinking about it too much, we perform an intuitive calculus on a new work or passage to test it for likeness to an authorial style we have previously internalized. The passages seem to us either authentic or not.

But what, say, of Hal, Hotspur, and Falstaff? They inhabit the same play, but each has a recognizable style that sets him apart from the other two. Can there be a single, identifiable Shakespearean language that unites their three very different kinds of speech? What could it be about the way they speak that would actually unite them, and separate them from characters created by other writers of the same time writing in the same genre, and even drawing on the same conventions of the wily villain, the vainglorious soldier, the braggart hero, and so on?

There are other impediments to identifying an authorial style in a systematic way. For instance, how can we be sure that some of the distinctive Shakespearean phrasings are not in fact common expressions from his own time? How confident are we that we can detect authorship as a steady patterning, rather than through occasional highlights? And when we explain our judgments on authorship to others, how can we do more than make some unsatisfactory generalizations, or offer some sample passages trusting that they will strike the same chord?

Consider the following extracts from three plays from the late sixteenth and early seventeenth centuries:

I meant indeed to pay you with this, which if like an ill venture it come unluckily home, I break, and you, my gentle creditors, lose. Here I promised you I would be, and here I commit my body to your mercies. Bate me some, and I will pay you some, and (as most debtors do) promise you infinitely.

15

This is a sleepy tune. O murd'rous slumber!
Layest thou thy leaden mace upon my boy,
That plays thee music? Gentle knave, good night;
I will not do thee so much wrong to wake thee.

But since you have made the days and nights as one,
To wear your gentle limbs in my affairs,
Be bold you do so grow in my requital
As nothing can unroot you.

There are numerous aspects of these passages that might help connect them with Shakespeare, even if we were not familiar with the passages themselves (from *2 Henry IV, Julius Caesar,* and *All's Well that Ends Well,* respectively[1]). They are all rich in metaphors; they are linguistically fanciful and playful; in manner, they are all more or less courtly and engaging. Their syntax is relaxed and varied, but always resolves into definite closures of structure and sense.

They share a further element linking them to regular Shakespeare practice that readers are less likely to notice: they all use the word *gentle*. This, it turns out, is a favourite Shakespeare word. It was equally available to him and to his contemporaries. It was by no means unusual, or neologistic, or archaic (*OED*). Yet *gentle* occurs nearly twice as regularly in Shakespeare plays as in Early Modern English dialogue generally. This is not just a matter of particular scenes, with a cluster of instances used for a special local effect, or by one character. It is a persistent preference, a minor but recurring thread in Shakespeare's linguistic fabric. To confirm this we can divide Shakespeare plays, and plays by others, into short sections, and then check how many (or how few) of the sections have an instance of the word. (In this way a particular cluster of occurrences is discounted: we are just counting whether there is an instance in a given segment, or not.) If we take 27 Shakespeare plays, and 109 plays from the period by other playwrights, and divide each into 2000-word segments, we find that while more than half of the Shakespeare segments have at least one example of *gentle*, the word appears only in 3 of every 10 of the others (Figure 2.1). It seems fitting, given this pattern of difference, that the word *gentle* was used of Shakespeare as a person. Ben Jonson calls him 'My gentle Shakespeare' in his commendatory poem in the First Folio. For Shakespeare's audience the word would have had associations first with the gentry and nobility, and only secondly with attributes of personal

---

[1] *2 Henry IV*, Epilogue, lines 10–16; *Julius Caesar*, IV.iii.267–70; *All's Well that Ends Well*, V.i.3–6. Lineation of Shakespeare plays and quotations from Shakespeare here and below are from G. B. Evans *et al.*, eds., *The Riverside Shakespeare*, 2nd edn (Boston: Houghton Mifflin, 1997).

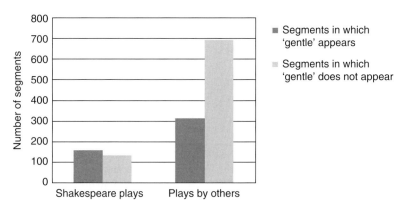

Figure 2.1 Appearances of *gentle* in segments of plays by Shakespeare and by others.

behaviour. In 1596 Shakespeare's father was granted a coat of arms, giving male members of the family the right to write 'gentleman' after their names. We might speculate that Shakespeare's preference for the word *gentle* is connected with this interest in family status.

Such speculations would never fully explain the motivations lying behind this or any other facet of Shakespeare's vocabulary. But in seeking an empirically based profile of this vocabulary, *gentle* is a beginning, pointing the way to a method that might be effective. What we need to do is to find more markers like this one, and to collect other markers that indicate that Shakespeare is not the author of a given passage. With a multitude of such markers we could transform the interestingly lop-sided distribution of Figure 2.1 into something more like a comprehensive picture. We would be hoping for success in separating all Shakespeare segments from all others, something on which we could build a reliable test for any segment of sufficient length.

Some such markers have already been identified in discussions of authorship. MacDonald P. Jackson, for instance, has observed that Shakespeare's characters use *yes* (rather than *yea* or *aye*) only where a special emphasis is required, or to respond to a negative, where other playwrights like Jonson and Fletcher adopted *yes* as the standard form.[2] In the present set of play segments, *yes* emerges as the strongest of all the markers of others' work as opposed to Shakespeare's. *Brave* is also high on the list. It occurs in one

[2] M. P. Jackson, 'Affirmative Particles in *Henry VIII*', *Notes and Queries*, 206 (1962), 372–4, cited in B. Vickers, *Shakespeare, Co-Author: A Historical Study of Five Collaborative Plays* (Oxford: Oxford University Press, 2002), p. 389.

in five segments of Shakespeare's plays, compared to two in five in the run of contemporary drama. To these we can add more instances of the distinctiveness of Shakespearean vocabulary. *Answer* and *beseech* come up much more often in Shakespeare dialogue than the dialogue of others. He had relatively little recourse to the word *sure* and to the plural form *hopes*. There is the beginning of an individual Shakespeare lexicon here, the first indications of a profile in word choice that marks him out from all his fellow dramatists.

A disputed passage in which some or all of *gentle, answer*, and *beseech* occur, and in which there are no instances of *yes, brave, sure*, and *hopes*, shows an affinity with known Shakespeare. If we add to these hundreds of other Shakespeare 'marker' words, we can be more confident in assigning a mystery passage to Shakespeare, or away from him. This is the basis for the method devised by John Burrows and called Zeta.[3] In the current chapter we present one variety of the Zeta test, a principle of selection to allow us to make use of hundreds of words that are unusually common in the author of interest, and of hundreds that are not, to make two axes of authorial differentiation.

We can begin by taking the set of plays by Shakespeare, and the other group of plays by his peers, and seeing if we can separate the two simply by tracking the appearances and absences of sets of words like *gentle* and *brave*. Our usual practice is to establish two sets, each of 500 words, one of which in this case will be markers of Shakespeare, and the other markers of the plays by his peers.

For this purpose we regard *hope* as a different word from *hopes*, and *beseech* as a different word from *beseeching*. We treat words the way a concordance does, rather than organizing them in the manner of a dictionary: the basic unit for our statistical work is thus the word-form rather than the headword. From one perspective this means we are missing a 'true' total for *hope* or *laugh*. On the other hand, this method means we are preserving an aspect of the detail of the language of the texts in our counts, and avoiding a series of decisions that might introduce their own arbitrariness and inconsistency.

As mentioned earlier, we work with 27 'core' Shakespeare plays, and 109 well-attributed single-author plays by others (there is a full list in Appendix A). We divide all these into segments each of 2000 words, ignoring speech, act, and scene boundaries. Residual portions we add to the end of the last segment of each play. We are aiming to examine the plays

---

[3] J. F. Burrows, 'All the Way Through: Testing for Authorship in Different Frequency Strata', *Literary and Linguistic Computing*, 22 (2007), 27–47.

down to quite small units – as it were at the level of the scene, rather than the level of the act or whole play – but using actual scene divisions would make for segments of wildly uneven length. Hence the decision to choose an arbitrary length in words, regardless of any other divisions within the play. In all, our set of plays yielded 291 Shakespeare segments and 1009 non-Shakespeare ones.

There are two different ways to assess the power of the method. The first is to see how well the counts of Shakespeare and non-Shakespeare marker words differentiate between the Shakespeare and non-Shakespeare segments. Is it true that the lowest-scoring Shakespeare segment still contains more of the Shakespeare words than the highest-scoring segment by another writer? On the opposite side, do all the segments in our set by Shakespeare's peers contain more of what we have declared to be non-Shakespeare words than any Shakespeare segment? If this complete separation is not achieved, how many exceptions are there? If the two sets have large numbers of scores that overlap each other, we will know that the diversity of vocabulary patterns within each of the two groups, and the degree of common ground between the two, have defeated our attempts to make a clear separation.

The second test is to see how well the method can discriminate between freshly introduced segments that we know are either by Shakespeare or by some other writer. These are segments that have not played any part in the selection of marker words, reflecting the ultimate goal of testing a new segment that is of disputed or unknown authorship. There is the danger that a method may be too closely tailored to the separation of the particular segments we use to choose the marker words, rather than (as we would wish) set up as a general method for distinguishing between any Shakespeare segment and any other. With this in mind we choose at random one indisputable Shakespeare play and one play confidently attributed to another playwright and put them aside for a second test. In effect, we strip these two plays of authorship and transform them into plays of unknown provenance, so that they can substitute for the anonymous or disputed plays and play sections that we will want to assign to an author.

For our first experiment, the lot fell to *Coriolanus*. We removed its 13 segments from the Shakespeare set, leaving 26 Shakespeare plays and the full set of 109 others. We then found the 500 words that are most characteristic of the slightly reduced Shakespeare set compared to the others. For this purpose the criterion for a 'characteristic' word was that it appeared in many of the Shakespeare segments and in few of the segments by others.

The formula we use for this purpose takes account of two quantities, the proportion of Shakespeare segments where the word appears, and the proportion of non-Shakespeare segments where it does not. Thus we count up all the Shakespeare segments containing the word, and divide this count by the total number of Shakespeare segments. Then we find the number of non-Shakespeare segments where the word does not appear, and divide that by the total number of non-Shakespeare segments. We then add these two proportions together to get a score that reflects the degree to which a given word is more common in Shakespeare than in the work of his peers. The highest possible score is 2, for words that appear in every Shakespeare segment (giving a score for that part of the index of 1), and in none of the non-Shakespeare ones (giving a score of 1 for that part also). The lowest possible score is zero, for words that never appear in Shakespeare and occur in every one of the segments by other authors. In practice we find no words at these two extremes; we simply choose the 500 words with the highest scores on this formula.

The word *gentle* appears at the head of the list, with a score of 1.24 (it appears in 69 per cent of the Shakespeare segments, and does not appear in 55 per cent of the segments by others). We have already discussed its lop-sided distribution between these two groups. Our cut-off for the full list is at 500. The word in this position is *heaven*, which has a score on the index of 1.03, coming much closer to the neutral score of 1 but still appearing more regularly in the Shakespeare segments. It is found in 71 per cent of the latter and in 68 per cent of the segments by other writers.

We then do the same thing in reverse to find our non-Shakespeare markers. This time we are seeking words that often appear in segments by other authors, but appear only rarely in segments by Shakespeare. This time *yes* heads the list (with a score of 1.27) and our last word is *discourse* (with a score of 1.03, the same as that for *heaven* in the other list).

We are concentrating on lexical words for this particular authorship test, words with semantic content like *gentle* and *brave*. There is a separate group of words, the function words, those with grammatical force rather than meaning, like *the* and *but*, most of which are too common for our purposes here. We are looking for words that are absent from some segments, whereas there are only a limited number of function words, and they occur very regularly, so that one can be sure of finding most of their number in any passage of reasonable length. (We employ this group in a second method, described later in this chapter.) It is convenient to establish a list of the function words and exclude them from the test from the beginning. There is a much larger range of different lexical words available and most of them occur irregularly and in small numbers. In our text of the 1604 *Hamlet*, for instance, there are nearly 160 words that occur 25 times or more, but more than 4500 that appear fewer than 25 times.

Having compiled lists of the Shakespeare and non-Shakespeare marker words in this way, we counted how many of them appeared in each segment. For this purpose, as before, one appearance was enough; the only distinction was between no instances and some. Each segment's count of Shakespeare words and non-Shakespeare words can then be compared to the counts for other segments.

To take one example, 84 of the 500 Shakespeare marker words appear in the first segment of *All's Well that Ends Well*. It does not have *gentle* but it does have three instances of *answer*, and so on down the full list of marker words. On the non-Shakespeare list this segment's score is 63: no instance of *brave*, but one of *hopes*, another prominent non-Shakespeare marker. (The particular numbers are only important in relation to the general pattern of such counts for Shakespeare segments and for segments by others.) We cannot rest simply with the totals of appearances, since some segments – the final segments of each play, which include the remainder after we have divided the total of words by 2000 word-units – are longer than others, and this needs to be taken into account. We therefore divide the number of marker words that appear in each segment by the total number of different words in that segment. For each segment, then, we ask two questions. Firstly, what proportion of the various different words it uses are Shakespeare 'favourites'? And, secondly, what proportion are words he generally avoids? Taking results for all 1298 segments like this we plot the counts on two axes, one for the Shakespeare and one for the non-Shakespeare markers. Figure 2.2 shows the results. This is an unfamiliar way to think about the plays. It is unusual to think of so many plays in a systematic relation to each other. It is odd to divide them up into even-sized portions. Out of all the myriad possible linguistic, literary, and dramatic aspects of the segments we have chosen just two to represent them in a chart, both counts of their word-use, a positive and a negative measurement of closeness to Shakespeare's overall vocabulary preferences. Yet these counts consolidate a great deal of information about individual word-use, and give us a common basis on which to compare all the segments. Each of the segments now has a place in a map that combines the two counts. We have established a region to which we can expect genuine Shakespeare segments to gravitate – the bottom right of the graph, defined by high scores on Shakespeare words, and low scores on the words he habitually neglects. The upper-left quadrant, correspondingly, is the

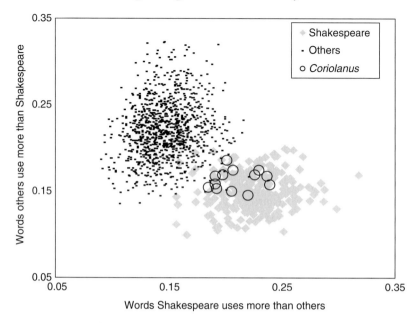

Figure 2.2 Lexical-words test: 2000-word Shakespeare segments versus 2000-word segments by others, with 2000-word segments of *Coriolanus*.

region where we expect segments by others will appear, with low scores on the Shakespeare words and high scores on the others.

If we look first at the two large sets of entries, the Shakespeare diamonds and the non-Shakespeare dots, we can see that the differences are large enough, and consistent enough across the two groups, to separate most of the segments. There are dots that appear in the area dominated by diamonds, but they are few in number and they are in the upper-left part of the cluster formed by the diamonds. Similarly, there are diamonds with scores that mean that they appear within the cluster of the dots, but these are isolated and well outside the heart of the dots' cluster. We can make a simple numerical estimate of the success rate by drawing an imaginary straight line between the two clusters.[4] Calculation shows that 17 of the non-Shakespeare segments fall to the Shakespeare side of this line, and five of the Shakespeare segments fall on the non-Shakespeare side, overall 2 per cent of the total, giving a success rate of 98 per cent. It is remarkable that one author's preferences in vocabulary are so consistent that counting

[4] For this purpose we use the perpendicular bisector of the line joining the centroids of the two clusters, as discussed in Chapter 3, below (p. 54).

words from two lists gives us a way of classifying the vast majority of them correctly.

The graph shows that neither of the two measures on its own would suffice to separate the two clusters. On the horizontal axis, which shows the counts of Shakespeare words, one can see by eye that the average Shakespeare count is much higher than the average non-Shakespeare one; but there is still a large overlap, a span occupied by both dots and diamonds. When we include the counts on non-Shakespeare markers – the vertical axis – though, the two groups separate almost completely. To tell the Shakespeare segments from the others, we need to know how many of the words that Shakespeare usually avoids appear in a given segment, as well as the number of his favourites. Once we have done this, the choices the authors habitually make within a shared vocabulary serve as a simple and powerful means of telling them apart. Admittedly, even with both counts in play, there are some exceptions, creating a band of the graph shared between the two groups. Given that there are 278 Shakespeare segments, and 1009 non-Shakespeare ones, though, this is an impressive performance. Combining the counts of Shakespeare and non-Shakespeare marker words gives us a simple way of distinguishing the two kinds of segment, which we can expect will fail in only a handful of cases.

If we turn to the *Coriolanus* segments, the circles, which played no part in drawing up the two lists of words, we see that they do indeed fall in Shakespeare territory. We can conclude that with this method we could assign a Shakespeare segment to Shakespeare even if it had played no part in arriving at the word lists, not with absolute certainty, but with considerable confidence.

We can try the same procedure again, this time including a randomly chosen play by a playwright other than Shakespeare, Thomas Middleton's *Hengist, King of Kent*. We compiled new lists, drawing on all twenty-seven Shakespeare plays this time, compared with a non-Shakespeare set without *Hengist*. The results are shown in Figure 2.3. The *Hengist* segments, like the *Coriolanus* ones, were free to fall wherever their counts of the marker words took them. Nine of the ten *Hengist* segments are placed in unambiguously non-Shakespeare territory, while one appears in a region shared between Shakespeare and the others. We are reminded that the segments used to establish the pattern of distinction between Shakespeare and the others do overlap. Grey diamonds appear well to the left and higher up than the main group, and black dots stray down and to the right. There is certainly a strong tendency to separate, but the evident variation within the two groups means that occasionally in a given segment Shakespeare

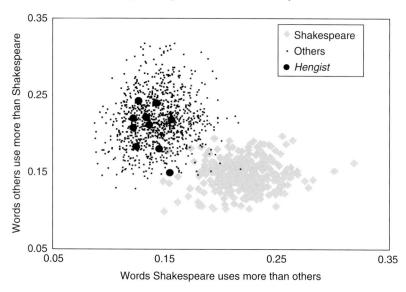

Figure 2.3 Lexical-words test: 2000-word Shakespeare segments versus 2000-word segments by others, with 2000-word segments of *Hengist*.

uses fewer of his favourite words, and more of those he normally eschews, so that on these measures it could on this basis be mistaken for a passage from one of his contemporaries. (The grey diamond in the upper-left-hand corner of the group is in fact the third segment of *All's Well that Ends Well*, extending from a point within I.iii.186 to a point within II.i.194.) In the same way one of the *Hengist* segments uses sufficiently few of the non-Shakespeare words, and at the same time just enough of the Shakespeare words, to overlap the Shakespeare group.

It is clear that the method can draw out patterns from the lexical words data that serve to distinguish Shakespeare segments from others, with effectiveness even in the more difficult case of test segments from outside the ones used to establish the groups of marker words. In the odd case, we must concede, a segment is not decisively placed in what we know to be the correct cluster. We have a method that is powerful but not infallible.

This is a crucial point. The results of computational stylistics are always matters of probability, not of certainty. Writers are free agents, and language is an endlessly flexible instrument. Writers tend to remain within a defined band of style, but this is a propensity, not an iron law. In the past, quantitative work in literary studies has sometimes suffered from exaggerating the reliability of its findings. In 1989, for example,

Donald W. Foster presented results that showed a newly discovered poem falling again and again within the Shakespearean range. After further elaboration by Foster, and a considerable controversy, the poem was subsequently included in several editions of Shakespeare's works. In the end, however, some of Foster's results did not stand up to scrutiny, and it proved that even on his chosen measures Shakespeare's style did not always match the style of the poem. The poem has since been definitively attributed elsewhere when an obviously superior candidate, John Ford, was found.[5]

Our method relies on the careful collection and weighing of data, and must be rigorously pursued. Even at its best it can mislead, by deceptively unequivocal results. The possibility of error must always be borne in mind. Yet none of this should obscure the main facts. The graphs confirm our intuitions that authorial individuality is powerful. They also establish, in a way readers' impressions can never do, that this effect is consistent and marked even in the mixed dialogue of plays produced in a highly collaborative and tightly interconnected theatre practice like the one Shakespeare knew.

The distribution of strategically chosen lexical words evidently offers the foundation for some useful authorial discrimination. It makes sense that writers have preferences for some words, and a tendency to neglect others. The analysis of large amounts of text shows how consistent and marked these patterns are throughout a career, even one as long as Shakespeare's. There are good reasons for looking for a second test as well. There will always be an element of error in any single method, and the graphs above show this, in those occasional data points of known origin that declare themselves as ambiguous, or frankly as members of the wrong side of the classification. After all, we are dealing with writers who are at liberty to imitate each other, to try new styles, and to write differently for a particular occasion or in a new genre, and we are trying to corral this vast conscious and unconscious literary activity with what are, at heart, very simple rules: either the segment in question uses a given word, or it does not. It is no wonder that success in discrimination is not complete. If we could find a second method, working independently of this one, so much the better. This also makes life more complicated, however. When

---

[5] D. W. Foster, *Elegy by W. S.: A Study in Attribution* (Newark, DE: University of Delaware Press, 1989); G. D. Monsarrat, 'A Funeral Elegy: Ford, W. S., and Shakespeare', *Review of English Studies*, 53 (2002), 186–203; B. Vickers, 'Counterfeiting' Shakespeare: Evidence, Authorship, and John Ford's 'Funerall Elegye' (Cambridge: Cambridge University Press, 2002); and H. Craig, 'Common-Words Frequencies, Shakespeare's Style, and the *Elegy* by W. S.', *Early Modern Literary Studies*, 8.1 (2002), available at http://purl.oclc.org/emls/08–1/craistyl.htm (last accessed 10 August 2008).

the methods fail to support each other, we are abruptly reminded of the residual uncertainty in each one (a French proverb says that 'Someone with a watch knows what time it is; someone with two watches is never sure'[6]). If the two methods agree, on the other hand, we start to build a really strong case.

The obvious place to look for a second computational-stylistics method is in the function words, those like *and* or *you*, which have vital grammatical functions but little or no semantic content. As we have already noted, these words, unlike the lexical words, are limited in number, and many of them are very abundant. They form a closed set, most of which will appear in almost any 2000-word segment of dialogue. The commonest of all, *the*, makes up one word in thirty in the plays we are analysing. In fact these words have been the commonest base data for computational authorship work. It is well established that writers use them at different rates, so that, if we combine a number of them together, they can offer effective authorial discriminations.[7] In this case calculating frequencies makes more sense than simply recording appearance and non-appearance.

To demonstrate a method based on frequencies of the function words we can examine a convenient series of problems where the solution is known with a degree of certainty. Brian Vickers, in *Shakespeare, Co-Author: A Historical Study of Five Collaborative Plays*, discusses five cases of putative Shakespearean collaboration in detail.[8] In each one a single collaborator is identified and the division of the play is clear-cut. Vickers details a strong scholarly consensus for each, and adds his own synthesizing and supplementing tests and discussion. It would seem safe to work on the basis that collaboration in these plays, and the details of the boundaries between parts, are so well established that they can serve as a test bed for the methods of the present book. We treat here *Titus Andronicus, Timon of Athens, Henry VIII*, and *The Two Noble Kinsmen*. We omit *Pericles*, where the collaborator, George Wilkins, has only one play to his name as independent work, and thus the method of establishing general stylistic differences over a wide sample cannot be applied. With George Peele (for *Titus Andronicus*), Thomas Middleton (for *Timon of Athens*) and John Fletcher (for *Henry VIII* and *The Two Noble Kinsmen*) there is a substantial canon to provide a basis for comparison with Shakespeare.

---

[6] D. Crystal, *As They Say in Zanzibar* (London: Collins, 2006), p. 51.

[7] D. I. Holmes, 'Authorship Attribution', *Computers and the Humanities*, 28 (1994), 87–106; J. F. Burrows, 'Textual Analysis', in *A Companion to Digital Humanities*, ed. S. Schreibman, R. Siemens, and J. Unsworth (Oxford: Blackwell, 2004), pp. 323–47.

[8] Vickers, *Shakespeare, Co-Author* (Oxford: Oxford University Press, 2002).

In the remainder of this chapter we will concentrate on these four cases, where we are almost sure Shakespeare collaborated with another author. This will demonstrate something of the technicalities of the methods and also give an indication of their effectiveness in an area that, on the face of it, presents great challenges for authorship study. In a collaboration the playwrights (we assume) are aiming at a single style for their play. They are working in the same genre, and on the same material. We can expect individual characteristics to be restrained. Writers may well be working outside their normal range and the demands of a particular assignment may well lead to departures from the patterns established over work in plays where they have a free hand.

In this demonstration we will use the same method in each case, forgoing the improvements that might come from adapting the methods to the particular instance for the sake of a benchmark test applied across the board. Having determined some rules for testing, we use them without variation to provide a strict estimate of their power to separate segments of known authorship. In later chapters we will adapt the methods to particular cases, taking account of genre and date in the authorial canons used to establish authorial signatures, bringing in additional statistical perspectives to wring more discriminating power out of the methods, and essaying some new methods adapted to the problem at hand.

The aim is to test methods, rather than to investigate, so we want sample material that is as uncontroversial as possible. With this in mind, we use whole scenes as defined in early editions, and only those that are generally regarded as the unaided work of one or other collaborator (in this Vickers is once again our guide). We also use only those that have 1500 words or more of dialogue, to minimize the effects of local variation. It is easy to see that very short passages can be dominated by a particular situation or subject, so that they depart from the persistent balance of elements that constitute a writer's style. As passages get longer, the local pressures tend to balance each other out and underlying habits and preferences assert themselves more strongly. Alvar Ellegård suggested that this sort of variation stabilizes at 4000 words in the kind of expository prose he was concerned with.[9] We have to balance the competing requirements of ideal sample length and applicability to our particular cases. A minimum of 1500 words yields us a number of scenes in each of our chosen plays, where a minimum of 4000 would yield none.

[9] A. Ellegård, *A Statistical Method for Determining Authorship: The Junius Letters, 1769–1772* (Gothenburg: University of Gothenburg Press, 1962), p. 33.

Table 2.1 shows the division of the 1594 Quarto of *Titus Andronicus* into scenes, with the length in words of each scene, as counted by our programs, and the attribution of each to Shakespeare or to George Peele, according to Brian Vickers' chapter in *Shakespeare, Co-Author* (pp. 148–243). An extra scene appears in Act III in the Folio version of the play, but this is excluded here to keep the focus on a single early printed version. Vickers' division builds on a long scholarly tradition of authorship work on the play. He draws on multiple markers of authorial difference, from the number of alliterations and the stress patterns of the verse to the number of polysyllabic words. We can proceed with the five scenes with more than 1500 words: I.i, attributed to Peele, and II.iii, III.i, V.ii, and V.iii, attributed to Shakespeare. This time instead of a comparison between Shakespeare and a mixed group of other writers we are interested in a Shakespeare–Peele contrast.

With the function words we cannot rely on counting appearances and non-appearances in segments as we did with the lexical words. We already know that many of the function words will appear in every segment. We need a procedure that works in frequencies and combines them so as to bring out more subtle patterns of use. We first select words that do show differences between the two authors (Shakespeare and Peele), and then use a mathematical technique to concentrate the discriminating power of the frequencies of the chosen words into a few composite factors.

A simple way to find the function words that are used most differently by two authors is Student's *t*-test.[10] This procedure is based on two of the fundamental statistical quantities, the mean or average and the standard deviation. The mean is simply the total of the counts for any variable divided by the number of counts. It is a summary of the underlying tendency of the group. In terms of prediction, it is the best guide to the count of any newly introduced sample from the same parent group. It is just a single number, however, and may conceal quite a wide variation: the same mean may have come about from a group of very similar values, or from a group that includes some very high and very low values. Hence the usefulness of the standard deviation, which measures the dispersion of values around the mean. The standard deviation is in the same units as the original variable (in the present work, the frequency, or proportional frequency, of a given word). It is calculated as the square root of the total variance, which is the average of the squared differences between the

---

[10] The test was proposed by W. S. Gossett (writing as 'Student') in 1908, and further developed by R. A. Fisher in 1926. See G. W. Snedecor and W. G. Cochran, *Statistical Methods*, 8th edn (Ames, IA: Iowa State University Press, 1989), pp. 53–8.

Table 2.1. *Division of* Titus Andronicus *between Shakespeare and Peele according to Vickers,* Shakespeare, Co-Author, *Table 3.11.*

Scene	Length in words	Author
I.i	3763	Peele
II.i	1038	Peele
II.ii	213	Peele
II.iii	2414	Shakespeare
II.iv	484	Shakespeare
III.i	2454	Shakespeare
IV.i	1030	Peele
IV.ii	1433	Shakespeare
IV.iii	947	Shakespeare
IV.iv	860	Shakespeare
V.i	1338	Shakespeare
V.ii	1670	Shakespeare
V.iii	1556	Shakespeare

samples (in our case, the segments) and the mean. The standard deviation has the property that in a statistically normal distribution approximately two-thirds of the values will lie within one standard deviation above or below the mean.

The *t* value of a variable is the difference between the means of the two groups, divided by the standard deviation of all the counts. The test compares the means of the two groups (in this case, counts for a given word in the Shakespeare and Peele groups of segments), takes standard deviations into account, and produces a composite measure of the strength and consistency of the difference. The variables with the highest *t* values, those in which we are most interested, will have large differences in means between the two groups and small overall standard deviations, implying a genuine difference in rates of use between the two groups.

This *t* value can be compared to a published probability table to estimate how likely the difference is to have come about by chance alone, taking into account the number of the samples. A low probability means that the two groups are markedly, and consistently, different in their frequencies. We tested 200 function words in our collection of 27 Shakespeare plays and 4 Peele ones. Of these, 55 were regarded by the *t*-test as consistently higher or lower in one author or the other, a difference expressed as a probability of less than one in 10 000 that the groups derive from the same parent population. (The absolute level of probability is in fact not of great interest here, since we are using the test primarily as a way to identify variables to be used in a further test.[11])

At the top of this list of the words that Peele uses more than Shakespeare are *and* and *thy*. At the top of the list of words that Shakespeare uses more than Peele are *it* and *very*. We might suspect some broader stylistic patterns behind this: Peele's dialogue prosier and more archaic in its grammatical forms; Shakespeare's including more casual and domestic exchanges. A method called principal components analysis, or PCA, can do a purely mathematical equivalent, comparing patterns of individual word-use to extract some composite 'factors', combinations of the original word-count variables.[12]

The PCA method seeks to find the strongest such factor, then the second strongest independent one, and so on. A strong factor is one that accounts for a large proportion of the total variance in a table of counts. This is a 'data reduction' method, since it aims to create a new composite variable, a so-called principal component, which represents a good deal of the underlying contrasts and similarities in the counts. If, for instance, we have a table of the heights and weights for the adult inhabitants of a given town, then we can make a new variable that is simply the sum of the two counts, and we will find that this combined variable represents with a good deal of accuracy the patterns of variation within the two original variables. Shorter people will tend to be lighter, and taller people heavier. The new variable we could call 'size'.[13] It will not account for all the variations in the height and weight table, since there are some short individuals who are heavy, and some tall individuals who are relatively light, but it will capture a basic fact about the table, one that in a sense is the most important fact in it.

Principal components analysis is most useful where there are numerous variables, rather than just two. We may have counts of rainfall, daily

---

[11] Thus the probability level does not translate into any very useful inference about these populations, and should be regarded as no more than a convenient threshold, especially as there is no presumption that the word-frequencies follow a normal distribution. The *t*-test was done on 2000-word segments, 301 from Shakespeare plays and 25 from Peele plays. We used the 'equal variance not assumed' results from the statistical package SPSS (version 16.0, copyright SPSS Inc., 1989–2007).

[12] The technique of PCA is well established and there are accounts of it in numerous textbooks on multivariate analysis: see, for example, C. Chatfield and A. J. Collins, *Introduction to Multivariate Analysis* (London: Chapman and Hall, 1980), pp. 57–79. In relation to textual analysis in particular, see J. N. G. Binongo and M. W. A. Smith, 'The Application of Principal Component Analysis to Stylometry', *Literary and Linguistic Computing*, 14 (1999), 445–65, and J. Burrows and H. Craig, 'Lucy Hutchinson and the Authorship of Two Seventeenth-Century Poems: A Computational Approach', *The Seventeenth Century*, 16.2 (2001), 259–82.

[13] This illustration derives from W. J. Krzanowski, *Principles of Multivariate Analysis: A User's Perspective* (Oxford: Clarendon Press, 1988), pp. 53–6.

maxima and minima of temperature, barometric pressure, wind speed, and so on for hundreds of locations across a continent over a year. We ask PCA to create the combination of these variables that represents the strongest 'latent' factor. The result might be one that corresponds with seasonal difference. We can then say that a lot of what is happening in the fluctuations in rainfall, temperature, and so on can be summed up in the difference between summer and winter. Then PCA can look for a second such composite variable. This might turn out to be one that is correlated with distance from the coast, or height above sea level. Either way we have found a way of summing up what is happening within the local variations in the table in some broad axes of difference.

Each principal component has a weighting for each variable. Variables that are irrelevant to the broad difference being isolated have low weightings; the most important ones have high weightings; and the ones that behave quite differently from each other are given opposite signs. Each sample (or segment) can then be given a score made up of the sum of its counts on each of the constituent variables, each one multiplied by its own weighting.

The lexical words method used for earlier experiments in this chapter simply adds counts of appearances of words together. PCA gives each word-frequency variable a weighting so as to highlight cumulative similarities and dissimilarities. The idea is familiar from stock market indexes or consumer price indexes, in which some elements are weighted more heavily than others to take account of their importance in the basket of stocks or consumer items.

In our case the variables are the frequencies of individual words. We chose the words that we know are used most differently by the two authors, and then asked the method to combine these word-variables so as to show the strongest underlying affinities and contrasts. Figure 2.4 presents the scores on the first two principal components for three groups of samples: 2000-word segments from the 27 confidently attributed Shakespeare plays in our archive, 2000-word segments from the 4 Peele plays we include, and the 5 eligible *Titus* scenes. The first principal component arrays the Peele segments (the black circles) to the left, and the Shakespeare segments (the grey diamonds) to the right. The Peele segments are also in the lower half of the graph, while the Shakespeare segments spread from top to bottom. The procedure has combined the information from the chosen word-variables and created two indexes. Each of the segments has a score on either index. When plotted together as in Figure 2.4 they provide a map that defines a Shakespeare region (to the right, characterized by high

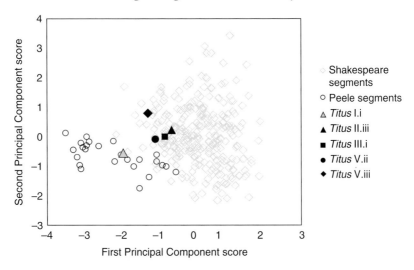

Figure 2.4 Function-words test: 2000-word Shakespeare segments, 2000-word Peele segments, and 5 scenes from *Titus Andronicus*.

scores on the first component) and a Peele one (to the lower left, characterized by low scores on both components). As with the lexical tests shown in Figures 2.2 and 2.3 in this chapter, this is a basis for classifying new segments as Shakespeare or Peele, depending on their use of the chosen function words. We are still using 2000-word segments of known authorship to provide the basis for classification, but this time we are contrasting one author with another, rather than one author with a larger mixed set of other authors.

The *Titus* scene usually ascribed to Peele – Act I, Scene i – marked with a grey triangle, is placed to the lower left of the graph. The other four scenes, ascribed to Shakespeare, and marked with solid black shapes, are all above it and to the right. A basis for a broad discrimination between the two authors is established by the two principal components, and on the basis of this one of the *Titus* scenes is placed with Peele and the other four with Shakespeare, a separation that is consistent with the division of the play shown in Table 2.1. One might wonder whether counts of these function words would vary so much within authors, from early works to late, or from one genre to another, or from any other cause, that overall authorial differences would be overwhelmed. Figure 2.4 shows that there is some overlap, some areas where circles are found mixed with diamonds, but generally the distinctions hold up. Moreover, in the case of the

Table 2.2. *Division of* Timon of Athens *between Shakespeare and Middleton according to Vickers,* Shakespeare, Co-Author, *Table 4.6.*

Scene	Length in words	Author
I.i	2087	Shakespeare
I.ii	2003	Middleton
II.i	295	Shakespeare
II.ii	1754	Shakespeare
III.i	497	Middleton
III.ii	711	Middleton
III.iii	363	Middleton
III.iv	835	Middleton
III.v	914	Middleton
III.vi	848	Middleton
IV.i	305	Shakespeare
IV.ii	422	Shakespeare and Middleton
IV.iii	4248	Shakespeare and Middleton
V.i	1860	Shakespeare
V.ii	130	Shakespeare
V.iii	88	Shakespeare
V.iv	678	Shakespeare

Titus segments, the method has discriminated between two authors' work within the same play and displays a pattern entirely consistent with the division between them presented in Vickers' book. As the two playwrights worked on their joint assignment, writing dialogue for the same characters in the same settings in a shared plot, their contrasting use of *and, thy, it, very* and the rest was nevertheless inscribing two deeply entrenched individual styles in their scenes.

We can deal more quickly with the three other collaborative plays. Vickers' book details a long tradition of scholarship on *Timon of Athens* that detects a second author besides Shakespeare in the writing of some scenes, and identifies this writer as Thomas Middleton. As with *Titus*, we have a neat hypothesis involving just two authors and many discrete sections. Table 2.2 presents the divisions with their lengths in our texts according to our counting procedures, and their authorship as Vickers records it. Once we have discarded the two scenes with mixed authorship, and the smaller scenes, we are left with I.i, I.ii, II.ii, and V.i. Of these I.i, II.ii, and V.i are attributed to Shakespeare, and I.ii to Middleton.

The *t*-test identifies eighty-seven function words as highly distinctive in use in the Shakespeare and Middleton sets. The highest values of all are for

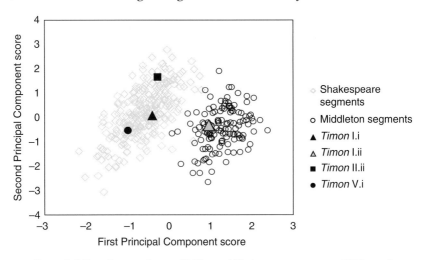

Figure 2.5 Function-words test: 2000-word Shakespeare segments, 2000-word
Middleton segments, and 4 scenes from *Timon of Athens*.

doth and *hath* (much more common in Shakespeare than in Middleton),
and for *that* as a demonstrative and *now* (more frequent in Middleton
than in Shakespeare).[14] Figure 2.5 shows the segments and scenes on the
first two principal components that combine the frequencies of all eighty-
seven words, using two different sets of weightings. The Shakespeare and
Middleton clusters have some overlap. One Shakespeare segment is placed
well into Middleton territory, for instance, with a score of 0.59 on the
first component, and −0.96 on the second. This is the second segment of
Romeo and Juliet, spanning I.ii.6 to I.iv.46. The scene from *Timon* attributed to Middleton (marked by a grey triangle) is placed in the Middleton
cluster, while the other three scenes (the solid black shapes) are well to the
Shakespeare side, consistent with the accepted ascription.

The last Shakespeare collaboration we will consider is with John
Fletcher. We begin with the history play *Henry VIII*, first performed in
1613 and first published in the Folio of 1623. In 1850 James Spedding
divided the play scene by scene between Shakespeare and Fletcher, and
this division has stood up remarkably well to a great variety of tests, as
Vickers shows (pp. 336–96). Table 2.3 shows this ascription with the
length of each scene in words in the text we use for counting. In Act V we

[14] H. Craig, 'Authorial Attribution and Computational Stylistics: If You Can Tell Authors Apart,
     Have You Learned Anything about Them?', *Literary and Linguistic Computing*, 14 (1999), 103–13,
     examines Shakespeare's and Middleton's contrasting styles in function-word use in detail.

Table 2.3. *Division of* Henry VIII *between Shakespeare and Fletcher according to Vickers,* Shakespeare, Co-Author, *Table 6.2 and p. 340 (for Prologue and Epilogue).*

Scene	Length in words	Author
Prologue	268	Fletcher
I.i	1866	Shakespeare
I.ii	1742	Shakespeare
I.iii	587	Fletcher
I.iv	941	Fletcher
II.i	1437	Fletcher
II.ii	1221	Fletcher
II.iii	898	Shakespeare
II.iv	1923	Shakespeare
III.i	1514	Fletcher
III.ii	3837	Shakespeare and Fletcher
IV.i	997	Fletcher
IV.ii	1430	Fletcher
V.i	1507	Shakespeare
V.ii	1845	Fletcher
V.iii	807	Fletcher
V.iv	651	Fletcher
Epilogue	132	Fletcher

have adopted the scene division of the *Riverside Shakespeare*, which follows the Folio in this case; some modern editions divide V.ii after line 34.[15] Spedding ascribed the first part of III.ii, up to the exit of the King at III.ii.203, to Shakespeare, and the rest of the scene to Fletcher.[16] In line with our policy of examining only scenes wholly by one collaborator for this test of our methods we have omitted III.ii from our analysis. As before, we identify the function words that are used most differently by the two authors. There are fifty-nine that are rated by the *t*-test in the top category. Fletcher uses *ye* and *all* much more than Shakespeare. Shakespeare uses the preposition *in* and the verb form *hath* much more than Fletcher. (*Ye* and *hath* have long been known as markers of the difference between Shakespeare's and Fletcher's styles.[17]) Figure 2.6 shows the results of a

---

[15] S. Greenblatt, W. Cohen, J. E. Howard, and K. Eisaman Maus, eds., *The Norton Shakespeare: Based on the Oxford Edition* (New York and London: Norton, 1997), p. 3118.

[16] Vickers, *Shakespeare, Co-Author*, p. 340.

[17] See A. C. Partridge, *Orthography in Shakespeare and Elizabethan Drama: A Study of Colloquial Contractions, Elision, Prosody and Punctuation* (London: Edward Arnold, 1964), pp. 149–53, cited in Vickers, *Shakespeare, Co-Author*, pp. 378–9. Partridge's findings were first published in his *The Problem of Henry VIII Re-Opened* (Cambridge: Bowes and Bowes, 1949).

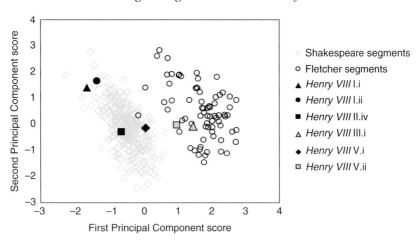

Figure 2.6 Function-words test: 2000-word Shakespeare segments, 2000-word
Fletcher segments, and 6 scenes from *Henry VIII*.

PCA using the full list of fifty-nine words. The known Shakespeare and
Fletcher segments are well separated. Just one – which we can identify
as the fifth segment of *The Faithful Shepherdess* – crosses the no-man's-
land between the two clusters.[18] The method assigns the *Henry VIII* scenes
tested according to the usual ascription, with III.i and V.ii both with the
Fletcher cluster.

As a last exploration of the efficacy of the methods in separating scenes
from a collaborative play we examine *The Two Noble Kinsmen*. The play
was first printed in 1634 and described then as the joint work of Fletcher
and Shakespeare. Table 2.4 lists the scenes of the play, with their length
in words and their authorship as summarized by Vickers as before. Most
of the scenes are too short for our purpose here. A 1500-word minimum
leaves us three: I.i, which Vickers gives to Shakespeare, and II.ii and III.vi,
which he gives to Fletcher.

We use the fifty-nine words already identified which satisfy the *t*-test
standard for difference in use between Shakespeare and Fletcher. We
can then include the three *Two Noble Kinsmen* scenes in a PCA with the
Shakespeare and Fletcher segments. Figure 2.7 shows the results for the
first two principal components, in the manner of Figures 2.4, 2.5 and 2.6.

---

[18] This segment begins within III.i.51 and ends within III.i.296, following the lineation in the
version in F. Bowers, ed., *The Dramatic Works in the Beaumont and Fletcher Canon*, 10 vols.
(Cambridge: Cambridge University Press, 1976), Vol. 3.

Table 2.4. *Division of* The Two Noble Kinsmen
between Shakespeare and Fletcher according to Vickers,
Shakespeare, Co-Author, *Table 6.28.*

Scene	Length in words	Author
I.i	1810	Shakespeare
I.ii	949	Shakespeare
I.iii	803	Shakespeare
I.iv	412	Shakespeare
I.v	108	Fletcher
II.i	496	Shakespeare
II.ii	2400	Fletcher
II.iii	744	Fletcher
II.iv	287	Fletcher
II.v	569	Fletcher
II.vi	343	Fletcher
III.i	1051	Shakespeare
III.ii	343	Shakespeare
III.iii	503	Fletcher
III.iv	249	Fletcher
III.v	1212	Fletcher
III.vi	2706	Fletcher
IV.i	1351	Fletcher
IV.ii	1346	Fletcher
IV.iii	878	Shakespeare
V.i	1392	Shakespeare
V.ii	1033	Fletcher
V.iii	1201	Shakespeare
V.iv	1159	Shakespeare

The scores for Act I, Scene i of *The Two Noble Kinsmen* place this scene well away from Act II, Scene ii and Act III, Scene vi of the same play. The method shows that I.i has a Shakespearean pattern of function-word use, while the other two scenes are placed with Fletcher segments. This corresponds with the attribution shown in Table 2.4. As with the other three plays discussed here, the results are entirely consistent with one well-supported theory about their creation. The method and the theory offer clear-cut mutual support.

The graphs of the present chapter provide a visual summary of the power of the two computational-stylistic methods. Both prove capable of abstracting patterns of word-use that are consistent enough to separate the segments of known provenance, often into almost completely distinct authorial clusters, sometimes into clouds of points that merge at their

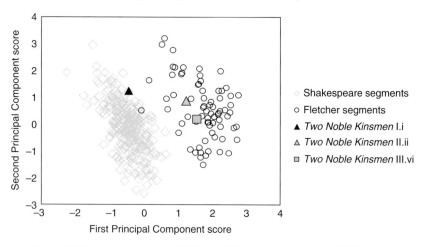

Figure 2.7 Function-words test: 2000-word Shakespeare segments, 2000-word
Fletcher segments, and 3 scenes from *The Two Noble Kinsmen*.

fringes. Neither method is absolutely reliable. Part of the reason for this
is the degree of overlap in these texts. The passages we are dealing with
share conventions, a limited set of genres, and a common heritage. They
were all written in an uninterrupted span for audiences in one city over
just two generations. Within this common ground they are all striving for
some innovation and development. This context of variation within broad
limits means that if we take hundreds of samples of dramatic dialogue the
length of a medium-sized scene, as we do here, we are almost bound to
find authors occasionally writing sufficiently unlike themselves, and sufficiently like each other, to defy the authorial boundaries that do divide the
vast bulk of one writer's work from the other's. But against this is a steady
pressure of differentiation, which gives us a very useful pair of tools for
assessing the origins of mysterious or disputed texts. It is worth remembering, too, that the fallibility of the methods individually can be reduced by
using both the methods on a single case, as we do in the studies presented
in succeeding chapters.

   The results shown here are evidence of forces operating within language
on a large scale: forces we could certainly have guessed at, but could never
have measured without the computer. For example, Shakespeare's characters, with a remarkable degree of consistency, use the words *gentle* and
beseech much more often than the characters of his contemporaries do.
Shakespeare's characters use *yes* less often. They are users of *hath* rather

than *has*. They are fond of the conjunction *that*, but not of *all* or *now*. Putting together these patterns of use, with those of other marker words, allows us to differentiate the plays as a group from plays by others (as the graphs show). It is remarkable that these regularities obtain even in the work of a famously diverse writer like Shakespeare, writing in a mode like drama, made up of multiple contrasting voices.

When we turn from the general patterns to particular cases we need to keep a proper scepticism, however. The right balance of confidence and caution in interpreting the results of methods like these can only come with repeated experiments with samples of known origin. These will help establish how much faith one should have in the findings, especially when they contradict the scholarly consensus, or one's own judgment as a reader. We aim to keep this in mind in the chapters that follow, and to continue to provide indexes of reliability from tests on samples whose origins we know. We can see from the experiments in this chapter that occasionally the methods get things wrong, or at least fail to give an unambiguously right answer. Most often, though, they get it right, arriving through their quite different means at the same conclusions as the consensus of the scholarly tradition. With this experience behind us we can move from problems where the answer is known to areas of doubt and dispute.

CHAPTER 3

The three parts of Henry VI

Hugh Craig

We begin by approaching perhaps the thorniest problem in attribution in the Shakespeare canon, involving the three history plays dealing with the reign of King Henry VI (1422–61 and 1470–1). The early evidence about authorship is mixed. None of the three plays is mentioned among those Francis Meres listed as Shakespeare's in 1598, although it is likely they had all appeared on stage by 1592.[1] They are all included in the 1623 Shakespeare Folio, however, which, as Michael Hattaway puts it, certainly represents an implicit claim by the editors of that volume that they are Shakespeare's work.[2] *1 Henry VI* was first printed in the Folio; *2* and *3 Henry VI* had appeared in earlier editions, as *The First Part of the Contention betwixt the Two Famous Houses of York and Lancaster* (1594) and *The True Tragedy of Richard Duke of York* (1595), both anonymous, and then together in a 1619 Quarto, in which they are both attributed to Shakespeare.

A series of editors since Lewis Theobald (1733) has been convinced that Shakespeare was just one of a number of collaborators on these plays. In his Shakespeare edition of 1790, Edmond Malone denied *1 Henry VI* to the poet on the grounds of its excessive use of classical allusion and its style of versification, and attributed the entirety of the text to Lodge; Greene; and the authors of *Selimus*, *Soliman and Perseda*, *The Spanish Tragedy*, and *Titus Andronicus* (which Malone thought was not by Shakespeare), as Andrew S. Cairncross reports.[3]

Through the next centuries there was a wide spectrum of scholarly opinion on the topic, from a belief that Shakespeare wrote only small sections of the plays, and merely revised others, to a conviction that he should

---

[1] S. Wells and G. Taylor, *William Shakespeare: A Textual Companion* (Oxford: Clarendon Press, 1987), pp. 111–13.

[2] William Shakespeare, *The First Part of King Henry VI*, ed. Michael Hattaway, New Cambridge Shakespeare (Cambridge: Cambridge University Press, 1990), pp. 42–3.

[3] William Shakespeare, *The First Part of King Henry VI*, ed. Andrew S. Cairncross, Arden Shakespeare (London: Methuen, 1962), p. xxix.

be regarded as responsible for the plays in their entirety. The grounds for doubts about Shakespeare's authorship included a perceived unevenness in quality and internal inconsistencies in the plots, as well as the classical allusions and verse styles Malone referred to. In the 1920s, however, Peter Alexander argued strongly that the plays were all Shakespeare's.[4] He also argued that *The First Part of the Contention* and *The True Tragedy* were not separate, non-Shakespearean plays, sources for the Folio plays, but alternate versions of them, probably memorial reconstructions by actors. A book by Madeleine Doran had independently argued this latter point.[5] These views were influential. John Dover Wilson's New Cambridge editions of the three plays (all 1952), however, went against the consensus in proposing detailed divisions of the plays among collaborators, and promoted the idea that in these plays Shakespeare was revising work originally written by others.[6] Cairncross's 1962 Arden edition of *1 Henry VI*, on the other hand, declared that the theory of collaboration that had prevailed in his predecessor H. C. Hart's Arden edition of 1909 was 'no longer in keeping with the progress of Shakespearean criticism'. Cairncross devoted his edition to 'examining the text as a text, and the play as a play by William Shakespeare' rather than 'conjecturing' the shares of Greene, Nashe, Marlowe, and the rest. He was convinced of the 'integrity' of the play, and (following Sir Edmund Chambers' famous 1924 lecture) rejected the work of the 'disintegrationists' (p. vii). Emrys Jones wrote in *The Origins of Shakespeare* (1977) that some scholars 'still incline to the view that Part One was written by more than one man' (p. 128), but evidently this school no longer predominated. Jones notes 'the peculiar blend of continuity and discontinuity' in the *Henry VI* plays, but attributes this to the local concerns of the dramatist; he does not mention the possibility of collaborative authorship in his discussion at this point (p. 136).[7]

The current state of play is best summed up as a bifurcation. Detailed discussion of the evidence for mixed authorship continues, alongside a prevailing scepticism and even impatience with such studies among editors. The best-developed hypotheses about collaborative authorship involve *1 Henry VI*, the first of the plays in terms of the action, though very likely

[4] P. Alexander, *Shakespeare's* Henry VI *and* Richard III (Cambridge: Cambridge University Press, 1929).

[5] M. Doran, Henry VI, Parts II and III: *Their Relation to the* Contention *and* True Tragedy (Iowa City: University of Iowa, 1928).

[6] William Shakespeare, *The First Part of King Henry VI*, ed. J. Dover Wilson (Cambridge: Cambridge University Press, 1952); *The Second Part of King Henry VI*, ed. J. Dover Wilson (Cambridge: Cambridge University Press, 1952); *The Third Part of King Henry VI*, ed. J. Dover Wilson (Cambridge: Cambridge University Press, 1952).

[7] E. Jones, *The Origins of Shakespeare* (Oxford: Clarendon Press, 1977).

not the first in order of composition. A distribution of the play among four authors, Shakespeare, Thomas Nashe, and two unnamed, was proposed by Gary Taylor in a lengthy paper.[8] A recent contribution by Brian Vickers has supported the attribution of Act I to Nashe, and the idea of a limited contribution by Shakespeare, but suggests that there is only a single collaborator beyond these two.[9] Paul J. Vincent has argued that the Folio version is Shakespeare's revision of an earlier play by Nashe and one other dramatist.[10] In an article in the *Times Literary Supplement* in 2008, Vickers further argues that Thomas Kyd was Nashe's collaborator on the first version of the play, which was later revised by Shakespeare.[11] On *2 Henry VI*, the state of play for those prepared to countenance the idea of collaboration is still much what it was for the *Oxford Textual Companion* in the 1980s, when Gary Taylor and Stanley Wells wrote that 'the problem [of authorship] cannot be solved without a thorough reconsideration of authorship throughout the dramatic output of the 1580s and early 1590s. Until such time the question of the authorship of the bulk of *Contention* should be regarded as open' (p. 112). On *3 Henry VI* the comment is that 'pending further investigation Shakespeare's responsibility for every scene of the play should be regarded as uncertain' (p. 112).

Editors generally reject this idea of a necessarily suspended judgment on authorship, and are sceptical about the prospects of reaching certainty. Roger Warren in his *2 Henry VI* edition (2002) is unwilling to accept that Taylor's study does anything more than establish a 'probability' that *1 Henry VI* is a collaboration, and questions one of the passages Taylor ascribes to Shakespeare, and one he ascribes elsewhere, based on Warren's own 'theatrical experience'.[12] In his edition of *1 Henry VI* (1990) Hattaway argues that it may never be possible to work out a proper ascription for the play 'as it is likely that at an early stage in his career Shakespeare was moving freely between the various verse registers that were being deployed in the plays in which he was probably acting'.[13] Occasionally editors who support the idea of a unitary Shakespeare authorship have neglected to carry their scepticism about evidence for mixed authorship to similar material

---

[8] G. Taylor, 'Shakespeare and Others: The Authorship of *Henry the Sixth, Part One*', *Medieval and Renaissance Drama in England*, 7 (1995), 145–205.

[9] B. Vickers, 'Incomplete Shakespeare; or, Denying Co-Authorship in *1 Henry VI*', *Shakespeare Quarterly*, 58 (2007), 311–52.

[10] P. J. Vincent, 'When Harey Met Shakespeare: The Genesis of *The First Part of Henry the Sixth*', Ph.D. dissertation, University of Auckland, 2005; see the summary on pp. 301–2.

[11] B. Vickers, 'Thomas Kyd, Secret Sharer', *Times Literary Supplement*, 18 April 2008, pp. 13–15.

[12] William Shakespeare, *Henry VI, Part 2*, ed. Roger Warren (Oxford: Oxford University Press, 2002), pp. 68–9.

[13] Shakespeare, *1 Henry VI*, ed. Hattaway, p. 43.

that may give support for Shakespeare attribution. Cairncross challenged the use of 'parallels of vocabulary' to non-Shakespearean authors on the ground that these links are poor evidence given the shared 'dramatic diction' of the age (p. xxxiii). Yet he had recourse to exactly the same sort of evidence when he claimed that *1 Henry VI* 'is full of Shakespeare's characteristic style and imagery' (p. xxxv).

Many current editions of the plays content themselves with summaries of unresolved questions about authorship and collaboration, and then revert to the convenient 'Shakespeare' as the effective point of origin. Contributors to *The Cambridge Companion to Shakespeare's History Plays*, edited by Michael Hattaway (2002), generally ignore the question of any shared authorship, and present Shakespeare as the authorial agency behind all aspects of all three parts of *Henry VI*.[14] Warren, in the Oxford edition of *2 Henry VI*, notes that doubts have been expressed over the centuries about the authorship of the *Henry VI* plays, doubts which arise mainly from a felt inferiority to other parts of the canon. He counters this with the likelihood that Shakespeare's early work was indeed uneven (pp. 67–8). In practice, he treats Shakespeare without qualification as the author, and refers freely to other works in the canon, or quotes those who do, for elucidation of the dramatic qualities of the play (pp. 3, 41, 52). It is common to remark, as Hattaway does in his edition of *1 Henry VI* in the New Cambridge series, that arguments for mixed authorship for these plays are not conclusive enough, and moreover that authorship is essentially irrelevant to readers and audiences in any case (pp. 42–3). We aim to reverse the first of these judgments in the present chapter, and to challenge the second.

Computational stylistics offers an opportunity to look afresh at the question of whether the *Henry VI* plays are collaborative, and, if they are, to whom their various parts should be assigned. We have to acknowledge that there are many difficulties in the way of any definitive division of plays of this period among putative authors. If authors worked together on a scene, the influence of the distinctive style of each, which is our only resource for attribution, is likely to be diluted. Again, if the practice was (as Dover Wilson and Vincent argue) close-worked revision of one author's work by a second, then stylistics is unlikely to be successful. There is, moreover, no ideal solution to the problem of how to divide plays

---

[14] Michael Hattaway, ed., *The Cambridge Companion to Shakespeare's History Plays* (Cambridge: Cambridge University Press, 2002). Phyllis Rackin's essay in the *Companion* on 'Women's Roles in the Elizabethan History Plays' (pp. 71–88), exceptionally, mentions Nashe's possible role in writing *1 Henry VI* (p. 74).

for analysis. The familiar act and scene divisions are generally a modern invention: *2 Henry VI*, for instance, has no acts or scenes in either the early Quarto or the Folio. Particular difficulties with these plays arise from the fact that they come from a period when individual authorship was less established than later. The fact that it was far less common to name an author on a play's title-page in the 1590s than later is a good indication of this.[15] Moreover, it may well be more difficult to detect the distinctiveness of individual styles in history plays of this period than elsewhere because the genre itself was just getting established in the early 1590s, writers were learning rapidly from each other, and strong influences like Kyd's, Marlowe's, and Shakespeare's, were felt everywhere.

Yet the new methods can give us a fresh approach to the problem independent of any one reader's judgment, and they can be tested so as to give a good idea of the degree of error that is built in. Absolute certainty, and a complete distribution of the elements of any one play among their authors, are unattainable at the methods' present stage of development, but we can, we believe, advance the argument on the basis of some solidly established stepping-stones.

We aimed first at a measure of the overall variation in style of the three plays. With this in mind we divided them into arbitrary 2000-word segments. This division means that there is no danger of bias through artfully chosen divisions, which might rely on unsound prior decisions about the likely points where authorship changed. With this method, also, variations in size between segments are kept to a minimum. A 2000-word segment generally provides a long enough sample for reliable attribution, long enough to even out some of the local idiosyncrasies of single short passages. The three plays provide ten, twelve, and eleven such segments respectively. This seems a sensible compromise between dependable attribution (for which the longer the passage the better) and a reasonably fine grain for the testing.

Using arbitrary blocks of text like this means that we often cut across what we might call 'natural' boundaries, like moments when characters '*Exeunt*' and new ones come on. These are the likeliest points at which one writer might hand over to another, so if the plays are collaborative, the 2000-word segments will probably contain some writing by more than one of the collaborators. We can take into account the possibility of segments of mixed authorship in our analysis, however, and read the results bearing in mind that an evenly divided authorship may lead to indeterminate

---

[15] A. B. Farmer and Z. Lesser, 'Vile Arts: The Marketing of English Printed Drama, 1512–1660', *Research Opportunities in Renaissance Drama*, 39 (2000), 77–165.

classifications of a segment, while a small admixture of a second author's writing will make an equally small difference in the scores for the segment concerned.

In general, using a simple measure of length in words for the blocks seems the right way to start a study like this, where there is no reliable external evidence on which to establish a segmentation that will match what actually happened in the writing process. In later phases of the process, when a pattern has been established, we move on to experimenting with segments bounded by scene divisions, to test emerging hypotheses about a division between authors.

We chose to examine how much the segments departed from Shakespeare norms, since the external evidence points to him, if anyone, as the author. Modest variation from these norms would fit the idea that Shakespeare in fact was the sole author, or responsible for most of the plays. If there were many segments remote from Shakespeare's usual style, on the other hand, we might suspect collaboration.

We used the 27 plays making up the core Shakespeare canon, and the 109 single-author, well-attributed non-Shakespeare plays from our corpus as control sets. We used one measure of 'Shakespeareanness' from a principal components analysis (PCA) using function words, and another from a test using lexical words.[16] The first question is whether any variation in style in these plays is unusual, suggesting mixed authorship, or is in fact much as one would expect from early Shakespeare plays. To establish a baseline we plotted the segments from a group of known Shakespeare plays on the two measures of likeness to Shakespeare. For this purpose we chose the three early history plays accepted as Shakespeare's, *Richard III*, *Richard II*, and *King John*; and three early comedies, *The Two Gentlemen of Verona*, *The Comedy of Errors*, and *Love's Labour's Lost*.[17] The results are

---

[16] The PCA measure combines information from three principal components (the three from the first ten with the highest correlation with a Shakespeare–non-Shakespeare dummy variable), using the word-variables identified by a *t*-test as having a probability less than 0.0005 that the two groups of observations are from the same parent population. The lexical-words test combines two scores, one based on a set of words that appear more regularly in Shakespeare and a second based on words that appear more regularly in the plays of his contemporaries. The known Shakespeare and known non-Shakespeare plays were divided into 2000-word segments. For each test we identified a Shakespeare centroid – a point whose coordinates are the average of values for the Shakespeare segments for each of the composite variables used – and a non-Shakespeare centroid, defined in the same way. For each test segment we found the difference between its distance from the non-Shakespeare centroid and its distance from the Shakespeare one. This difference we regarded as the 'Shakespeareanness' of the segment.

[17] To make sure they were being treated exactly like the *Henry VI* segments, we withdrew all the segments of each play in turn from the process of finding Shakespeare markers among the function and lexical words.

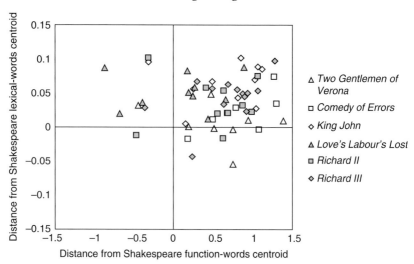

Figure 3.1 Distances from Shakespeare centroids on function words and on lexical words for 2000-word segments of 6 Shakespeare plays. The procedures are as in Table 3.1, except that for each test the test play is withdrawn from the Shakespeare set.

in Figure 3.1. Segments with high, or Shakespeare-like, scores on the PCA function-word measure are to the right, and those with high scores on the lexical-words measure are towards the top of the graph. Segments that are high on both measures are in the upper-right quadrant. Here the two tests are in accord that the segment is closer to a Shakespeare pattern than to a non-Shakespearean one. Forty-three of the fifty-eight segments, around three-quarters of them, are in this quadrant. A segment that is low on both tests will appear in the lower-left quadrant. There is just one of these, the sixth segment of *Richard II*. The graph gives us a summary of the variation in canonical early Shakespeare: mostly, the segments conform to the general Shakespeare pattern; occasionally, a segment does not, to the extent that it is classified as non-Shakespearean by both the function-words and the lexical-words tests. Looked at another way, the graph offers an estimate of how well the tests perform in overcoming the variation in the segments to classify them nevertheless as Shakespeare's. Each segment is treated exactly as if it was a disputed text of unknown authorship: neither it, nor any of its fellows from the same play, has any part in selecting the word-variables used to classify it. Regarded separately, each test assigns fifty-one out of the fifty-eight segments correctly (i.e., there are seven segments below the horizontal axis, and seven to the left of the vertical axis). The correct assignations are different for the two methods, however. All the *Comedy of Errors* segments are to the right, correctly assigned by the function-words procedure, while two of them are below the *x*-axis, i.e. misclassified by the lexical-words test. All the *Love's Labour's Lost* segments are above the line, on the other hand, correctly classified by the lexical-words method, while three of them are to the left, misclassified by the function-words test. Clearly, the methods are more reliable used together than separately: the solitary grey square in the lower-left quadrant tells us that we can expect the combined methods to classify a known Shakespeare segment as 'not by Shakespeare' about once in fifty-eight trials. Figure 3.1 suggests that, when a play is entirely by Shakespeare, we can expect its segments to fall mostly in the top-right quadrant, occasionally in the lower-right or upper-left quadrant, and only rarely in the lower-left quadrant of a combined test like this.

Figure 3.1 is also one answer to the question of how distinguishable or otherwise is one author's style in a field like Shakespearean drama, and whether authorial individuality in language is an objective fact, or a comfortable shared delusion. We establish a fixed point of reference for this style for each method – a centroid – and then test how far from this point portions of the author's texts fall when they are treated as if they were anonymous. The text portions do scatter, but not so far that any but the odd case comes to resemble the work of the generality of the author's peers, especially when two tests are used together. Almost always there are enough shared elements in Shakespeare's language to overcome the centrifugal pressures of local likeness to other writers in character, situation, turns of phrase, genre, and so on.

We can now examine results for each of the *Henry VI* plays one by one. Figure 3.2 plots the results for *1 Henry VI* segments on the same axes as those of Figure 3.1. Only two of the ten *1 Henry VI* segments are assessed by both methods as closer to the Shakespeare pattern than to the non-Shakespearean one, and appear in the upper-right quadrant. Three are in the lower left, warranted by both methods as non-Shakespearean. In general, the segments are more dispersed across the Shakespeare versus non-Shakespeare divides than any of the early canonical plays we tested, as a comparison with Figure 3.1 will show. (The scales are the same in both graphs.) The most obvious conclusion is that *1 Henry VI* is mixed in authorship: part by Shakespeare, part by another author or by other authors. To put this another way, if *1 Henry VI* is all by Shakespeare, then in it his writing departs much more from his underlying regular patterns of style, and of vocabulary, than he does in other plays he wrote about the same time.

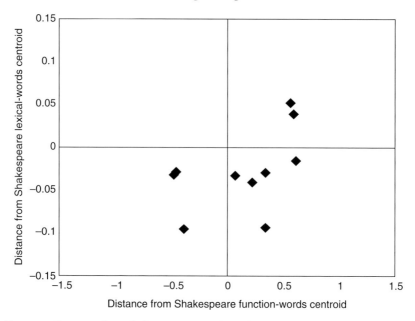

Figure 3.2 Distances from Shakespeare centroids on function words and on lexical words for 2000-word segments of *1 Henry VI*.

Figure 3.3 shows the results for *2 Henry VI*. The *2 Henry VI* segments, like the *1 Henry VI* ones, are generally placed lower and further to the left compared to the known Shakespeare ones. There are more in the upper-right quadrant than for *1 Henry VI*, three as against two (the fourth circle, appearing on the horizontal axis, has a lexical-words score just below zero), but there are again three segments in the lower-left quadrant (the diamond on the vertical axis has a score just above zero). Again, this is a quite different pattern from the canonical plays tested in Figure 3.1, a pattern that suggests mixed authorship.

The *3 Henry VI* segments, on the other hand, are less widely scattered (Figure 3.4). There is only one *3 Henry VI* segment in the doubly non-Shakespeare quadrant. Six of the eleven segments are closer to Shakespeare on both tests and appear in the upper-right quadrant. This is a more dispersed pattern than the most dispersed of the canonical plays in this experiment, *Richard II*, which has seven of its ten segments classified as Shakespeare on both tests, and one of its ten classified as doubly non-Shakespeare, but the results are not so different that one would say that the play is clearly collaborative by these measures.

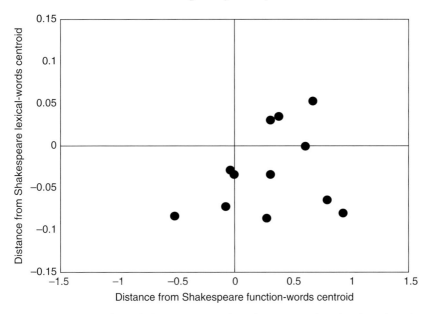

Figure 3.3 Distances from Shakespeare centroids on function words and on lexical words for 2000-word segments of *2 Henry VI*.

This attempt to find an overall measure of variation from Shakespeare norms has something in common with the methods used by Ward E. Y. Elliott and Robert J. Valenza. They have carried out an extended study of the Shakespeare canon in relation to the hypothesis that the real author of these works is the Earl of Oxford. They work with multiple numerical tests designed to fail texts that fall outside consistent Shakespeare ranges. They have two summary measures, one the number of tests failed, and the other a single composite distance from Shakespeare norms. Their conclusion is that while all three parts of *Henry VI* fall outside the limits established by a core set of his works, *2 Henry VI* is in a group of plays that are 'only slightly outside Shakespeare's composite boundaries' and that 'could well be by him alone or almost alone'.[18] Elliott and Valenza only treat the three plays as wholes, however, and they advise that their methods 'work better on poems than plays' and 'much better on single-authored than on co-authored texts' (p. 358).

---

[18] W. E. Y. Elliott and R. J. Valenza, 'Oxford by the Numbers: What Are the Odds that the Earl of Oxford Could Have Written Shakespeare's Plays?', *Tennessee Law Review*, 72.1 (2004), 323–453 (p. 398).

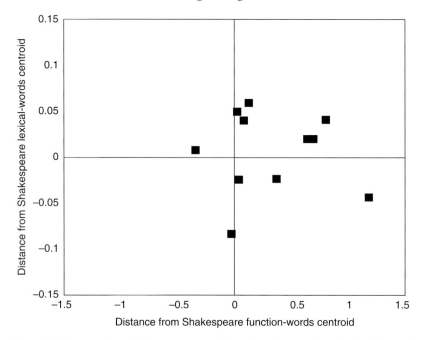

Figure 3.4 Distances from Shakespeare centroids on function words and on lexical words for 2000-word segments of *3 Henry VI*.

Figures 3.1 to 3.4 give a consolidated result from two separate tests, working on large background sets, close to 300 segments of Shakespeare, and over 1000 by other dramatists. The variation of the regular Shakespeare plays, their departure from Shakespeare norms, is within limits, while some *1* and *2 Henry VI* segments stray outside these. The most obvious explanation is that this is the result of mixed authorship. Only one *3 Henry VI* segment is judged to be non-Shakespearean by both methods; on the other hand, six of the eleven score close to the Shakespeare centroid on both tests. In all, these segments are not so decisively different from the regular Shakespeare pattern that we see in Figure 3.1. They do not invite further investigation in the same way, and we have not pursued the question of the authorship of this play any further.

The first two parts of *Henry VI* are decidedly mixed in their pattern, with parts less attached to Shakespeare than are the parts of plays we believe are entirely by Shakespeare. This is consistent with Shakespeare's playing a role in their creation, but only as part of a shared enterprise. The

Table 3.1. *Distances of 2000-word segments of* 1 Henry VI *from Shakespeare centroids.*

Segment	First and last lines	Closeness to Shakespeare on function words	Closeness to Shakespeare on lexical words
1	I.i.1–I.ii.79	−0.45	−0.03
2	I.ii.80–I.iv.89	0.34	−0.09
3	I.iv.89–II.iii.24	−0.48	−0.03
4	II.iii.24–II.v.66	0.61	−0.02
5	II.v.66–III.ii.2	0.34	−0.03
6	III.ii.2–III.iv.33	0.23	−0.04
7	III.iv.33–IV.ii.56	0.59	0.04
8	IV.ii.56–IV.vii.40	0.56	0.05
9	IV.vii.40–I.iii.140	0.07	−0.03
10	I.iii.140–end	−0.38	−0.10

Both centroids are based on a comparison between 2000-word segments from 27 Shakespeare plays and 2000-word segments from 109 plays by others. The function-word centroid is from a PCA using 69 Shakespeare marker words identified by a *t*-test. The distance is the Euclidean distance from the centroid in 3 dimensions, using the first 3 principal components. The lexical-words centroid is from scores for 500 Shakespeare marker words and 500 non-Shakespeare marker words identified by an index of comparative regularity of occurrence in the two sets.

indication from the graphs is that Shakespeare is indeed involved in the authorship of these plays, but as part of a collaborative effort.

Table 3.1 shows the scores for individual segments of *1 Henry VI* on the 'Shakespeareanness' measures used in Figure 3.2: i.e. the values that we used to plot the segments. It also identifies the first and last line of each segment according to the divisions and lineation of the *Riverside Shakespeare* (second edition). Segment 8 is highest on the lexical-words measure (it is the top diamond in Figure 3.2) and is one of the three highest on the function-words test. It is thus judged securely Shakespearean by the method. It covers almost all of the action involving Lord Talbot and his son and their deaths in the siege of Bordeaux, which runs from the beginning of IV.ii to the death of Talbot after IV.vii.32. Edmond Malone, writing in the eighteenth century, thought that these scenes were probably the only part of the play written by Shakespeare, judging from the fact that they were in rhyme, and were 'somewhat of a different complexion from the rest of the play'.[19] Dover Wilson and Taylor on quite independent grounds attribute

[19] E. Malone, *A Dissertation on the Three Parts of King Henry VI: Tending to Shew That Those Three Plays Were Not Written Originally by Shakespeare* (London, 1787), p. 46.

them to Shakespeare. Cairncross says these scenes 'express a deeper emotion than the rest and produce memorable touches' (p. lv).

These scenes were celebrated soon after they were first performed. In *Pierce Penilesse His Supplication to the Divell*, entered in the Stationers' Register on 8 August 1592, Thomas Nashe records a strong audience reaction to this section of the play:

> How would it haue ioyed braue *Talbot* (the terror of the French) to thinke that after he had lyne two hundred yeares in his Tombe, he should triumphe againe on the Stage, and haue his bones newe embalmed with the tears of ten thousand spectators at least (at seuerall times), who, in the Tragedian that represents his person, imagine they behold him fresh bleeding.[20]

Segment 7, the second-highest diamond in Figure 3.2, is also Shakespearean according to both these tests. It covers the latter part of the short III.iv, the whole of IV.i, and the first part of IV.ii. These are scenes in which Talbot figures prominently, as do the red and white roses of the houses of Lancaster and York. The highest score on the function-words test is actually Segment 4, with a lexical-words score just below zero. It includes the whole of II.iv (as well as the last part of II.iii, and the first part of II.v). Most readers of the play have been struck with the distinctness and quality of II.iv, set in the garden of Temple Hall, where Richard Plantagenet and the Duke of Somerset pick a white and a red rose as emblems of their factions, and are followed by their supporters (the Earl of Warwick, Vernon, and a lawyer pick white roses, and the Earl of Suffolk a red one). The dialogue is taut, there are speeches bristling with menace, and the symbolism of the roses is clear-cut and memorable. There has been near-universal agreement on stylistic grounds that this scene was written by Shakespeare.

Cairncross mentions II.iv and the Talbot battle scenes, along with II.v, the death of Mortimer, and V.iii.45–195 – Suffolk's wooing of Margaret – as generally claimed for Shakespeare by those who see the play as collaborative (p. xxix). This coincidence between scenes included in segments identified as closest to Shakespeare in style and the views of commentators suggests that we should move directly to testing the larger divisions proposed by Taylor. He divides the play into Act I (Thomas Nashe); Acts III and V (a second dramatist, 'Y'); Act II, barring II.iv, and IV.i (a third dramatist, 'W'); and the II.iv and IV.ii–IV.vii.32 already discussed (attributed to Shakespeare; pp. 162, 168). This omits only the latter part of IV.vii, from IV.vii.33 to the end of the scene. We can test the four composite

---

[20] Cited in Taylor, 'Shakespeare and Others', p. 151. Nashe does not mention *1 Henry VI* by name, but, as Taylor points out, this play is the only one we know of depicting the death of Talbot (p. 151).

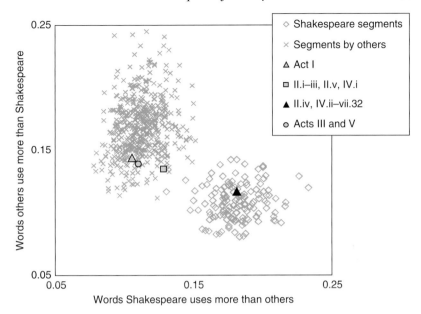

Figure 3.5 Lexical-words test: Shakespeare versus non-Shakespeare 4000-word segments, with four portions of *1 Henry VI.*

sections of the play in a test based on the lexical words that separate 4000-word Shakespeare segments from non-Shakespeare play ones of the same size, as in Figures 2.1 and 2.2 in the previous chapter. Figure 3.5 shows the results. The procedure places the parts of the play Taylor assigned to Shakespeare – the Temple Garden and Talbot scenes – close to the centroid of the Shakespeare cluster. The other three divisions are with the non-Shakespeare cluster. This gives no certainty about the exact boundaries of the scenes we should ascribe to Shakespeare, but broadly Taylor's hypothesis about the ascription to Shakespeare is confirmed. There seems little doubt that Shakespeare had a hand in the play, and little doubt that others were involved also. Act I of the play is the furthest from the Shakespeare cluster and would seem to be definitely non-Shakespearean.

John Dover Wilson made the case for Nashe's part in *1 Henry VI* in his introduction to the Cambridge edition of 1952 (pp. xxi–xxxi). Dover Wilson adduced parallels in sources and wording between the play and Nashe's works, as well as matches in the form of stage directions, and attributed the whole of Act I to him. Taylor has added a number of 'linguistic preferences', such as a liking for the '-eth' verb ending, to the evidence for Nashe's authorship of Act I (pp. 176–7).

If Nashe did write Act I of the play, he wrote no other history play or part of a history play that we know of. His only known dramatic production is *Summer's Last Will and Testament*, which the *Annals of English Drama* classifies as a comedy; it is a masque-like series of appearances by allegorical figures representing aspects of the seasons. What Nashe did produce in quantity were satirical, topical, and allusive prose works. Thus where Shakespeare has a large corpus of plays, including histories, to provide an indication of what his style might have been like in writing for a play such as *1 Henry VI*, for Nashe we can only extrapolate from essentially non-dramatic works. We prepared three prose works, the *Pierce Penilesse* already quoted, *Strange News, Of the Intercepting Certaine Letters* (1592), and *The Unfortunate Traveller* (1594) for the purpose, together a little over 100 000 words, and divided them into 4000-word segments. We did the same for the 49 well-attributed single-author plays in our corpus dated by the *Annals of English Drama* before 1600. We reserved *Summer's Last Will and Testament* as a test piece. As usual, we found 500 markers of one of the text sets (the Nashe prose works) as against the other set (the plays by other writers before 1600) and 500 markers of the plays by others as against the Nashe prose texts. We then counted how many of the markers appeared in each sample in the analysis and divided the result by the total number of different words in each sample. On this basis, how well do the prose works serve to identify a Nashe style in his solitary play? Figure 3.6 shows the results. To establish a boundary between the 'Nashe' and 'not Nashe' areas of the graph we found the centroid of each cluster, the point representing the average of the cluster's values on each dimension, and then plotted the perpendicular bisector of the line between the two centroids. In the graph we show just the bisector line, the dashed diagonal line. Any datapoint that falls on this line would have scored zero in the analyses in Figures 3.1 to 3.4: i.e. is exactly equidistant from the two centroids. Two of the four segments of *Summer's Last Will and Testament* are classified as by Nashe (the asterisk markers overlapping each other), two not. Clearly the scores for the parts of this play on Nashe and non-Nashe words draw them toward the Nashe cluster, but not decisively so. Compared to the non-Nashe segments, they score at the higher end on Nashe words, and to the lower end on non-Nashe words; but these scores are lower, and higher, than any Nashe prose segment. Act I of *1 Henry VI*, which appears in the graph as a black triangle, is classified with the plays by others rather than with Nashe prose, and is further from the bisector line than any of the *Summer's Last Will and Testament* segments. On the other hand, it is closer to the Nashe cluster than any of the other Taylor divisions, and it might be

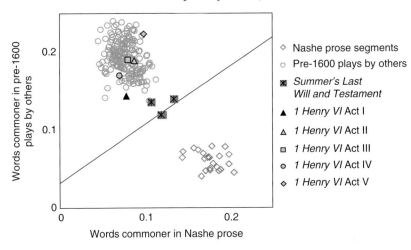

Figure 3.6 Lexical-words test: 2000-word Nashe prose segments versus 2000-word segments of pre-1600 plays by others, with 2000-word segments of *Summer's Last Will and Testament* and acts of *1 Henry VI*.

possible to see a trace of Nashe influence in its placement in the lower part of the non-Nashe cluster. There is nothing unusual about its count of the words that characterize the Nashe prose works as against the early drama, but it does have relatively few of the words that are scarcer in the Nashe prose works.

The placement of the Nashe play segments suggests that the need to rely on prose segments for a Nashe signature creates difficulties in classifying drama by his hand. We can reduce the strain on the method a little by comparing the Nashe prose segments with play segments from just one author. Figure 3.7 is a Zeta test of the three Nashe prose works against Shakespeare plays from before 1600. As before, we can test the discriminating power of the procedure by including the segments of *Summer's Last Will and Testament* as if they were of unknown authorship. Act I of *1 Henry VI* is on the Shakespeare side of the bisector line, but closer to it than any other Shakespeare segment or any of the other acts of *1 Henry VI*. The four *Summer's Last Will and Testament* segments are now on the Nashe side of the bisector. It would not be possible from this to rule out Nashe as author of Act I, but it does not confirm him as the author either. The division by acts shows that there is no other act more likely to be by Nashe. The Nashe hypothesis survives, then. If *1 Henry VI*, Act I is by Nashe, then this assignment led him to draw less on the vocabulary of his

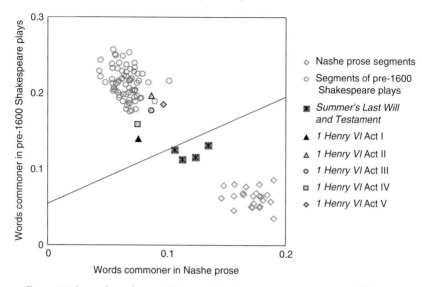

Figure 3.7 Lexical-words test: 2000-word Nashe prose segments versus 2000-word segments of pre-1600 Shakespeare plays, with 2000-word segments of *Summer's Last Will and Testament* and acts of *1 Henry VI.*

prose works than he does in *Summer's Last Will and Testament.* In fact, Act I of the history play is quite low on the words that Nashe uses in the prose works, but that Shakespeare doesn't use in his pre-1600 plays: lower than many segments of Shakespeare plays. Where it most resembles Nashe is in its low score on the words that Shakespeare uses more than Nashe.

The most recent contribution on the authorship of *1 Henry VI* is the 2008 article by Vickers already mentioned. He presents numerous close parallels in phrasing between the play and Kyd's works, drawing for this purpose not only on *The Spanish Tragedy* and *Cornelia* (Kyd's translation of Robert Garnier's *Cornélie*) but also on *Soliman and Perseda*, which many authorities have accepted as Kyd's. He also presents new evidence connecting Kyd with *Arden of Faversham* and *King Leir*, reviving some older authorship proposals. (The authorship of *Arden of Faversham* is the subject of Chapter 4, below.)

In our tests we have found no affinities between Kyd and *1 Henry VI.* Figure 3.8 shows a lexical-words test contrasting Kyd (represented by *The Spanish Tragedy* and *Cornelia*) with the 134 plays in our corpus by other authors. The segments of *1 Henry VI* are placed in the non-Kyd cluster. They are clearly differentiated from Kyd in both dimensions. On the words

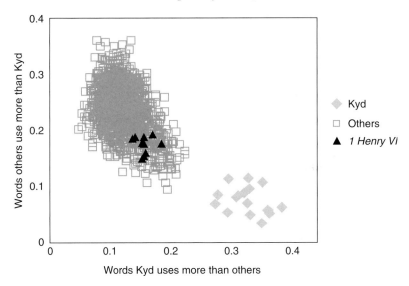

Figure 3.8 Lexical-words test: 2000-word segments from 2 Kyd plays versus 2000-word segments from 134 plays by others, with 2000-word segments from *1 Henry VI*.

that generally appear more often in the Kyd segments the *1 Henry VI* segments all score lower than any canonical Kyd segment (looking along the *x*-axis). They all score higher than any Kyd segment on the words Kyd uses less often than his contemporaries (referring to the *y*-axis).

Admittedly, Kyd's canon does present difficulties for our methods. There are just two Kyd plays where authorship is unquestioned, and one is a translation and a closet play. The situation is better than with Nashe, but not much. The methods we use in this book are most reliable where there is a sizeable group of plays that can be confidently attributed to a given candidate author. Kyd's two unquestioned plays are really too few for trustworthy results, certainly when compared to a very large assortment of plays by various other authors. We have twenty-seven Shakespeare plays of mixed genre in the 'core' Shakespeare set, and on that basis it is reasonable to presume that any characteristics that are broadly true for this group are authorial. Even if we have four plays, as with Greene, we are moving beyond accidental and local characteristics to something more general. With only two plays in a canon we can only say that we have found characteristics shared between those particular plays.

To meet some of these difficulties we also carried out tests with a Kyd set expanded for the occasion to include *Soliman and Perseda*, to broaden the basis for a Kyd authorial signature (at the cost, of course, of relying on a less well-authenticated canon). We also reduced the comparison set, excluding plays dated by the *Annals of English Drama* at 1600 or later, to make the two rival groups less lopsided.[21] This gave us three more tests, the two-play Kyd set compared to the smaller comparison set, and the three-play Kyd set compared to the full comparison set and the reduced one. In all three of these new tests the *1 Henry VI* segments remained firmly with the non-Kyd cluster.

In Chapter 2 we presented classifications that placed test scenes with their known authors, or at least in line with what is now received opinion. In the case of Kyd and *1 Henry VI* our results present a direct contradiction of an authorship hypothesis coming from a respected scholar and supported by a carefully established case. To explain how this might have come about we need to contrast the methods used on the two sides.

The primary approach in our book begins with an authorial pattern established from texts of known provenance. We select function-word markers and lexical-word markers by contrasting sets of work of known authorship, whether it be one author against another or one author against many. We then measure how closely the disputed text follows these patterns of use. The method Vickers presents in his article, and which he sometimes relies on in his other authorship work, as in linking *A Lover's Complaint* to John Davies of Hereford,[22] is quite different. The scholar seeks phrases and combinations of words that are shared by the disputed text and the text or texts of a given author, but are very rare elsewhere. On this latter question, digital archives can offer decisive confirmation. The researcher can establish rarity beyond question by demonstrating, for example, that a given phrase does not appear in any of a fixed set of 50 or 500 comparable texts. The method proceeds on the assumption that if there are enough of these phrases and combinations, and they are of sufficient quality as parallels – strikingly similar in the way in which they are used in their texts, for instance – then shared authorship is the only credible explanation. One of the advantages of this method is that the parallels can be presented to readers, who can then judge for themselves. Is it really believable that such complicated and distinctive phrases and word combinations can have come about

---

[21] The numbers of plays and segments in the various sets are as follows: original Kyd set, 2 plays, 17 segments; expanded Kyd set, 3 plays, 25 segments; pre-1600 non-Kyd set, 48 plays, 416 segments; full non-Kyd set, 134 plays, 1281 segments.

[22] B. Vickers, *Shakespeare, 'A Lover's Complaint', and John Davies of Hereford* (Cambridge: Cambridge University Press, 2007), pp. 204–66.

merely through imitation, or similar subject matter, or through shared language habits?

This is an argument from rarity, rather than (as with the function-word and lexical-word tests in the present study) from patterns in commonness. Vickers' method starts with the language of the disputed text and then moves to the language of the putative author (or, in some of the published versions, to the language of various candidate authors). In Vickers' article it is also an absolute argument, rather than a relative one. It is possible to collect parallel phrases from test texts of known provenance, as for example MacDonald Jackson and Vincent have done,[23] and then to assess whether the patterns in the particular case are indeed exceptional, but Vickers does not do this in his Kyd article. We are presented simply with a collection of parallels with Kyd.

The parallel-passages method is attractive for literary scholars, since it pays attention to actual passages, rather than to wider patterns, and since, as already mentioned, it allows readers to make their own assessment of the evidence. Intuitively it is plausible: of course writers will have characteristic turns of phrase, word pairings or extended phrases that are highly peculiar to themselves. In many cases, one must concede, it will give a true result. The disputed text may indeed be by the author with whose canon it shares a large number of striking phrases. We believe, however, that it is a method that may also produce some false classifications. Used with no comparative data, it may be seriously deceiving. Who can tell if a similar list of rare shared phrases could be assembled with a different author? On the negative side, how often would a text we know is by a given author fail to yield a satisfactory list of parallels with that author's other work? The method relies on what Vickers calls 'the accumulated evidence of highly individual usages in thought and words occurring too often for coincidence'[24]; this can be restated, in Elliott and Valenza's words, as 'Christmas trees full of unique quirks equals proof.'[25]

As it happens, Thomas Merriam has already applied a parallel-passages technique to the authorship of *1 Henry VI*, but he was seeking links with Marlowe rather than Kyd.[26] He examined V.iii.1–44, in which Joan de

---

[23] See for example M. P. Jackson, 'Determining Authorship: A New Technique', *Research Opportunities in Renaissance Drama*, 41 (2002), 1–14, and Vincent, 'When Harey Met Shakespeare', pp. 303–24.

[24] Vickers, *Shakespeare*, p. 205.   [25] Elliott and Valenza, 'Oxford by the Numbers', p. 339.

[26] T. Merriam, 'Faustian Joan', *Notes and Queries*, 245 (2002), 218–20. I am grateful to Dr Ruth Lunney for directing my attention to this article. Jackson presents a long list of the triple-word matches he has found between *Arden of Faversham* and *2 Henry VI*, showing (among other things) that there is nothing necessarily unusual about the matches Vickers found between Kyd plays and *Arden*, *1 Henry VI*, *King Leir* and so on ('New Research on the Dramatic Canon of Thomas Kyd',

Pucelle summons up devils, pleads unsuccessfully for their help, and is captured by the Duke of York on the battlefield. Merriam found that this passage shares many unusual phrases with the Marlowe canon. The longest is 'aid me in this enterprise' (*1 Henry VI*, V.iii.7), which appears verbatim in *Doctor Faustus* (line 1334),[27] but nowhere else in the drama of the period, according to Merriam's researches in the Chadwyck-Healey *Literature Online* website.[28] Another of Merriam's examples is 'regions under earth' (*1 Henry VI*, V.iii.11). In *2 Tamburlaine* we find the words 'the region under earth' (IV.iii.32); Merriam reports that there is no parallel phrase in Shakespeare or in any other play of the period collected in *Literature Online*. Joan fears that France will be forced to 'vail her lofty-plumed crest' (*1 Henry VI*, V.iii.25). In *Doctor Faustus*, as Merriam points out, Marlowe writes 'my plumed crest' (line 1778), and in *1 Tamburlaine* 'loftie Crestes' (I.i.145). Merriam's interest at this point is in Shakespeare, and he points out that there are no phrases combining *lofty* or *plumed* with *crest* or *crests* in Shakespeare plays outside *1 Henry VI*. Elsewhere he finds just one parallel, the 'plumed crest' of the anonymous *Selimus* (p. 218). We can confirm that there are no instances in our set of 130 non-Marlowe plays either.

There are more of these to be found if we search *1 Henry VI* beyond Merriam's chosen passage. '[W]e will make thee famous through the world', says the Bastard to Joan in the play (III.iii.13); Tamburlaine says to Bajazeth 'Thy fall shall make me famous through the world' (*1 Tamburlaine*, III.iii.84). *Famous* does not appear within five words of *world* anywhere else in the 130 plays in our set by authors other than Marlowe. As far as we can tell this is a phrasing peculiar to Marlowe and to *1 Henry VI*. In the latter play, Gloucester tells the Bishop (later Cardinal) of Winchester that the King is not 'exempt / From envious malice of thy swelling heart' (III.i.25–6). Not surprisingly, it is rare for writers to associate *envious*, *malice*, and *heart*; they do not appear together anywhere in our set of 130 plays by any playwright other than Marlowe. In *The Massacre at Paris*, however, Marlowe writes 'To stop the malice of his envious heart' (I.i.30). The phrase 'monstrous treachery' appears in *1 Henry VI* (IV.i.61) and in *Edward II* (V.vi.97) and nowhere else in our reference set of plays. There is of course no obvious place to draw the line in such matters. There

Research Opportunities in Medieval and Renaissance Drama, 47 (2008), 107–27). I am most grateful to Professor Jackson for allowing me to see this article before it was published.
[27] References to Marlowe here and below are from Christopher Marlowe, *The Complete Works*, ed. F. Bowers, 2 vols. (Cambridge: Cambridge University Press, 1973).
[28] *Literature Online*, http://lion.chadwyck.co.uk (Cambridge: Chadwyck-Healey, 1996–).

are some parallels (like the pairing 'scarlet robes', occurring in *1 Henry VI* at I.iii.42 and in *1 Tamburlaine* at V.i.524, and not appearing any-where in the set of 130) that fulfil the same conditions of rarity but do not speak of common authorship, despite the brute fact of the silence of the comparison set.

It may be, indeed, that we do not yet know enough about the under-lying regularities of phrasemaking in language to provide a proper context for instances of very rare phrases. Are there perhaps more of these than we have allowed for? Is it perhaps not so unexpected to come across pair-ings or triplets of words that are in two texts but not in a very large set of others? If there are more of these pairings and triplets available than we thought, i.e. a much larger total number, then it becomes more likely that parallel but rare passages will occur in any two texts even if by different authors.

The instances collected above may or may not offer evidence for Marlowe's hand in *1 Henry VI*. They do cast doubt on the force of the par-allel passages Vickers presents in his article, however. Certainly it would seem perilous to argue from a set of such parallels alone for authorship. Then if the text may have multiple authors there is another set of com-plications. If a given section has no such parallels, does that argue for a different author? How long should a section go without a significant par-allel before we suspect a second author? Such questions of segmentation bedevil any method, of course, but weigh especially heavily on a method that relies on rarities.

In his article Merriam does not rest with the parallel-passages evi-dence. He concedes that the phrases and lexical words he cites might be reasonably considered as 'echoes' of Marlowe by another writer, and goes on to show that there are also affinities between his chosen passage and Marlowe's plays in the use of a set of the function words. Merriam tests the function-word use of this passage in a PCA and finds it to be charac-teristic of Marlowe's, rather than Shakespeare's, pattern (pp. 218–9). Here Merriam anticipates the methods of the current study.

Merriam's contention, suggested by his title, 'Faustian Joan', is that Marlowe wrote some at least of the passages involving Joan de Pucelle. This is an inviting hypothesis to test. Merriam's chosen passage is too short for the methods we are using here, however. It is not much over 300 words of dialogue in total. Nevertheless, if we make the hypothesis a little more general, and consider all the sections in the play where Joan appears, we can assemble three substantial samples. The sections in I.ii.22–150, I.v, I.vi, and II.i of the play cover the introduction of Joan and her early successes. Together they yield 2214 words. Further on, III.ii.1–114, III. iii, and IV.vii deal with her struggle with Talbot's forces, and yield 2350 words. Joan's appearances in Act V, namely, V.ii, V.iii.1–44 (the passage Merriam tests), and V.iv, yield 1803 words in all.

Merriam, in his PCA, sets up a contrast between Shakespeare and Marlowe to test *1 Henry VI*, V.iii.1–44. This is important, given that there are many who regard Shakespeare as the sole author of the play, but for those already convinced of the collaboration theory it leaves open the question of whether a third writer would be a still better candidate. The ideal contrast is not between Marlowe and Shakespeare, but between Marlowe and his rival dramatists as a group. With this in mind we carried out a lexical-words test setting the six well-attributed Marlowe plays, *Doctor Faustus*, *Edward II*, *The Jew of Malta*, *The Massacre at Paris*, and *1* and *2 Tamburlaine*, against 130 plays by others from the period (all the single-author, well-attributed plays available in our archive). For this test, in line with experiments already presented, we selected two sets of marker words, one where Marlowe scored higher than his contemporaries, and one where he scored markedly lower. The three sets of passages including Joan de Pucelle were included. Figure 3.9 presents the results. The centroids of the Marlowe and non-Marlowe segment groups are shown as black dots. They are joined by a solid line; the dotted line, serving as a boundary between the areas where we expect a Marlowe segment to appear and those where we expect segments by others to occur, bisects the line between the centroids at right angles. The middle and later Joan sequences are on the Marlowe side of the line and the early sequence on the other side. This corroborates Merriam's hypothesis. Two of the three Joan sequences use words Marlowe favours, and avoid words he also neglects, sufficiently to align them with his 44 segments rather than the 1254 by other writers.

The test relies for one half of its operation on Marlowe marker words, words he uses more than his contemporaries. The full list we employ for the purpose comprises 500 words. The middle group of Joan de Pucelle passages has 104 of these, bringing it well within the Marlowe range and differentiating it sharply from the pattern of work by others, even material of comparable genre like Greene's *James IV*, Peele's *Edward I*, or Shakespeare's *Richard III*.[29] The marker words are arranged in our tables according to the balance between use in Marlowe and use elsewhere, beginning with some that appear (for instance) in close to half of the Marlowe segments,

---

[29] The score we use is the total of marker words that appear, divided by the total of different words used in the segment. The score for the passages with Joan de Pucelle is 0.20; average scores for segments of the other plays mentioned are 0.15, 0.16, and 0.18 respectively.

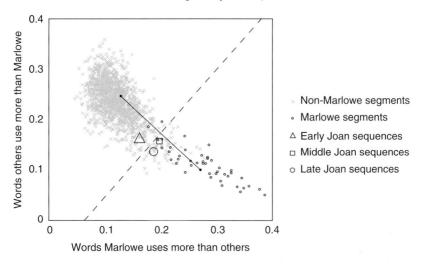

Figure 3.9 Lexical-words test: 2000-word segments by Marlowe versus 2000-word segments by others, with three sequences involving Joan de Pucelle from *1 Henry VI*.

but in only a handful of the non-Marlowe ones, or alternatively in almost all the Marlowe segments but in no more than half of the others. Here, to illustrate, are the words that appear in the middle Joan sequence and that are also in the top fifty of the Marlowe marker words, listed from the most distinctively Marlovian down:

gold arms realm pride slain sword golden overthrow death base damned foe field yield cruel stay conquering hell countries words terror

The function words allow us a way of cross-checking this finding. We can pit Marlowe against a series of other authors and then test the Joan sequences on the same analysis, in the manner of the studies of collaboration presented in Chapter 2. Table 3.2 shows the difference between the distance from the Marlowe centroid and the distance from the centroid of each of five other author clusters for each of the three sequences. The authors beyond Shakespeare are from Taylor's list of possible collaborators in *1 Henry VI*.[30] A positive score shows that the distance between the sequence in question and the non-Marlowe centroid is greater than the distance from the Marlowe centroid. The scores indicate that the first two sequences are closer to Marlowe than to any of the six other authors.

---

[30] Taylor himself rules out Chettle and Lodge from among his list; Yarington, as he says, may be only a scribe ('Shakespeare and Others', p. 173). Munday, Nashe, and Porter have only one play each in our corpus so must be omitted.

Table 3.2. *Measures of closeness to Marlowe of three Joan de Pucelle sequences on function words.*

	First sequence involving Joan: I.ii.22–150, I.v–II.i	Second sequence involving Joan: II.iii.1–114, III.iii, IV.vii	Third sequence involving Joan: V.ii–V.iii.44, V.iv
Greene	1.11	1.17	0.08
Heywood	0.11	1.61	0.64
Kyd	0.60	1.02	1.19
Peele	1.16	0.41	−0.34
Shakespeare	0.18	0.48	0.51
Wilson	1.12	1.72	0.78

Six PCAs were run, using word-variables with a *t*-test probability of <0.05 that the two authorial groups were from the same parent populations. The difference between the distance to the centroid for another author and the distance to the Marlowe centroid is shown. A positive score indicates the sequence is closer to the Marlowe centroid. The first two principal components were used.

The third is closer to Marlowe than to all but Peele. There is, therefore, a strong case on our measures for seeing Marlowe as the author of one part at least of the play. (We were not able to find any strong evidence elsewhere for Peele's participation in *1 Henry VI*.) Marlowe has been proposed before as part-author of the play, by Allison Gaw, but his evidence depended on the belief that *The First Part of the Contention* and *The True Tragedy of Richard Duke of York* were separate plays, both by Marlowe (Gaw here followed C. F. Tucker Brooke).[31] More positively, Taylor says that there are only three plays of the right period that provide parallels with the way the scenes are marked in Act III (into four scenes), and most of the modern Act V (irregularly divided), in the Folio, namely the two parts of *Tamburlaine* and *Locrine*; but he then immediately dismisses Marlowe as a possible author for parts of the play, with the comment that even advocates like Gaw 'could find almost no evidence anywhere' for the attribution (pp. 177–8).

Taylor does not himself present any evidence against the attribution, beyond citing F. G. Hubbard's discussion of patterns of repetition and parallelism in the drama of this period. Taylor reports Hubbard as arguing

---

[31] A. Gaw, *The Origin and Development of* 1 Henry VI: *In Relation to Shakespeare, Marlowe, Peele, and Greene* (Los Angeles: University of Southern California Press, 1926). On Tucker Brooke's theory, see p. 10; pp. 87–92 offer parallels between parts of *1 Henry VI* and the plays Gaw believed to be by Marlowe. Gaw does not ascribe the Joan la Pucelle scenes to Marlowe (see the table on p. 159). Gaw's attributions are discussed in Taylor, 'Shakespeare and Others', p. 178.

that the abundance of these features in *1 Henry VI* rules out Marlowe's authorship, since they are quite uncharacteristic of his known work. In this case Taylor seems to have been misled by the fact that Hubbard includes *1 Henry VI* in a table enumerating various forms of repetition and parallelism in early Shakespeare plays, just after a discussion that notes that *2 Henry VI*, *3 Henry VI*, and *Richard III* exhibit 'Senecan characteristics' of repetition and parallelism that tend to be absent from Marlowe's plays.[32] The table shows that *1 Henry VI* has in fact fewer of these elements than the other three, so Hubbard's rule for excluding Marlowe as author does not apply to it. Taylor (p. 178) cites Hubbard as if he had included *1 Henry VI* as one of those who are unlike Marlowe in this respect. However, it is true that Hubbard does note one instance of an unusual kind of repetition – 'Repetition of a word or words with an added epithet' – in *1 Henry VI*, and indeed within what is in our analysis the sixth segment, at III. iii.50 (p. 363). Hubbard finds a number of other instances in Peele and in *Locrine* (p. 374) but none in Marlowe (p. 376).[33]

Scholars have often noted parallels between *1 Henry VI* and Marlowe's practice and style. Taylor's identification of a similar style of scene division in Acts III and V and the *Tamburlaine* plays has already been mentioned. He also remarks that the way sources are used in *1 Henry VI* is 'surprisingly similar' to Marlowe's methods in *Tamburlaine, Part 2*: 'in both cases, in order to make a play from historical materials already exploited in another play or plays, the author was forced to compound materials from widely separated dates, played havoc with anything resembling historical sequence, and simply invented a good deal' (p. 151). The fact of Marlowe's influence on the play is generally accepted, but this is a different matter from authorship. Indeed, the fact that Marlowe's contemporaries imitated his style in their plays has led to a certain impatience with any suggestion that he may actually have written parts of plays beyond the seven plays that bear his name. Taylor's dismissal of Marlowe as a candidate for *1 Henry VI* has already been mentioned. In his thesis, Vincent deals with Merriam's attribution of a passage from *1 Henry VI* to Marlowe in a footnote, arguing that Merriam's 'elaborate, "non-traditional" attribution technique proves only that all of Marlowe's contemporaries extensively plundered his

---

[32] F. G. Hubbard, 'Repetition and Parallelism in the Earlier Elizabethan Drama', *PMLA*, 20 (1905), 360–79; table and discussion on pp. 376–7.

[33] Overall, looking at Hubbard's tables, *1 Henry VI* does yield more repetitions and parallelisms than an average Marlowe play, but not to any very marked degree: it is higher than the Marlowe average in five of the columns, lower in four, and the same in one (pp. 376, 377). In any case, the overall pattern ceases to have much application if we are only concerned with Marlowe's authorship of a part or parts of the play.

dramatic vocabulary, especially that of the *Tamburlaine* plays, a fact that has long been recognized by "traditional" attribution scholars' (p. 286 n. 33). Vincent here overlooks the fact that Merriam includes function-word tests as well as the lexical-words tests, which rely on the content words that others could 'plunder' from Marlowe. He himself presents an authorship test based on pairs of words shared between a scene of *1 Henry VI* and one of a selected group of authorial canons, and not appearing else-where in the group. Marlowe is one of his authorial canons, so his method is open to the same objections arising from Marlowe's influence which he makes to Merriam. The figures he presents in his appendix indicate that for seven scenes of *1 Henry VI*, Marlowe is the author with the largest number of rare phrases in common, and that for another two scenes he has the equal largest number with one other author (pp. 303–20).

Vincent is emphatic that this does not mean that Marlowe is the author of these scenes (p. 286). Yet making Marlowe an exception in this way does at the very least entail an admission that Vincent's method fails in a con-siderable proportion of the scenes of the play. One might then ask, would it fail in other instances as well? Might not the influence of Shakespeare, or Kyd, also be so strong as to invalidate a test by rare phrases? If the method is unreliable with Marlowe, why do we assume it is reliable elsewhere?

One writer's influence on another takes various forms, from involun-tary contagion to conscious imitation, parody, allusion, plagiarism, and so on. It presents a challenge to any method that works by detecting affinities in style. In the methods presented in this book this challenge is met from the beginning. Let us assume that Peele was influenced by Marlowe in his early plays, and this took the form of using a number of unusual words that were especially associated with Marlowe. In establishing sets of marker words that distinguish the two writers, our method identifies words that appear much more often in Peele than in Marlowe, and much more often in Marlowe than in Peele. A word that Marlowe often uses, but Peele has adopted, will be discarded because Peele's use will mean that in this com-parison it is not a word peculiar enough to Marlowe to be included.

For authorial influence to matter, it would have to be markedly greater in the particular segment being tested than in the segments used to estab-lish the lists. A generally pervasive influence, such as Marlowe's is often alleged to be, should not defeat the method, but a particular local influ-ence (such as the pressures of a collaboration) might. With a very large set like Shakespeare, admittedly, this idea of inoculation against influ-ence has less force. Assuming Marlowe's influence is restricted to one sub-set of Shakespeare's plays, then the adoption of Marlowe words in those plays might not weigh sufficiently against all the other plays that escaped Marlowe's influence.

With function words the workings of influence are harder to hypothesise, but it is still conceivable that a characteristic sentence construction could be transmitted and in turn affect frequencies of function words. Fortunately the experiments described in the latter part of Chapter 2 do address the question directly. In cases where we might most suspect authorial influence, cases where we are confident that there are two writers working together, methods based on function-word use are still able to keep a clear distinction between styles. Here one would think the expectation of influence is stronger than in the case of Marlowe and *1 Henry VI*. There are good reasons to hold that Fletcher might wish to imitate Shakespeare in *Henry VIII* or *The Two Noble Kinsmen*. (Our experiments have in fact shown that Fletcher's lexical word use in *Henry VIII* aligns some of his sections of the play with Shakespeare rather than his own work.) Shakespeare was the senior writer, and there must be some premium on a shared style for a single play or a single character. There is no comparable reason, as far as one can tell, for those working on *1 Henry VI* to imitate Marlowe's style.

We would wish to challenge two views implicit in dismissals of Marlowe's authorship: firstly, that he is somehow impossible as a candidate; and secondly, that his influence on others was so extraordinary as to invalidate stylistic evidence for his authorship, wherever it appears, and however strong it seems to be. There are valid objections to the function-word evidence presented here, such as the possibility that there is an author not present in our archive who might be a yet stronger candidate. But the notion that, on this occasion, and only on this occasion, an author like Shakespeare was so imbued with Marlowe's characteristic vocabulary and syntax that he could pass for Marlowe, is harder to accept.

Let us assume for a moment that Joan la Pucelle, in the middle of the play at least, is indeed the creation of Marlowe. Our perspective on her immediately shifts. Her alliance with fiends and witches, her scoffing rhetoric, her acting under disguise, are then those of a Marlovian villain. Her origins and ambitions come into focus: she is the daughter of a shepherd, aspiring to wield exceptional power based not on inheritance but on native wit and daring. If Marlowe also wrote the earlier scenes in which she appeared, what critics have called her 'Marlovian rhetoric'[34] there is indeed just that. If Marlowe wrote the later scenes in which she is involved,

---

[34] Shakespeare, *1 Henry VI*, ed. Hattaway, p. 24.

her abrupt descent into witchcraft and fornication would find parallels in
Doctor Faustus in particular.[35]

Computational stylistics can help clear a little of the uncertainty with
1 Henry VI, then. The play is a collaboration. Shakespeare wrote the
Temple Garden scene and the scenes depicting Talbot's last battle, but
no other substantial portion. It seems very likely that Marlowe wrote the
middle part of the strand of the play involving Joan of Arc. These two
playwrights may have written more than these named sections; other playwrights may well have been involved, including Nashe. Here we move
into an area of doubt computational stylistics cannot yet resolve. But our
experiments can offer an unequivocal assertion on mixed authorship for
the play, and identify parts written by Shakespeare and by Marlowe.

Table 3.3 lists the PCA and Zeta 'Shakespeareanness' measures for the
2000-word segments of *2 Henry VI*, the same ones presented graphically
in Figure 3.3. There are three segments with positive scores on both measures, Segments 7, 8, and 12; Segment 6 almost qualifies, with a lexical-
words score very close to zero. Segment 6 is the black disc on the *x*-axis
in Figure 3.3. The datapoints in the graph that are more properly in the
upper-right quadrant, moving from left to right, are Segments 7, 12, and
8. Among these perhaps the one that is easiest to credit to Shakespeare
from a reader's point of view (though it is not the highest-scoring on either
of the measures of Table 3.3) is Segment 7. It encompasses the latter part
of York's speech in III.i, and the first part of III.ii. Most of it is concerned
with a complex series of reactions to the murder of Humphrey, Duke
of Gloucester. There is a long speech from Queen Margaret seeking to
turn King Henry's sympathy from Gloucester to herself (III.ii.73–121).
The segment includes references to 'sheets' (III.ii.174) and (avian) 'kite[s]'
(III.ii.193 and 196). Edward A. Armstrong notes that there is a series of
passages in canonical Shakespeare plays in which kites and beds or bed
furnishings are mentioned within a close compass. He suggests that
Shakespeare associated the kite with disease and death, and thought of
beds in terms of death-beds, so that death connected the two in his mind
in an unconscious association.[36] He regards this connection as one of the
most striking examples of idiosyncratic image-clusters in Shakespeare,
listing eight passages in eight different plays (of which *2 Henry VI* is one)
in which it occurs (p. 13).

---

[35] Hattaway, *ibid.*, compares Joan's 'bravura obscenity' at V.iii.23, directed at the fiends, with
Faustus's treatment of the devil in Act 1 of *Doctor Faustus* (p. 24).

[36] E. A. Armstrong, *Shakespeare's Imagination: A Study of the Psychology of Association and Inspiration*
(London: Lindsay Drummond, 1946), pp. 11, 15.

Table 3.3. *Distances of 2000-word segments of* 2 Henry VI *from Shakespeare centroids, based on the same two tests as in Table 3.1.*

Segment	First and last lines	Closeness to Shakespeare on function words	Closeness to Shakespeare on lexical words
1	I.i.1–I.ii.2	0.001	−0.034
2	I.ii.2–I.iii.150	0.279	−0.086
3	I.iii.150–II.i.105	0.938	−0.080
4	II.i.105–II.iii.79	0.802	−0.065
5	II.iii.79–III.i.113	−0.034	−0.029
6	III.i.113–III.i.365	0.612	−0.001
7	III.i.365–III.ii.233	0.313	0.030
8	III.ii.233–IV.i.36	0.679	0.053
9	IV.i.36–IV.ii.160	0.316	−0.034
10	IV.ii.160–IV.vii.121	−0.073	−0.072
11	IV.vii.121–V.i.13	−0.507	−0.083
12	V.i.13–end	0.383	0.035

Vincent has examined the distribution of the alternative spellings 'o' and 'oh' in the play.[37] The 'oh' forms are concentrated in what modern editors designate as Act III, which is quite distinctive in this way from Acts I, II, and IV (Act V has a more mixed pattern). The two compositors set both forms in their stints. Vincent suggests that this pattern indicates that there were at least two different authors in the play. He suggests that other evidence, such as a dearth of the pronoun *ye* and peculiarities in classical allusions, make Act III distinct from the rest of the play and associates it with Shakespeare. From Table 3.3 we can see that Segments 6, 7, and 8, which emerge as the most 'Shakespearean' of the segments on our tests, include all but the first 100 or so lines of Act III. The evidence converges to support the idea that the play is a collaboration, that one of the collaborators was Shakespeare, and his contribution is mainly in what is designated Act III in modern editions.

Dover Wilson regarded Greene, along with the three fellow-scholars addressed in *Greene's Groatsworth of Wit* (Peele and Marlowe, and probably Nashe), as the main candidates for a share in the authorship of *2 Henry VI*. We assessed each of these four authors' claims by a series of lexical-words tests, observing where the *2 Henry VI* segments clustered in an analysis of the author's works contrasted to those of others. In the Greene, Nashe,

---

[37] P. J. Vincent, 'Unsolved Mysteries in *Henry VI, Part Two*', *Notes and Queries*, 48 (2002), 270–4.

and Peele tests all the segments were grouped with the 'other' texts. In the Marlowe test Segments 10 and 11 clustered with the Marlowe segments.

The two segments cover the whole of IV.iii–x, with the last part of IV.ii and the first part of V.i (Table 3.3). All of the complete scenes that are included involve what the 1594 Quarto title-page calls 'the notable rebellion of *Iacke Cade*'. Is it possible that the Cade scenes are by Marlowe rather than by Shakespeare? Certainly they are detachable from the rest of the play. Some characters in them are shared with other sections – the King, Queen Margaret, and Buckingham, in particular – but the majority appear only in IV.ii–ix: Cade himself and the rest of the rebels, Sir Humphrey and William Stafford, Lord Say, Lord Scales, and Alexander Iden. York declares his stratagem in urging Cade to rebellion in his soliloquy at the end of III.i, and Iden reports the death of Cade in V.i.64–82, immediately after York has declared that he has returned from Ireland to oust Somerset and fight Cade, but these are the only references to the rebellion outside Act IV. Warren points out that the Cade York describes in his soliloquy is quite different from the one the audience sees in the next act (p. 53). York's Cade is an athletic warrior against the Irish, a trusty secret agent, 'headstrong' (III.i.356) but able to resist any torture (III.i.376–8). The Cade of Act IV displays none of these traits to any marked degree, and introduces some new ones. He is a dangerous demagogue, pursuing an anarchic revolutionary logic to bloodthirsty ends. In the end he is weakened by starvation and succumbs in single combat to a better-fed and better-born opponent.

We tried various experiments to identify Marlowe's hand across the play. Table 3.4 shows the results. The table consolidates the evidence from twelve tests. We looked at function words as well as lexical words and used comparisons with various groups of plays by others, as well as with Shakespeare plays. We always used the full Marlowe set of plays as a reference point but for the comparison set we tried selecting only plays dated by the *Annals* before 1600, and only history plays dated before 1600, to take account of the effects of chronology and genre.[38] We aimed to answer questions such as: Does the likeness of some segments of *1 Henry VI* to Marlowe extend to function-word patterns as well as lexical-words ones? Do the affinities that sometimes appear really stem from the fact that

---

[38] The text sets were as follows: Marlowe, 6 plays, 44 segments; non-Marlowe plays, 36 authors, 130 plays, 1254 segments; non-Marlowe plays before 1600, 15 authors, 44 plays, 389 segments; non-Marlowe history plays before 1600, 8 plays, 3 authors, 88 segments; 27 Shakespeare plays, 291 segments; 15 Shakespeare plays before 1600, 153 segments; and 6 Shakespeare history plays before 1600, 69 segments.

Marlowe's plays are closer to *1 Henry VI* in date than the comparison set, or are closer to the typical concerns of the history play than the others?

The first three tests were discriminant analyses using our usual set of 200 function words. Discriminant analysis combines the information in multiple variables, much like PCA, but where PCA identifies the most important factors in the data regarded as a single collection, discriminant analysis aims to maximize the difference between pre-defined classes within the observations. We used a form that classified each segment with one or other of the 36 authors represented in our full archive of 136 plays: in this case, the 36 authorial groups of segments. Any test segment can be classified with any of the 36 groups. The table only records whether a segment was ascribed to Marlowe or to one of the others; in this case that cell of the table contains a tick. Each of these progressively narrowed tests assigned segments of *2 Henry VI* to Marlowe, not always the same segments, though Segments 9, 10, and 11 were always classified with Marlowe. We then ran lexical-words tests contrasting the Marlowe segments with the three different sets of segments by others. In these tests Segment 10 was classified as Marlowe twice, and Segment 11 three times.

The second set of tests contrasted the Marlowe segments with Shakespeare ones. We first ran PCAs with function words selected to discriminate between the Marlowe plays and the full set of Shakespeare plays, the Shakespeare plays before 1600, and the Shakespeare history plays before 1600. We classified test segments as 'Marlowe' (and ticked the appropriate cell of the table) if their scores on the first two principal components put them closer to the Marlowe centroid than to the non-Marlowe one. Eight segments were classified as Marlowe on all three tests. On the narrowest test, comparing the six Marlowe plays with the six early Shakespeare history plays, Segments 6, 7, and 8 were classified as 'Shakespeare' and the rest as 'Marlowe'. Finally, we ran our usual lexical-words tests for the three varieties of the Marlowe–Shakespeare contrast. This time the number of *2 Henry VI* segments assigned to Marlowe increased as the focus narrowed, reaching a total of four for the comparison with early Shakespeare history plays. Looking across Table 3.4 as a whole we see that Segment 11 was always classified with Marlowe, and Segment 10 almost always. Function-word tests give a much larger share of the play to Marlowe than do the lexical-words ones. Narrowing the basis of comparison by date and genre does not materially alter the overall pattern of affinities with Marlowe, which are concentrated in Segments 10 and 11 but evident elsewhere as well. The likeness of this *Henry VI* play to Marlowe's style is certainly persistent.

Table 3.4. *Segments and sequences of 2 Henry VI classified as Marlowe or non-Marlowe, and Marlowe or Shakespeare, by various tests.*

Texts used	All plays	All pre-1600 plays	All pre-1600 history plays	Marlowe versus all non-Marlowe plays	Marlowe versus non-Marlowe pre-1600 plays	Marlowe versus non-Marlowe pre-1600 history plays	Marlowe versus Shakespeare plays	Marlowe versus Shakespeare pre-1600 plays	Marlowe versus Shakespeare pre-1600 history plays	Marlowe versus Shakespeare plays	Marlowe versus Shakespeare pre-1600 plays	Marlowe versus Shakespeare pre-1600 history plays
Method	Discriminant	Discriminant	Discriminant	Lexical words	Lexical words	Lexical words	PCA	PCA	PCA	Lexical words	Lexical words	Lexical words
Segment 1	✓	✓									✓	✓
Segment 2			✓				✓	✓	✓			
Segment 3	✓	✓					✓	✓	✓			
Segment 4							✓	✓	✓			
Segment 5							✓	✓	✓			
Segment 6							✓	✓	✓			
Segment 7							✓					
Segment 8							✓	✓	✓			
Segment 9	✓	✓	✓				✓	✓	✓			
Segment 10	✓	✓	✓	✓	✓	✓	✓	✓	✓	✓	✓	✓
Segment 11	✓	✓	✓	✓	✓	✓	✓	✓	✓	✓	✓	✓
Segment 12	✓	✓	✓				✓	✓	✓			
IV.ii–x	✓	✓	✓	✓	✓	✓	✓	✓	✓	✓	✓	✓
IV.iii–x	✓	✓	✓	✓	✓	✓	✓	✓	✓		✓	✓

Those classified as Marlowe are marked with a tick. The discriminant analysis tests use 200 function words and classify segments by author (36 authors are included in the full set, 15 in the pre-1600 set, and 3 in the pre-1600 history play set). The lexical-words tests use the 500 words that appear more regularly in one of the comparison sets and the 500 that appear more regularly in the other. The PCAs use those variables with probability <0.0005 on the *t*-test that they are from the same parent population for each text set.

Segments 10 and 11 do not include IV.ii, which is the first Cade scene. We ran the same tests with the sequence IV.ii–x, the complete set of Cade scenes, and also the sequence IV.iii–x. The bottom rows of Table 3.4 show that the longer sequence is only classified as Marlowe by one of the lexical-words tests, the one comparing Marlowe with pre-1600 Shakespeare history plays. The likeness of Marlowe in style and vocabulary that is so strong in IV.iii–ix, which makes up almost all of segments 10 and 11, does not extend to IV.ii. This is a little perplexing.

However, Marlowe clearly has a large hand in the latter part of the Cade sequence. Cade is plausible as a Marlowe character. Like Joan in *1 Henry VI*, he is of humble parentage but aspiring to supreme political power. This is a Marlovian theme, familiar from the shepherd Tamburlaine who comes to conquer most of the known world in *1* and *2 Tamburlaine*. Both Joan and Cade construct fantasies of noble birth: Joan denies her father to his face three times, and claims she is 'descended of gentler blood' (*1 Henry VI*, V.iv.8); Cade declares that his bricklayer father was the son of Edmund Mortimer, Earl of March, and was stolen as a child by a beggar-woman (*2 Henry VI*, IV.ii.132–46).[39] Cade at his death continues to spout defiance like a good Marlovian hero, albeit in comic and even earthy prose: 'Let ten thousand devils come against me, and give me but the ten meals I have lost, and I'd defy them all. Wither, garden, and be henceforth a burying-place to all that do dwell in this house, because the unconquer'd soul of Cade is fled' (IV.x.60–5). The Cade scenes include two displays of severed heads: Queen Margaret cradles the head of the Duke of Suffolk in IV.iv, and the rebels put the heads of Lord Saye and Sir James Cromer on poles and make them kiss in IV.vi. Then, in V.i, William Iden presents Cade's head to the King. Margaret E. Owens suggests that this extravagant stage imagery recalls stagecraft like Marlowe's at the end of *Edward II*, where the new King addresses the severed head of the younger Mortimer: 'So insistent is the verbal and visual imagery of decapitation in *2 Henry VI* that one might be tempted to speculate that the dramatist(s) took a deliberate risk, indulging in an exercise in theatrical audacity of a kind we more typically associate with Marlowe.'[40] The key issue is whether the Cade scenes were written by Marlowe, or by a fellow-dramatist fallen under his spell. Thomas Cartelli (without the advantage of computational-stylistics results) assumes the latter. He sees Marlovian

---

[39] D. C. Gerould notes the parallel between Joan and Cade (without making any reference to Marlowe), but claims wrongly that Cade denies his father: 'Principles of dramatic structure in *Henry VI*', *Educational Theatre Journal*, 20 (1968), 376–88 (p. 382).

[40] 'The Many-Headed Monster in *Henry VI, Part 2*', *Criticism*, 38.3 (1996), 367–82 (p. 379).

influence dispersed throughout the play. *2 Henry VI* was 'both composed and performed in the shadow of the Tamburlaine plays'; it is 'virtually saturated in Tamburlainean statements of proud self-assertion'.[41] Cartelli's examples are from York and from Suffolk as well as from Cade (pp. 86–7). In his detailed analysis he emphasizes the differences between Cade and Tamburlaine. The rebels in *2 Henry VI* and in *The Life and Death of Jack Straw* (a subsequent play based on the Cade rebellion) may aspire like Tamburlaine to heroism and power but:

> [t]he pretensions of such characters to be 'Lords within ourselves' are ... nothing more than pretensions, and are mocked by the playwright who depicts them and by history alike ... the potential for audience engagement with rebellious figures that is at least authorially discouraged in plays like *Jack Straw* and *2 Henry VI* is sustained in Marlowe's treatment of Tamburlaine and his confederates. (p. 74)

Cartelli notes, however, that Cade is given some telling lines of Tamburlaine-like attack on the ideology of aristocratic privilege, which are 'significant interventions in the discursive dominance of the ruling class' (p. 86), instances of 'resistance to ... social enslavement', which Cartelli sees echoed outside the Cade scenes as well (p. 87). His conclusion is that 'Shakespeare himself, at the time of *2 Henry VI*'s composition, was too immersed in the Tamburlaine phenomenon to sustain a consistent critical detachment' (p. 88).

The present argument is that it was in fact Marlowe rather than Shakespeare who was the origin of these reflections of Tamburlaine in a rebel fifteenth-century clothier. There is always the danger of bending a response to suit what emerges from an empirical study; but once the suggestion has been made, we can see a range of attitudes and emotions in these scenes that is more extreme, more reckless than we usually associate with Shakespeare. Warren (without at this point speculating on authorship) notes that the 'tone' of the Cade scenes is sometimes 'elusive' in performance, an unfamiliar balance between 'comic and violent elements' (p. 51). Cade's seemingly unstoppable early success against the established forces of order, his exuberant barbarity, and the tinge of farce that this brings to the operations of power in an organized society, would find more analogues in Marlowe than in Shakespeare.

Commentators have often found it difficult to assimilate the Cade scenes to the broader Shakespeare canon. In the current Arden edition of *2 Henry VI* Ronald Knowles refers to the remarkable 'play of ideas within farce'

---

[41] T. Cartelli, *Marlowe, Shakespeare, and the Economy of Theatrical Experience* (Philadelphia: University of Pennsylvania Press, 1991), p. 86.

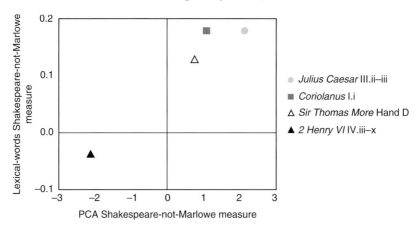

Figure 3.10 Four play sections with mutinous crowds evaluated on two measures of resemblance to Shakespeare rather than Marlowe. The *x*-axis is the difference between the distance to the Marlowe centroid and the distance to the Shakespeare centroid for the first two components of a PCA based on Shakespeare–Marlowe marker words identified by a *t*-test. The *y*-axis is the difference between the distance to the Marlowe centroid and the distance to the Shakespeare centroid for the two measures of a lexical-words test, proportional scores for 500 Shakespeare-not-Marlowe markers and proportional scores for 500 Marlowe-not-Shakespeare markers. The centroids in both cases are based on scores from 2000-word segments from 27 Shakespeare plays and 6 Marlowe plays.

in this sequence (p. 10), and the challenge it has always posed to critics.[42] He says that 'the dramatic power of lower-class rebellion in *2 Henry VI* was to remain unsurpassed, even in comparison with Shakespeare's later representation of plebeian disorder in *Julius Caesar* and *Coriolanus*' (p. 74). We can put Knowles's comparison on a computational-stylistics footing, and set the section of the Cade scenes we have identified as by Marlowe – *2 Henry VI* , IV.iii–x – alongside the scenes of Mark Antony, Brutus, and the Roman crowd, and the latter's savage capture of the poet Cinna (*Julius Caesar*, III.ii–iii), and the first scene of *Coriolanus*, where Menenius confronts another restive assembly of plebeians. We can add the Hand D addition of *Sir Thomas More*, another scene of popular rebellion, mentioned later by Knowles in this context (p. 74) and the subject of Chapter 7, below. Figure 3.10 shows the scores of these four sections on a PCA measure of 'Shakespeare-not-Marlowe' style, based on function words, and a

[42] William Shakespeare, *King Henry VI, Part 2*, ed. Ronald Knowles (London: Thomas Nelson, 1999), pp. 65–7.

Zeta test of 'Shakespeare-not-Marlowe' vocabulary. The *Sir Thomas More* addition and the sequences from the two Shakespeare Roman plays are positive on both measures, and so fall in the upper-right, Shakespearean quadrant. The Cade sequence is in the lower-left quadrant, well separated from the other three. It is negative on both measures, more like Marlowe in style and diction than like Shakespeare.

If Shakespeare wrote these scenes, he was imitating Marlowe's diction and syntactic habits as well as responding to his transgressions against decorum and social stability, his rampant individualism in attitudes and dramatic characterization. This is not beyond the bounds of possibility, but the weight of evidence presented in the tables and graphs makes it unlikely. The Cade scenes stray beyond the bounds of Shakespearean style in a way quite unlike other early plays we know to be Shakespeare's. They fit Marlowe's patterns quite closely, on the other hand.

As we have mentioned, there are many scholars of these plays who have declared themselves indifferent to the question of whether they were written by one playwright, or by more than one. Yet a new confidence that two of the plays at least are collaborative does make a difference in many of the issues that have preoccupied scholars of the *Henry VI* plays. Emrys Jones comments that the view that *1 Henry VI* is a collaboration 'has possibly damaging implications for the idea that Shakespeare designed a play sequence of three or four Parts' (p. 128). Cairncross thought that the copy for *1 Henry VI* was 'a transcript of the author's manuscript, carrying some annotations by the stage-adapter or prompter'; this licensed a thorough-going programme of emendation, aiming to recover authorial readings from errors of transmission (p. xxvi–vii). The particular application of parallels from Shakespeare plays is weakened if collaborative authorship is established. On the other hand, the evidence presented so far does not bear directly on the debate over whether *1 Henry VI* was written after the other two parts.

In other areas the notion of collaboration does have wide implications. It makes it more than ever unsatisfactory to cloak what seems indeed to be a shared creative effort under a single entity, 'Shakespeare'. The two dramatic centres of interest in *1 Henry VI*, Lord Talbot and Joan la Pucelle, may well derive in many of their crucial scenes not from a single creative origin but from the two most potent dramatic forces of the early 1590s, Shakespeare and Marlowe, with their contrasting rhetorical styles and their quite different means of purchase on the attention of playgoers. It seems that in *2 Henry VI* another powerful episode, the Cade rebellion, derives from Marlowe, while other elements, like the fraught interactions within the court after the assassination of Gloucester, can be confirmed as Shakespearean.

Most of the findings we present in this book are closely in accord with scholarly consensus, or at least with one well-populated strand of a scholarly debate. In the case of *1* and *2 Henry VI* we offer some results like this, but also some less conventional propositions. Marlowe's hand in these two plays has been proposed before, but not in precisely this form, to the best of our knowledge. Any departure from the work of centuries of good readers must be presented with due hesitation. We think, though, that the evidence is strong enough to warrant Shakespeareans giving a hearing to the possibility that we should look to Marlowe rather than to Shakespeare as the source of many of the Joan la Pucelle and Jack Cade scenes.

CHAPTER 4

Authoring Arden of Faversham

Arthur F. Kinney

'You don't expect me to know what to say about a play when I don't know who the author is, do you?' Flawner Bannal asks in *Fanny's First Play* by George Bernard Shaw; 'If it's by a good author, it's a good play, naturally.'[1] For over four centuries now, the anonymous *Arden of Faversham* (*c.* 1588–92) has been thought an exceptionally good play by most critics, who date it sometime shortly after the 1587 edition of Holinshed's *Chronicles* and who acknowledge its influence on other plays at the dawn of the great decade of Elizabethan, and Shakespearean, drama. According to the logic of Flawner Bannal, it should therefore have an exceptionally good author – someone like Thomas Kyd or Christopher Marlowe, or perhaps even Shakespeare himself: a ready-made challenge for an application of computational stylistics.

The play dramatizes the bloody killing of Thomas Arden, a minor servant in the government of Henry VIII and Edward VI; a customs officer at the port of Faversham, Kent; and the recipient of the abbey lands of Faversham following the dissolution of the monasteries. He was killed by his wife Alice, her lover Mosby, and two hired assassins as he played backgammon in the parlour of his home. The death was first recorded in the *Breviat Chronicle* for 1551:

This year on S[aint] Valentine's day at Faversham in Kent, was committed a shameful murder, for one Arden a gentleman was by the consent of his wife murdered, wherefore she was burned at Canterbury, and there was hanged in chains for that murder and at Faversham (two) hanged in chains [one of them Arden's man-servant Michael Saunderson, who was hanged, drawn, and quartered], and a woman burned [Elizabeth Stafford, Alice Arden's day-servant], and in Smithfield [in London] was hanged one Mosby and his sister [Susan] for the murder also.[2]

---

[1] As quoted by M. P. Jackson, 'Shakespearean Features of the Poetic Style of *Arden of Faversham*', *Archiv für das Studium der neueren Sprachen und Literaturen*, 230 (1993), 279–304 (p. 279).
[2] Quoted from P. Hyde, *Thomas Arden in Faversham: The Man Behind the Myth* (Faversham: The Faversham Society, 1996), p. 92.

Thus six people were executed to even the score. The goods of the criminals, valued at £184 10s 4½d, along with some jewels, were forfeited in the Faversham treasury; the city of Canterbury received 43s for executing George Bradshaw and for burning Alice Arden alive. Only two persons involved in attempting to kill Arden, the painter William Blackbourne and the hired assassin Shakebag, who probably actually did the killing, escaped punishment.

The play depicts eight separate attempts on Arden's life. Mosby plans to kill him with a poisoned portrait; his wife poisons his broth; the dispossessed landlord Greene, along with his hired assistants Black Will and Shakebag, attempt to kill him in a London street (when one of them is struck by a market awning), at his London lodgings, on the road to Rochester, and later in the fog. Mosby and Alice attempt to provoke a fight with Arden when he sees them together, Black Will proposes they stab Arden at the fair, and then they all descend on him at home when he is playing a game of tables. The play suggests several motives: Arden's arrogance as a political servant rewarded with monastic lands, his apparent disinterest in his marriage, his wife Alice's passion for her lover Mosby, Mosby's own desire to inherit Arden's wealth, Mosby's social ambitions. Economic negotiations and exchanges are emphasized in the play: Arden's man-servant Michael agrees to murder his master in exchange for Mosby's sister Susan; the painter Clarke offers to supply the poison in return for Susan; Greene wants back money from land he feels Arden took from him wrongfully; and the enlisted assassins agree to kill Arden for a fee, a fee that increases as the play progresses and their early efforts fail. *Arden of Faversham* thus enacts a private history that Holinshed thought had wide public resonance.

Nor was he alone in such an estimate. In 1577 Edward White entered a book in the Stationers' Register entitled *A Cruel Murder done in Kent*, probably based on the sensational story of Thomas Arden, and this was apparently followed by a play, *Murderous Michael*, staged at the court of Elizabeth in 1579, but neither text survives. The London merchant-tailor Henry Machyn entered the story of Thomas Arden in his diary and John Stow published it in his *Annals of England* (1592, 1631); Thomas Heywood refers to it in *Troia Britannica* (1609); John Taylor uses it as an example of God's vengeance on murderers; and the whole story was told in another popular oral form, a ballad published in 1633 as '[The] complaint and lamentation of Mistress Arden of [Fev]ersham in *Kent*, who for the love of one *Mosby*, hired certain Ruffians [a]nd Villains most cruelly to murder her Husband; with the fatal end of her and her Associates'. The legacy was later revived in London as a puppet show (1736) and a ballet at Sadler's Wells (1799).

The play of *Arden of Faversham* has also endured as a major play despite lacking an identifiable author. There were four editions published in England between 1592 and 1633. In the past century alone, it has appeared first in Ashley Thorndike's *Minor Elizabethan Drama*, Volume 1, in 1910 and several subsequent editions; in Felix E. Schelling's *Typical Elizabethan Plays* (1927); and in E. H. C. Oliphant's *Shakespeare and His Fellow Dramatists*, Volume 1 (1929) and his *Elizabethan Dramatists Other than Shakespeare* (1931). The work is also included in *Elizabethan and Stuart Plays*, edited by C. R. Baskervill, Virgil B. Heltzel, and Arthur H. Nethercot (1934); *Five Elizabethan Tragedies*, edited by A. K. McIlwraith (1938); *Elizabethan Drama*, edited by John Gassner and William Green (1967); and *Three Elizabethan Domestic Tragedies*, edited by Keith Sturgess (1969). Separate texts have appeared in The Malone Society publications (1947 for 1940), edited by Hugh MacDonald and D. Nichol Smith; in the Revels edition, edited by M. L. Wine (1973); and in the New Mermaids edition, edited by Martin White (1990). The play has also been re-edited in two recent editions: in *Renaissance Drama: An Anthology of Plays and Entertainments*, edited by Arthur F. Kinney for Blackwell (2000, 2005), and *English Renaissance Drama*, edited by David Bevington, Lars Engle, Katharine Eisaman Maus, and Eric Rasmussen for Norton (2002). The play has an enviable record of translation as well: by Diego Angeli in *Opere attribute a Shakespeare*, Volume 1 (1934); by Mario Praz in G. Baldini's *Teatro elisabettiano* (1948); by Pierre Messiaen in *Théâtre anglais: moyen âge et XVIe siècle* (1948); by Felix Carrier (1950); by Laurette Brunius and Loleh Bellon (1957); and by Miklós J. Scenczi in G. Somlyó's *Anglo reneszánsz drámák*, Volume 1 (1961).[3] (A century earlier, François-Victor Hugo had turned the play into French.) No other anonymous play of Shakespeare's time has compiled such a record.

Yet 'no one knows who wrote it', Bill Bryson writes in his 2007 biography of Shakespeare.[4] Subsequently Brian Vickers assigned authorship of the entire play to Thomas Kyd.[5] But the overwhelming favourite candidate has been Shakespeare. In 1952 Sydney Cockerell reported in the *London Times* about dining with Algernon Swinburne at Watts-Dunton's No. 2,

---

[3] Much of this information is taken from T. P. Logan and D. S. Smith, eds., *The Predecessors of Shakespeare: A Survey and Bibliography of Recent Studies in Renaissance Drama* (Lincoln: University of Nebraska Press, 1973).

[4] B. Bryson, *Shakespeare: The World as Stage* (New York: Atlas Books, 2007), p. 18.

[5] B. Vickers, 'Thomas Kyd, Secret Sharer', *TLS*, 18 April 2008, p. 13.

The Pines. He made some remark, now forgotten, that the relatively deaf Swinburne took to be a reference to *Arden of Faversham*. 'For the rest of the meal', Cockerell recalled, 'I listened entranced to an eloquent discourse on that remarkable play, which he emphatically declared to have qualities of genius that could be found in Shakespeare alone.'[6] Others have agreed. 'Again and again, an image calls to mind his early work, especially in the Histories', observes M. B. Smith in *Marlowe's Imagery and the Marlowe Canon* (1940), and cites as examples words drawn from archery, riding, birding, and gardening, and the frequent references to animals.[7] But caution is in order, as M. L. Wine writes in his introduction to the Revels text, because of the reportorial nature of the text. 'To judge from the better portions of the text', he continues, '*Arden* is written in predominately end-stopped iambic pentameter verse. But so is almost every extant play from this period, including those by Shakespeare, Marlowe, and Kyd' (p. lxxxv).

Despite the difficulty in locating distinctive Shakespearean habits of mind and language in *Arden*, there have been those from the seventeenth century to our own who linked his name to the anonymous play. The work is one of a group labelled 'the Shakespeare apocrypha' by Tucker Brooke, and it shares with that group, according to Brooke, a critical history that falls into three stages. In the first period, stretching from the close of the sixteenth century to the eighteenth century, attribution relied on non-literary, sometimes paratextual matters – the claims on the title-pages (which could be false), entries in the Stationers' Register (which could be blocking entries rather than authentic ones), or book lists drawn up as advertisements by enterprising booksellers. A second period – one he associates with such Shakespearean editors as Capell, Steevens, and Malone – was just the reverse. Scholars relied not on evidence outside the texts but the literary qualities of the texts themselves, including shared common words, parallel passages, and even commonality of tone. The identification of texts relied on literary sensitivity and discernment. The third period, beginning in the nineteenth century, attempted to be more scientific. 'The trend of the time', Brooke writes,

was more towards more exact knowledge, towards the careful consideration and classification of minutiae; for the first time an attempt was made, and with a good measure of success, to establish definite criteria for style and spirit, whereby

[6] This anecdote is taken from J. M. Carroll and M. P. Jackson, 'Shakespeare, *Arden of Faversham* and "Literature Online"', in *Shakespeare Newsletter*, 54.1 (Spring 2004), 3–6 (p. 3).
[7] Cited by M. L. Wine in his introduction to the Revels edition of *Arden of Faversham* (Manchester: Manchester University Press, 1973), pp. xix–xcii (p. lxxxv).

the work of one dramatist might be distinguished from that of another. The most tangible, but surely not the sole result of the effort is the development of the 'metrical tests'.

Still, '[t]he new system, however, [was] at least as liable to abuse as that which it superseded'.[8]

Attributing authorship to *Arden of Faversham* was first undertaken by Edward Archer in a playlist he established in 1656. He listed plays in three columns – the play title in column one, the author in column two, and the genre in column three – and alongside *Arden of Faversham* appeared the name of Richard Bernard, a Puritan clergyman who had translated Terence. The citation was in 'An Exact and perfect Catalogue of all the Plaies that were ever printed' in an appendix of *The Old Law*. But in 1945, W. W. Greg returned to the manuscript behind that publication to find that the columns had become misaligned; what Bernard's name went with was a translation of Terence's *Andrea*, the entry following *Arden*, and in realigning the columns the authorship attributed to Arden became 'Will. Shakespeare'.[9] Archer's listing did not influence others for long; in 1661, the bookseller Francis Kirkman, working with Archer's list, removed the attribution, making the play once again anonymous. He had on his side, after all, the First Folio of Shakespeare's *Works* of 1623, which did not include the play. Still, such an attribution has always shown a certain resilience, and the Faversham historian Edward Jacob printed a version of the play in 1770 'With a Preface, in which some Reasons are offered in favour of its being the earliest dramatic Work of Shakespeare now remaining, and a genuine Account given of the Murder, from authentic Papers of the Time.'[10] For such connections Stephen Jones had little patience. In his *Biographia dramatica* (1812) he calls Jacob's preface, with its Shakespeare attribution, 'ridiculous' (II.36).[11]

'The deadly parallel', as Oliphant labelled it, has been aligned with external evidence for other attributions of *Arden*'s author. Kyd and Marlowe are cases in point. 'In Kyd's case', according to Wine,

most of the 'parallels' are to *Soliman and Perseda*, the authorship of which is extremely debatable, and, to a lesser degree, to *The Murder of John Brewen*, a pamphlet of 1592 about an Arden-type murder which is now completely discredited as Kyd's. Advocates of either [Kyd or Marlowe] have cited 'typical' words and

[8] C. F. Tucker Brooke, *The Shakespeare Apocrypha* (Oxford: Clarendon Press, 1929), p. ix.
[9] W. W. Greg, 'Shakespeare and *Arden of Feversham* [*sic*]', *Review of English Studies*, n.s., 21.82 (April 1945), 134–36.
[10] Hyde, *Thomas Arden in Faversham*, p. 5.
[11] Stephen Jones, *Biographia dramatica*, 3 vols. (London, 1812), Vol. II, p. 36.

phrases and have employed the usual 'tests', but they have brought us no closer to certainty. Marlowe's origins in Kent and the probability of Kyd's having been for a time a scrivener (and thus familiar with legal terminology) and a servant (like Mosby) in a large household counter Shakespeare's possible interest in the Arden name; the known circumstance of Kyd and Marlowe's sharing a chamber in 1591 takes on the glow of external evidence for joint authorship [something Oliphant seriously advanced]. (p. lxxxvii)

There have been other candidates, too, in George Peele, Robert Greene, Anthony Munday, Samuel Rowley, Robert Yarrington, Thomas Heywood, George Wilkins, and – perhaps to no surprise – the seventeenth Earl of Oxford (and the sixth Earl of Derby). There seem to be no bounds, in fact, to the urge to speculate. William Archer, writes Wine, thought the play might even 'have been written by some local gentleman (like the Lord Cheiny introduced in it), who took a special interest in this particular theme, and made no other excursion into letters' (p. lxxxviii). Even more far-fetched is the introduction (in 1633) of a person named Cloy who may never have existed.[12]

Despite scrambling for evidence that will guarantee one attribution of authorship or another, Kyd and Marlowe, the early Shakespeare's most accomplished contemporaries, have long been considered leading candidates as sole or joint authors of *Arden of Faversham*. The idea of joint authorship by Kyd and Marlowe, urged in a private letter to Brooke and more publicly as well by Oliphant, was taken up but with a twist by Charles Crawford, who suggested the work was by Kyd who deliberately imitated Marlowe (1903); Felix Schelling agreed in *Elizabethan Playwrights* (1925). H. B. Charlton and R. D. Waller, in their edition of Marlowe's *Edward II* (1933), think Kyd borrowed from that play in writing *Arden*. In a contribution to *Notes and Queries* (1940), William Wells

---

[12] 'The anonymous "Notes on Sales. Arden of Feversham [*sic*]", *Times Literary Supplement* (*TLS*), 2 August 1923, p. 524, discovers a new clue for authorship of the play in the sale catalogue (1792) of Dr John Monro's library, which recorded "Cloy's Tragedy of Arden of Faversham, 1633". Why was the play attributed to "Cloy"? It is unlikely that he was the former owner of Monro's copy. (See V. Scholderer, "*Arden of Faversham*", *TLS*, 1 February 1936, p. 96, who thinks "Cloy" was the earlier owner, and the name an inaccurate transcription of "Wm. Oldys" (the eighteenth century antiquary).) W. J. Lawrence, "The Authorship of *Arden of Faversham*", *TLS*, 28 June 1934, p. 460, offers evidence that there existed an itinerant entertainer called Bartholomew Cloys in the early Caroline period, but there might have been other Cloys. (This article reminds C. L. Stainer, "*Arden of Faversham*", *TLS*, 12 July 1934, p. 492, of the John Cloy mocked in Jonson's *Tale of a Tub*.) E. H. C. Oliphant, "*Arden of Faversham*", *TLS*, 18 January 1936, p. 55, believes a Cloy existed who might or might not have contributed to *Arden*' (Logan and Smith, *The Predecessors of Shakespeare*, p. 244). The reference might instead be to the ballad, which was also published in 1633. An anonymous reader of this book for Cambridge University Press suggests he 'is almost certainly Bartholomew Cloys [who] had presented a puppet version – the puppet Arden was popular, and Cloys was a puppeteer'.

agreed that was the case but added Marlowe's *Massacre at Paris* to Kyd's resources. The bandwagon continued. J. M. Robertson in *The Shakespeare Canon* (1925) and T. S. Eliot in 'Seneca in Elizabethan Translation' (1927) also claim *Arden* was written by Kyd, while Kyd's legal knowledge makes him a candidate for Percy Allen, along with Shakespeare and Marlowe, in *Shakespeare, Jonson, and Wilkins as Borrowers* (1928). In *And Morning in His Eyes* (1937) Philip Henderson acknowledged the aid of Shakespeare and Marlowe, but considered that *Arden of Faversham* remained largely Kyd's accomplishment. Others agreeing that Kyd is a possible or the probable author include Kenneth Muir (1938–43), Alan S. Downer (1950), A. P. Rossiter (1950), Willard Farnham (1956), W. Bridge-Adams (1957), Wilfred T. Jewkes (1958), and José Axelrad and Michèle Willems (1964). But Philip Edwards – the editor of the Revels text of *The Spanish Tragedy* (1959) and the author of *Thomas Kyd and Early Elizabethan Tragedy* (1966) – has strong reservations: he misses 'the Seneca-Garnier cast of *The Spanish Tragedy*' in *Arden* and thinks correspondences may be considered reminiscences. Others have expressed their doubts, too: F. W. Bateson, Zdeněk Stříbrný, Arthur Freeman.

The most recent claimant for Kyd's sole authorship is Brian Vickers, who cites as his sole predecessors Crawford, Walter Miksch (1907), H. Dugdale Sykes (1914), P. V. Rubow (1948), and Felix Carrère (1950): a letter to the *Times Literary Supplement* one week later added F. G. Fleay (1891) and Ronald Bayne (1897).[13] Vickers argued for the use of a version of computational stylistics and set forth his criteria for making attributions: 'They must not consist of single words, for common words are widely shared, and rare ones are easily copied. Since the unique characteristic of natural languages is their ability to combine words in syntactic-semantic sequences, an author's individuality will be more visible if we can identify his preferred grouping of words, consecutive clusters of three or more' (p. 13), thus dismissing the combination that we use so that one means of identification is confirmed or denied by another. Instead Vickers looks only for distinctive groups of words (what we refer to as 'strings of words') limited to the canon of a single author. Some of the phrasal pairings he discovers, for instance, 'Ile none of that', 'there is no credit in', and 'thou wert wont to' are commonplaces. Vickers did not test these phrases against collections of proverbs or various commonplace books, and limited his evidence for their uniqueness only to 'Elizabethan drama before 1596' (p. 14). He calls this repetition of phrases in the work of a single author 'self-plagiarism', since he is drawing on a new software called 'Pl@giarism',

---

[13] A. C. Green, 'Arden ...' *TLS*, 23 April 2008, p. 6.

but even this term is misleading; in 1621 plagiarism meant then, as now, 'wrongful appropriation or purloining, and publishing, as one's own, ideas [or works] of another' (*OED*). Vickers does not mean conscious or unconscious stealing; he means repetition of conscious or unconscious habits of thought and expression. His less proverbial instances are even more doubtful: 'How now My Lord, what makes you rise so soone?' is called a plagiarism of 'Had I been wake you had not rise so soone' (p. 14). The sentiments are similar in language, but they do not say the same thing. In both instances, Vickers would use them as, incontrovertibly, 'not commonplace but idiosyncratic phrases' (p. 14).

Unlike the case with Thomas Kyd, Christopher Marlowe has generally been advanced as a collaborator on *Arden*, rather than its sole author. This is the view of J. M. Roberston in *An Introduction to the Study of the Shakespeare Canon* (1924) and Frederick S. Boas in *Christopher Marlowe: A Biographical and Critical Study* (1940), where he makes a case for Marlowe grounded on his writing habits, not unlike Vickers for Kyd, citing correspondences between Marlowe's plays and *Arden*. Anonymity is not a problem but an analogy. 'If *Arden* is anonymous in all its editions, so is *Tamburlaine*.' John Bakeless concludes in Volume 2 of his magisterial biography of Marlowe (1942) that 'There is something of [Marlowe] in [*Arden*], whether it is stray samples of his handiwork, deliberate thefts, or unconscious echoes.' He may have in mind some of the linkings that Brooke argued in 1922 were borrowings from *Edward II*. T. W. Baldwin, in *On the Literary Genetics of Shakspere's Poems & Sonnets*, even uses connections between *Edward II* and *Arden* to date both that play and *The Massacre at Paris* as plays following *Arden* in composition.[14]

But Swinburne was not alone in his uninterrupted defence of Shakespeare as the author of *Arden of Faversham* at Watts-Dunton's No. 2, The Pines. In the words of Jayne M. Carroll and MacDonald P. Jackson, he was supported by

[t]he fine editor of Shakespeare, Charles Knight, the great German scholar Nicolaus Delius, the literary historian W. J. Courthope, and the play's French translator, François Victor Hugo [who] upheld [the attribution] with various degrees of conviction, while many other commentators, including Henry Tyrrell, John Addington Symonds, A. H. Bullen, and Alfred Mézières were inclined to believe that Shakespeare had been involved with the script of *Arden of Faversham* as part-author, reviser, or corrector. Even sceptics were apt to detect speeches and lines with 'a Shakespearean ring' to them.[15]

---

[14] This history of attributions is taken from Logan and Smith, *The Predecessors of Shakespeare*, pp. 241–6.

[15] Carroll and Jackson, 'Shakespeare, *Arden of Faversham*', p. 3.

They may have in mind the dramatic and poetic intensity of the play's language. Here is Michael, Arden's servant, torn with conflicted loyalties:

> My master's kindness pleads to me for life
> With just demand, and I must grant it him;
> My mistress she hath forced me with an oath
> For Susan's sake, the which I may not break,
> For that is nearer than a master's love;
> That grim-faced fellow, pitiless Black Will,
> And Shakebag, stern in bloody stratagem –
> Two rougher ruffians never lived in Kent –
> Have sworn my death if I infringe my vow,
> A dreadful thing to be considered of. (iv.62–71)

Black Will and Shakebag, the clownish characters with clownish names that seem to point to Shakespeare, are here threatening, unbalancing Michael's oaths to his master, to Susan, and to them. Mosby's later speech focuses more on the self than the situation:

> Well fares the man, howe'er his cates do taste,
> That tables not with foul suspicion;
> And he but pines amongst his delicates
> Whose troubled mind is stuffed with discontent.
> My golden time was when I had no gold;
> Though then I wanted, yet I slept secure;
> My daily toil begat me night's repose;
> My night's repose made daylight fresh to me . . .
> But whither doth contemplation carry me?
> The way I seek to find where pleasure dwells
> Is hedged behind me that I cannot back
> But needs must on although to danger's gate. (viii.7–14, 19–22)

Such speeches convey not only character and mood but masterful assurance.

Here, finally, is Alice, in the early stages of awareness that Mosby may not be the passionate lover she has assumed all along:

> Wilt thou not look? Is all thy love overwhelmed?
> Wilt thou not hear? What malice stops thine ears?
> Why speaks thou not? What silence ties thy tongue?
> Thou hast been sighted as the eagle is,
> And heard as quickly as the fearful hare,
> And spoke as smoothly as an orator,
> When I have bid thee hear or see or speak.
> And art thou sensible in none of these? (viii.123–30)

Even the syntactical ordering here cannot prevent the power of the language.

H. A. Kelly writes in *Divine Providence in the England of Shakespeare's Histories* (1970) that 'Shakespeare's great contribution was ... to unmoralize [the] moralizations of his contemporaries' and thus create a kind of characterization that 'eliminates simplistic evaluations of complex moral situations'.[16] Wine agrees and adds that the complexity of situation finds its parallel in the complexity of *Arden*'s structure, linking it with Shakespeare's early tetralogy:

The episodic structure of *Arden* and of the plays in the tetralogy (more so the *Henry VI* plays) involves characters in an intricate web in which their own weaknesses concur with Fortune to bring about their ruin and the ruin of others. The good are weak, ineffectual, or naïve. Gloucester can no more save Henry from himself than Franklin can save Arden from himself. And the evil, through self-betrayal and distrust of one another, destroy themselves. The role of Providence in all these plays is extremely difficult to assess. It is not at all clear that Henry's loss of his kingdom is divine retribution upon the Lancastrians; it is equally not clear that Arden's murder is in any way a fulfillment of Reede's curse. A voice that echoes King Henry's at the worldly Cardinal Beaufort's death-bed seems pervasive throughout *Arden* and the early Histories: 'Forbear to judge, for we are sinners all' (*2 Henry VI*, III.iii.31). Reality is too complicated. (p. xci)

Again and again, Wine locates connections between the tetralogy and *Arden*, noting the common words and shared phrasing, the similarities in the prose style of Jack Cade (though, as we have argued in Chapter 3, these scenes may well be by Marlowe rather than Shakespeare) and that of Black Will and Shakebag (p. lxxxix).

MacDonald P. Jackson, whose Oxford B.Litt. thesis on 'Material for an Edition of *Arden of Faversham*', partly redacted in 'Shakespearean Features of the Poetic Style of *Arden of Faversham*', provides what is still the richest analysis of *Arden*'s style as it relates to Shakespeare. Jackson's thesis is that 'The poetry of Shakespeare's maturity is the most vital and concentrated linguistic medium ever devised.'[17] He follows Philip Edwards in distinguishing Shakespeare's style from that of others by emphasizing the fact that

Shakespeare makes sound, sense, and image work together to maximum effect and in such a way as continually to extend the range of experience gathered into his plays. Shakespeare's poetic language is concrete, packed with sensuous content, catering to the inner ear and eye, stimulating the imagination through metaphor. Shakespeare's natural tendency is always to present [quoting Edwards] 'a concept, a quality, an abstraction, in terms of what is visual, physical, familiar'.[18]

---

[16] As cited by Wine, *Arden of Faversham*, p. xci.   [17] Jackson, 'Shakespearean Features', p. 281.
[18] P. Edwards, *Shakespeare: A Writer's Progress* (Oxford: Oxford University Press, 1986), p. 76; cited by Jackson, 'Shakespearean Features', p. 281.

So in *Macbeth* he speaks not of darkness but of 'the blanket of the dark', not of control but of 'the belt of rule', not of compassion and tenderness but of 'the milk of human kindness'. In each case the common word – 'blanket', 'belt', 'milk' – ties the general idea to a concrete visual image. (p. 281)

If *Arden* is by Shakespeare, however, it is not mature but early Shakespeare. The style is not altogether there, although the identifiably consistent practices largely are. Image-clusters in his earliest work derive, most often, from gardening or from animals, from riding or hunting or birding – the same images and image-clusters that distinguish *Arden of Faversham*.

Yet the early Shakespearean nature of the poetic style of *Arden of Faversham* is best illustrated not by mere citation but by analysis of the qualities of particular passages, according to Jackson.

As they wait to ambush Arden on Rainham Down, Dick Green instructs Black Will and Shakebag in an elaborate figure:

> Well, take your fittest standings, and once more
> Lime your twigs to catch this weary bird.
> I'll leave you, and at your dag's discharge
> Make towards, like the longing water-dog
> That coucheth till the fowling-piece be off,
> Then seizeth on the prey with eager mood.
> Ah, might I see him stretching forth his limbs
> As I have seen them beat their wings ere now. (ix.38–45)

There is nothing comparable to that vivid, detailed, and homely sporting image in the plays of Marlowe, Kyd, Peele, Green, Lyly, Lodge, Nashe, Wilson, Munday, or the other non-Shakespearean dramatists known to have been writing in the decade before *Arden of Faversham* was published. For something similar we have to turn to Shakespeare, as in *1 Henry IV*, IV.ii.45–52:

> How are we park'd and bounded in a pale,
> A little herd of England's timorous deer,
> Maz'd with a yelping kennel of French curs!
> If we be English deer, be then in blood,
> Not rascal-like, to fall down with a pinch,
> But rather, moody-mad; and, desperate stags,
> Turn on the bloody hounds with heads of steel,
> And make cowards stand aloof at bay.

It is the concrete particularity of these two hunting images that makes them quite alien to Shakespeare's predecessors and early contemporaries (p. 282–3). Jackson cites further examples in *2 Henry VI*. The images tend to cluster in more extended and more complex ways than in Kyd, Marlowe, or any other playwright suggested for the authorship of *Arden*. At its most advanced, even in the early playwriting years, the words of Arden also form intricate chains of meaning that reinforce and compli- cate one another, as in Arden's complaint to Franklin about his wife's behaviour (iv.1–20).

There are other features of *Arden*, too, which also seem to point spe- cifically to the talents and techniques of Shakespeare, even the early Shakespeare. One is the use of an unfolding soliloquy or monologue in which a character's insight develops before us. We have seen this in speeches of Michael, Mosby, and Alice. Jackson also finds it in dialogue as well, as in the dialogue about love between Alice and Mosby when, in viii.45–69, both of them say more and less than each of them realizes. The author of *Arden of Faversham* also uses action to reveal inner motives and revealing actions that the character him-/herself, as well as others from the play, may not discern. A case in point is Michael. From nearly the start he is torn between his inbred loyalty to Arden and the promise of Susan, Mosby's sister and Alice's serving maid, if he will only aid in their plan to murder Arden. He has made oaths of loyalty to both parties.

A final characteristic of *Arden of Faversham* that seems Shakespearean is its deliberate ambiguity. How are we to take it? The eight repeated attempts on Arden's life keep building suspense, keep us expecting the worst, keep us watching the consequences of failure on the parts of Alice and Mosby and the wearing effects it has on them. The play is more serious and revealing than a bare outline of plot might suggest. At the same time, each botched attempt seems to flirt with farce, turning the assassins into near-harmless clowns. How, then, are we to take this drama as it replays to an audience already well aware of the notorious story of Thomas Arden? The one voice of reason throughout the play, the one who never seems endangered nor bewil- dered, shamed nor guilt-ridden, is Arden's friend and confidant Franklin. And it is Franklin who delivers the Epilogue, who wraps up everything for us. He begins by narrating the consequences of the play's events:

> Thus have you seen the truth of Arden's death.
> As for the ruffians, Shakebag and Black Will,
> The one took sanctuary, and, being sent for out,
> Was murdered in Southwark as he passed
> To Greenwich, where the Lord Protector lay.
> Black Will was burned in Flushing on a stage;
> Greene was hangèd at Osbridge in Kent;
> The painter fled, and how he died we know not. (Epilogue, 1–8)

In a critical commentary on the play in *Shakespeare Survey*, Alexander Leggatt remarks on these lines that

Shakebag, who kills in passing, is killed in passing – literally. Black Will dies as the ferryman predicted, but he is burned, not hanged. The omen was only half effective. Greene is hanged; and with the rhythm thus established we expect to hear of the painter Clarke's execution in the next line; instead of which the playwright tells us that he doesn't know everything [although history could have told him]. It would have been so easy to slip in another execution; but the playwright does not want things to be that neat. Even in the final mopping-up, something eludes us.[19]

Franklin continues:

> But this above the rest is to be noted:
> Arden lay murdered in that plot of ground
> Which he by force and violence held from Reede,
> And in the grass his body's print was seen
> Two years and more after the deed was done. (Epilogue, 9–13)

This too is deeply equivocal. Arden is murdered, but on that ground he violently held from Reede; he is thus a victim of murder and complicit in causing that murder. The reality of the situation is not in his bloody corpse, but in the two years of an accusing imprint of his body – and perhaps in the success of the murder itself as well as the execution of its perpetrators. They suggest a providence that brings about justice and teaches a lesson long, long after events have become history. Is the play about human frailty or Godly providence? 'Indeed', writes Leggatt, 'much of the play's fascination stems from the way it keeps us guessing about the kind of play it is' (p. 122). This very ambiguity, this open-endedness, is also a feature of Shakespearean drama that his contemporaries do not share.

Most recently, MacDonald P. Jackson, in *Shakespeare Quarterly* (Autumn 2006), has argued forcefully for Shakespeare as the sole author of Scene viii of the play.[20] Like his predecessors, Jackson rehearses a number of lexical and syntactic parallels between lines in *Arden* and in the works of Shakespeare, especially the early works. In this scene, which he calls 'superbly shaped [with a] range of tones [that] is extraordinary' (p. 250), he relates words and strings of words to *The Rape of Lucrece* and a corpus of 132 plays in the Chadwyck-Healey electronic database *Literature*

---

[19] A. Leggatt, '*Arden of Faversham*', *Shakespeare Survey*, 36 (Cambridge: Cambridge University Press, 1983), pp. 121–33 (p. 132).

[20] M. P. Jackson, 'Shakespeare and the Quarrel Scene in *Arden of Faversham*', *Shakespeare Quarterly*, 57.3 (Autumn 2006), 249–93.

Online to prove that Shakespeare was the sole author.[21] At the end of an exhaustive comparison and textual analysis, he argues, following the lead of Keith Sturgess, that Shakespeare is also the author of Scene vi.

There is, therefore, strong evidence for Shakespeare's involvement in *Arden*. Computational stylistics can test this involvement from a new perspective, and can explore further the possible divisions of the play between putative authors. We have taken as our task that of attributing authorship throughout the play. But in this we are presented with an attribution problem of the most difficult kind. There is no external evidence about authorship of any part of it. The writers involved could be one, or two, or more. As with all such completely open authorial questions, we must assume single authorship of sections of the play to find an authorial signature. Testing, at our present stage of developing methods, must be based on an individual style displayed in work elsewhere; the alternative – writers collaborating or revising each other's work – would make attribution almost impossible. Even the question of how to divide the text is difficult. The 1592 Quarto, the only substantive text, is not divided into acts or scenes. Modern editions like the Revels edition by Wine or the Blackwell edition by Kinney divide the play into eighteen scenes and an epilogue. Each of the scenes ends with an '*Exeunt*', and so there are clear-cut 'natural' divisions, but unfortunately most of these scenes are too short for any reliable analysis.

In the face of these challenges, we decided to test primarily for likeness or unlikeness to Shakespeare's acknowledged style. (None of our preliminary testing provided us with any other promising candidates; we deal with the two most often supported, Marlowe and Kyd, later in the chapter.) Shakespeare has been proposed as recently as last year, his authorship is the main concern of this book, and the canon of well-attributed sole-author Shakespeare plays is large enough to provide a useful stylistic basis. We decided to work with the established scene boundaries to begin with, but to build up longer sequences based on our preliminary findings with the scenes.

We started with a variant of Burrows' Zeta method, drawing on the distribution of lexical words. Its base data are counts of the lexical words that appear regularly in a group of texts (here, Shakespeare's plays, divided into segments) but only rarely in a second group (segments from plays by other writers dated by the *Annals of English Drama* between 1580 and 1619), and counts of the complementary list of words rare in Shakespeare but common in the other group. In our variation on the method each list consists

---

[21] *Literature Online*, http://lion.chadwyck.co.uk (Cambridge: Chadwyck-Healey, 1996–).

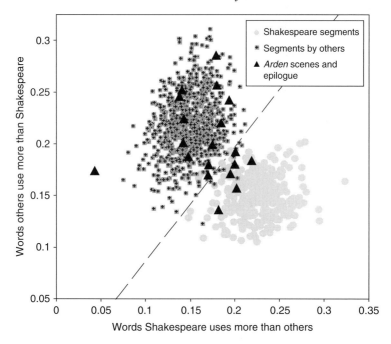

Figure 4.1 Lexical-words test: 2000-word segments from Shakespeare versus 2000-word segments from plays by others, with scenes from *Arden of Faversham*.

of 500 words, the 500 with the greatest contrast in distribution between the Shakespeare segments and others. *Gentle, beseech, answer, spoke,* and *purpose* head the list of words Shakespeare used much more than his contemporaries; *yes, care, hopes, sure,* and *brave* are the first in the list of words that are less frequent in his plays than in others.

Each segment is given a score based on the number of Shakespeare marker words that appear in it, divided by its total number of different words, and a similar score for the non-Shakespearean markers. In Figure 4.1 we have used the two scores as two axes of a scatter-plot. The Shakespeare segments are marked by grey circles and the ones from non-Shakespeare plays by small black crosses. There are 291 Shakespeare segments and 1067 by others. The dotted diagonal line divides what is deemed to be the Shakespeare part of the graph area from the non-Shakespeare part. It was constructed by finding the centroid for each cluster, a point with average scores for the cluster on the two scales, and then drawing a line bisecting the line (not shown on the graph) between the two centroids, at right angles to it.

Table 4.1. *Key to scenes from* Arden of Faversham
plotted in Figure 4.1.

(a) *Scenes on the Shakespeare side of the bisector line
in Figure 4.1.*

Scene	Words	Score on x-axis	Score on y-axis
iv	831	0.202	0.157
v	524	0.182	0.136
vi	363	0.218	0.184
vii	247	0.200	0.180
ix	1286	0.201	0.192
xvi	179	0.195	0.171

(b) *Scenes on the non-Shakespeare side of the bisector line
in Figure 4.1.*

Scene	Words	Score on x-axis	Score on y-axis
i	5230	0.142	0.201
ii	938	0.185	0.220
iii	1724	0.170	0.180
viii	1312	0.148	0.188
x	844	0.138	0.246
xi	268	0.170	0.170
xii	606	0.140	0.252
xiii	1260	0.175	0.199
xiv	3544	0.143	0.224
xv	108	0.179	0.286
xvii	118	0.043	0.174
xviii	320	0.194	0.242
Epilogue	149	0.179	0.256

Of these two 'training' sets of segments, the ones we used to select the two lists of word-variables, just a few from each cluster fall on the 'wrong' side of the line. The vast majority are correctly assigned. We then plotted all eighteen scenes from *Arden of Faversham*, and its Epilogue, on the same two axes, collecting scores for each one for the two lists of words, and dividing each one, as before, by the total number of different words used in that section of the play. These are the black triangles in Figure 4.1. Table 4.1 shows the scenes in two groups, those which fall either side of the dividing line in Figure 4.1. It gives the total number of words used in each scene, and its x- and y-coordinates in the graph, to help identification.

Some of the scenes are very short, and their placement cannot be regarded as reliable. Even for larger scenes, there is an element of error, as we have emphasized through this book. Nevertheless, this analysis gives us an indication of the likeness of these portions of the play to Shakespearean vocabulary patterns. In general, the pattern of Figure 4.1 shows that Shakespeare did write parts of *Arden of Faversham*, but did not write the whole. The two largest scenes, where we can place most reliance, Scenes i and xiv, are in the upper left, or non-Shakespearean, part of the graph (Scene xiv is the third triangle down in the column of five triangles to the left of the cluster of crosses, and Scene i is the fourth triangle down in this column). Six smaller scenes are placed below the dotted line and with the Shakespeare segments.

We can join some of the scenes together, guided by the results in Figure 4.1, so as to divide the play into a smaller number of sections made up of contiguous scenes. This should make for a more reliable assessment, though one that carries a greater risk of combining more than one author's work in a single segment. Scenes i to iii fall into the non-Shakespearean part of Figure 4.1 and together comprise 7892 words. Scenes iv to vii are all in the Shakespeare part of the graph, and amount to 1965 words altogether. Scene viii is on the non-Shakespeare side, but at the lower end of the cluster; Scene ix is just over the boundary into Shakespeare territory. If we join these two we make a third section of the play of 2598 words. The remaining scenes are all on the non-Shakespeare side, save for the short Scene xvi. If we join all these together we make a fourth section of 7396 words in all.

We can calculate scores for these sections on the same basis as before and plot them with the original 2000-word segments (Figure 4.2). The first section, Scenes i to iii, marked by the black circle, falls well into the non-Shakespeare part of the graph. The next section, Scenes iv to vii, marked by the black triangle, is some distance away, within the Shakespeare cluster. The third and fourth sections, the black diamond and black square, are placed in the non-Shakespeare group. The divided authorship of the play is confirmed.

We cannot be sure that we have the boundaries right. It is impossible to tell if short scenes are rightly placed in one grouping or another. Indeed, even the conventional scene divisions may be misleading, since authors may have written only parts of scenes. Nevertheless, we have divisions of the play that are defensible and easily understood, and we can test these further to cross-check the hypothesis of authorship divided between Shakespeare and one or more others, and of the concentration

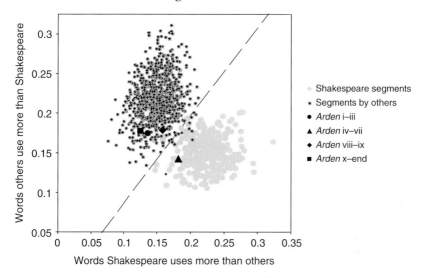

Figure 4.2 Lexical-words test: 2000-word segments from Shakespeare versus 2000-word segments from plays by others, with groups of scenes from *Arden of Faversham*.

of Shakespeare's part in the middle of the play. Figure 4.3 shows a principal component analysis (PCA) using the function words that mark Shakespeare's work as different from others', and including as texts the four larger *Arden* divisions and whole plays by Shakespeare and others from the 1580–1619 period.[22] The Shakespeare plays appear to the left, and the plays by others to the right. The non-Shakespeare plays are widely spread across the vertical axis, whereas the Shakespeare plays are in a narrower band in this dimension. There is some overlap of the two groups, an area where we find both circles and crosses, but it is clear that the first principal component, the horizontal axis, separates most Shakespeare plays from most non-Shakespeare ones. On this axis the second *Arden* group, Scenes iv to vii, is to the extreme left – the Shakespeare end – of the plot. It seems that this section is like Shakespeare in its use of function words as well as in its vocabulary. The third group, comprising Scenes viii and ix, is in the

---

[22] Twenty-seven Shakespeare plays and the eighty-five well-attributed single-author plays in our archive dated by the *Annals* in the target period were included. The word-variables are the twenty-six from our usual list of 200 function words which the *t*-test identified as having a probability of less than 0.001 that the two sets of observations came from the same parent population. The words that are more common in Shakespeare are *almost*, *by* (adverb), *hath*, *did*, *not*, *so* (conjunction and adverb of manner), *something*, and *very*. The words more common in the other plays are *all*, *amongst*, *both*, *can*, *dare*, *may*, *must*, *now*, *only*, *perhaps*, *somewhat*, *still*, *these*, *those*, *to* (infinitive), *unto*, *ye*, and *yet*.

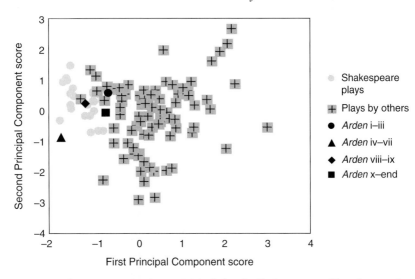

Figure 4.3 Function-words test: PCA of plays by Shakespeare and by others, with groups of scenes from *Arden of Faversham*.

middle of the Shakespeare group. This modifies the result of Figure 4.2. We must record an open verdict on its authorship: it is somewhat unlike Shakespeare in vocabulary, but close to an average Shakespeare score in function-word use. The other two Arden groups are just beyond the edge of the Shakespeare group, with scores higher (just) than any Shakespeare play on the first principal component, but within the non-Shakespeare cluster. This confirms the lexical-words results for these two sections.

We are confident therefore that Shakespeare wrote part of *Arden of Faversham*. We can move to some comparisons with single other authors, along the lines of the work on collaboration in Chapter 2. Marlowe and Kyd, as we have noted earlier in the chapter, have been the other two best supported candidates for authorship of *Arden of Faversham*. Both are represented in our archive, but while there are six well-attributed Marlowe plays, making a sound basis for comparison with other authors, there are only two Kyd plays of undoubted sole authorship: *The Spanish Tragedy* and *Cornelia*. Lukas Erne has made the case that *Soliman and Perseda* should be added to the Kyd canon,[23] so, in the interests of testing the associations between Kyd and *Arden of Faversham* as fully as possible, we decided to run two sets of comparisons between Kyd and Shakespeare, one with *The*

23 L. Erne, *Beyond* The Spanish Tragedy: *A Study of the Works of Thomas Kyd* (Manchester: Manchester University Press, 2001), pp. 160–6.

Spanish Tragedy and *Cornelia* alone representing Kyd, and one with an expanded Kyd group including *Soliman and Perseda* as well.

We turned first to our usual lexical-words test, which begins by identifying a large group of words that appear more often in one writer than in the other, and another group that appear more often in the second writer than the first. We establish the typical ranges for the two authors through counts of these words in 2000-word 'training' segments from plays we know are by one writer or the other. On this basis we can test sections of disputed authorship. We compared Shakespeare to Marlowe, to the two-play Kyd, and to the three-play Kyd. In the event, in each of the three tests, the four *Arden* sections were placed on the Shakespeare side of the bisector line we established to mark Shakespeare from non-Shakespeare parts of the graph. In the two Kyd comparisons all the 'training' segments were placed on the correct side of the bisector line. In the Shakespeare–Marlowe test, all the 'training' segments but one fell to the correct side of the line (the exception was the seventh segment of *The Jew of Malta*, which was placed just to the Shakespeare side).

These tests thus gave no support for the idea that Marlowe or Kyd were collaborators in writing *Arden of Faversham*. To explore this further we turned to our other source of data for the plays, the counts of function words. For each of the three comparisons, we proceeded as in the one-on-one tests of Chapter 2. We identified function words with characteristically higher or lower counts in one writer as compared to the other and then used these words for a PCA of the 'training' sets of 2000-word segments and the four *Arden* sections. Figure 4.4 shows the results for the Shakespeare–Marlowe test. The two clusters of known Shakespeare and Marlowe segments overlap a good deal. Our main interest is in the first, third, and fourth *Arden* sections, marked by the black circle, diamond, and square. The square is well outside the Marlowe cluster, much more like Shakespeare on these measures. The circle and the diamond are at the outer edge of the Marlowe cluster, but well within the Shakespeare one. None of them is marked out as strikingly like Marlowe as against Shakespeare. Marlowe does not appear to be the, or a, collaborator in the play. The triangle falls in a shared territory, and is about equally close to Shakespeare as to Marlowe patterns on this test.

Figure 4.5 shows the same test, this time with the two-play Kyd set compared to Shakespeare. All four sections are outside the Kyd cluster, and within the larger Shakespeare one. Again, there is nothing encouraging for Kyd's candidature here. Finally, we tested Shakespeare segments against an enlarged hypothetical Kyd group (Figure 4.6). One of the

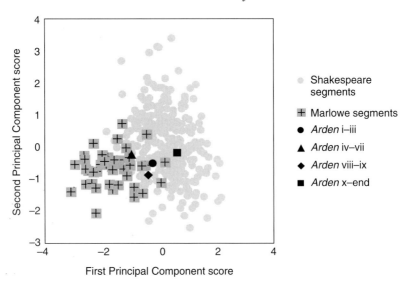

Figure 4.4 Function-words test: PCA of 2000-word segments from Shakespeare and from Marlowe plays, with groups of scenes from *Arden of Faversham*.

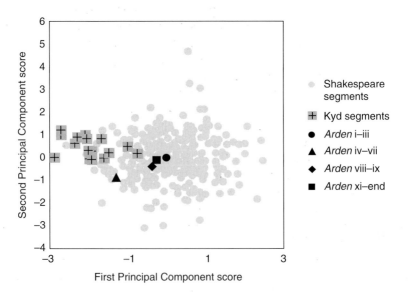

Figure 4.5 Function-words test: PCA of 2000-word segments from Shakespeare plays and from well-attributed Kyd plays (*Cornelia* and *Spanish Tragedy*), with groups of scenes from *Arden of Faversham*.

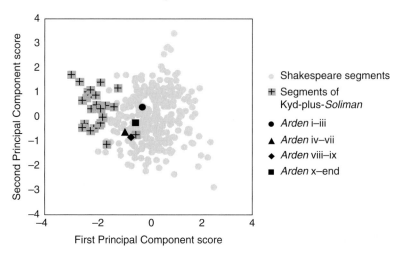

Figure 4.6 Function-words test: PCA of 2000-word segments from Shakespeare plays and from a hypothetical enlarged Kyd grouping (*Cornelia, Soliman and Perseda,* and *Spanish Tragedy*), with groups of scenes from *Arden of Faversham.*

crosses – the second segment of *Soliman and Perseda* – is placed away from the new Kyd-plus-*Soliman* cluster. The four sections of *Arden* are also all placed well away from the main cluster of crosses, more like Shakespeare than like Kyd-plus-*Soliman*. They have scores that associate them with the second segment of *Soliman,* but there is no pattern of association with the new Kyd grouping. Our tests show no sustained affinities between the *Arden* sections and the work of Marlowe or Kyd, either in vocabulary or in function-word use. We suggest that the quest to find Shakespeare's partner or partners in the *Arden* enterprise must look beyond these two.

Our conclusions on Shakespeare's putative authorship of *Arden of Faversham* are more positive. We were able to test the attribution in two quite independent but mutually reinforcing ways. Given that the results broadly confirmed each other, we can be confident in our conclusions: *Arden of Faversham* is a collaboration; Shakespeare was one of the authors; and his part is concentrated in the middle section of the play. We can in addition hazard that Shakespeare's portion lies within the sequence beginning at Scene iv in the modern division of the play and ending with Scene ix. While this confirms MacDonald P. Jackson's recent proposal, we can now extend it considerably while nevertheless supplying probable boundaries to Shakespeare's part in the play.

CHAPTER 5

Edmond Ironside *and the question of Shakespearean authorship*

Philip Palmer

In 1932, Muriel St Clare Byrne drew the following distinction between authentic authorial style and the conventional 'tricks' of the commercial theatre: 'The Mundays and the Chettles have their tricks of expression, but because they are just tricks they or anybody else can use them. Tricks are catching: style is not'.[1] Byrne's simple observation reveals a manifest truth about authorship attribution and the Early Modern English stage. It is perplexing that so many subsequent critics have ignored her useful advice. This is especially true when considering the fraught role of internal evidence in many failed attribution projects, which have employed suspect methodologies in order to highlight affinities in 'tricks' between anonymous plays and known playwrights. The case of the anonymous *Edmond Ironside* serves as a prime example of this practice. The only critics who have attributed an author to the play – E. B. Everitt and Eric Sams – failed to build their arguments on anything stronger than verbal parallels. These features of a dramatic text typically reflect the mere 'tricks' of theatrical convention rather than the subtle linguistic nuances of authorial style.

Yet one has to give Everitt and Sams credit for trying to build an authorship case on the dearth of evidence the play provides. When trying to prove authorship for a play such as *Ironside*, for which no definite date, publication, or performance record exists, internal substantiation is the only way to proceed. After a long period of disfavour following Samuel Schoenbaum's *Internal Evidence and Elizabethan Dramatic Authorship* (1966),[2] the use of such evidence in the field of attribution studies has rebounded in recent years owing to computational stylistics. Developments in this exciting new field mean that it makes sense to reassess anonymous plays that have slipped into critical oblivion. My chapter will apply

---

[1] M. St C. Byrne, 'Bibliographical Clues in Collaborate Plays', *The Library*, 4th series, 13 (1932), 21–48.

[2] S. Schoenbaum, *Internal Evidence and Elizabethan Dramatic Authorship: An Essay in Literary History and Method* (London: Edward Arnold, 1966).

computational stylistics to *Edmond Ironside* in order to shed more light on its anonymous authorship and corroborate earlier arguments that Shakespeare did not write the play. Although it may seem unnecessary to exhume the arguments of Sams and Everitt – simply because they have been so convincingly debunked by earlier critics – this case study holds great import for exploring the methods of computational stylistics and its manifold applications to Early Modern literature.

Critics have produced a variety of responses – ranging from conservative to controversial – to the question of authorship and *Edmond Ironside*. For almost the first 100 years of scholarship surrounding the play, critical attention focused exclusively on its dramatic characteristics, the state of the manuscript, and source material – thereby sidestepping the more risky arguments of dating and authorship. Yet the tenuous claims of two twentieth-century scholars positing Shakespearean authorship of the work would dramatically alter the play's critical landscape. Despite the considerable amount of literature reacting to the work of Everitt and Sams, many critics have begun to move away from the question of *Ironside*'s authorship entirely. It appears that recent critical approaches to the play – usually expository in nature – hearken back to more conservative treatments given earlier in the century.

The first scholar to provide commentary on the play, albeit cursory and inaccurate commentary, was the mid-nineteenth-century scholar J. O. Halliwell-Phillipps.[3] His conclusion of 1647 as *Ironside*'s date of composition seems far-fetched to anyone familiar with the conventions of the play. It is probable that Halliwell-Phillipps was simply thrown off by the mid-seventeenth-century actors' names scrawled in the manuscript's margins. A. H. Bullen concurred with this date in an introduction to his 1887 edition of the play in an equally cursory treatment of the topic.[4]

The critics of the early twentieth century were the first to make concerted efforts to study the play and its date. Both Madeleine Hope Dodds and F. S. Boas posited 'around 1590' for the date of the play's composition. Strong similarities between *Ironside*'s dramatic techniques and those of plays written in the 1590s formed the foundation for their dating arguments. In a 1924 article, Dodds discussed the play's influence on Anthony Brewer's *The Love-Sick King*, claiming that an acting troupe descended from the Lord Admiral's Men revived the play for performance.[5] Since

[3] J. O. Halliwell-Phillipps, *A Dictionary of Old English Plays* (London: J. R. Smith, 1860), p. 82.

[4] A. H. Bullen, ed., *Old English Plays, New Series* (London: Wyman and Sons, 1887–90), Vol. II, p. 420.

[5] M. H. Dodds, '*Edmond Ironside* and *The Love-Sick King*', *MLR*, 19 (1924), 158–68.

Dodds was much more preoccupied with *Ironside*'s seventeenth-century afterlife, it is no surprise that she simply stated her opinion of the play's date before moving away from questions of the play's origins. Boas investigated the placement of *Edmond Ironside* within the Egerton 1994 MS collection, now in the British Library, in addition to analysing the play's interpolated stage directions, the latter of which mention seventeenth-century actors. He drew the conclusion that a company in the 'fourth decade of the seventeenth century' must have performed the play.[6] Despite his emphasis on the play's seventeenth-century life, Boas did assign it an early date of composition, mainly because of the 'neo-Senecan' stage conventions and themes found throughout the text. Boas also mentioned that *Edmond Ironside* is written in a script unlike any other play in MS Egerton 1994. He concluded that the play, along with the early *Thomas of Woodstock*, was revived to join *The Captives* and *The Two Noble Ladies* as the small repertoire of a seventeenth-century travelling company (p. 104).

The first printed edition of the play, published by the Malone Society in 1927, contains a brief but informative discussion by Eleanor Boswell.[7] She too dated the play to the early 1590s and attributed its seventeenth-century performances to a provincial group. She was the first scholar to draw attention to the play's main theatrical reviser, whom Randall Martin identifies as Hand A in his 1991 edition of *Ironside*.[8] Boswell concluded that the chief hand in the MS probably belonged to a playhouse scribe familiar with legal handwriting and terminology. The nature of the handwriting moved Boswell to label the scribe 'a broken-down scrivener's clerk'. Like Boas, Boswell suggested that *Edmond Ironside* could be related to the lost plays *Knewtus* and *Hardicanute*, performances of which Henslowe mentioned in the autumn of 1597. She also dedicates a small portion of her introduction to the actual content of the play, pointing out several of its theatrical conventions in addition to the playwright's idiosyncrasies and shortcomings. Like her predecessors, Boswell makes no attempt to attribute the play to an author.

The next couple of decades showed little dissent from the opinions of Boas and Boswell. Both W. W. Greg and E. K. Chambers paid little attention to the play and mainly reiterated the work of previous critics.[9]

---

[6] F. S. Boas, *Shakespeare and the Universities* (Oxford: The Shakespeare Head Press, 1923), pp. 111–42.

[7] E. Boswell, ed., *Edmond Ironside* (Oxford: Oxford University Press, 1927).

[8] R. Martin, ed., *Edmond Ironside and Anthony Brewer's* The Love-Sick King (New York: Garland, 1991), p. 356.

[9] Greg provides a more detailed bibliographical analysis of the play MS than Boswell in his *Dramatic Documents from the Elizabethan Playhouses* (Oxford: Oxford University Press, 1931), pp. 256–61.

However, Greg's bibliographical analysis did reveal that the MS is a prompt copy from the playhouse penned by 'a not very intelligent scribe'. Greg also concluded 'there is no evidence of censorship' in the MS.[10] A few years later Robert Boies Sharpe diverged from the dating consensus of the previous decades and suggested 1598 as the date of composition. He drew his conclusion from what he interpreted as a topical reference to the Earl of Essex in the play's dissembling character Edricus. According to Sharpe, strong confluences exist between Edricus's character and court opinion of Essex in 1598.[11] In 1942 Alfred Hart's discussion of the play in terms of theatrical excision largely ignored the topics of authorship and dating.[12]

No student of *Ironside* endeavoured an attribution argument until E. B. Everitt wrote his controversial book *The Young Shakespeare* in 1954.[13] This work disturbed the status quo of cautious conservatism associated with the play and incited unfavourable critical responses. Everitt contended that several anonymous Elizabethan plays, including *Ironside*, were written by William Shakespeare. In the case of *Ironside*, Everitt also argued that the MS is a holograph copy. He built his argument from evidence gathered almost entirely from verbal parallels. His lack of caution while using such a methodology implies that he failed to take the advice found in Byrne's 'Bibliographical Clues in Collaborate Plays' published two decades before.[14] Everitt's attribution of the play to Shakespeare served less to solve the play's authorship question and more to prove once and for all what Shakespeare was up to in the 'lost years'. In order to accomplish his goal, Everitt took the 'lumping' approach to authorship attribution – a strategy that seeks to add works to a given author's canon – as a means of filling in biographical gaps.[15] Everitt's views were not well received. No fewer than five rebuttals appeared within the decade following publication of his

---

The specificity of his study excluded any discussion of dating or authorship. Chambers toes the party line in his three-sentence description of the play found in *William Shakespeare: A Study of Facts and Problems*, 2 vols. (Oxford: Oxford University Press, 1930), Vol. I, p. 111.

[10] Greg, *Dramatic Documents*, p. 258.

[11] R. B. Sharpe, *The Real War of the Theaters* (Boston: D.C. Heath and Co., 1935), pp. 100–1.

[12] A. Hart, *Stolne and Surreptitious Copies: A Comparative Study of Shakespeare's Bad Quartos* (London: Melbourne University Press in association with Oxford University Press, 1942), pp. 126–7.

[13] E. B. Everitt, *The Young Shakespeare: Studies in Documentary Evidence*, Anglistica, 2 (Copenhagen: Rosenkilde and Bagger, 1954).

[14] See n. 1. Her essay deals mainly with questions of authorship concerning *The Downfall of Robert Earl of Huntington* and *The Death of Robert Earl of Huntington*. However, Byrne does provide 'golden rules' for using parallels in attribution arguments. She also exhibits scepticism concerning any traces of individual style in plays that are heavily edited, or collaborative, or both.

[15] Harold Love explains lumping and splitting in his insightful and invaluable *Attributing Authorship: An Introduction* (Cambridge: Cambridge University Press, 2002), pp. 219–20.

controversial work.[16] Some called his work 'dangerously retrogressive' and 'a feast of speculation'.[17]

One of these reviewers, Irving Ribner, did more than simply criticize Everitt's argument. Building upon Madeline Hope Dodds's supposition about the play's performance in the seventeenth century, Ribner claimed that the *original* Lord Admiral's Men first performed *Ironside* in the late sixteenth century.[18] This argument would make Ribner the first critic to attribute the play's original performance to a particular theatrical company. For the next couple of decades, various critics discussed the play, but usually only in passing. In 1958 Bernard Spivack studied the play's depiction of the transformed Vice figure. He also placed the work in the context of the Elizabethan chronicle history play.[19] Ten years later David Bevington connected the play with the Essex controversy of 1598, thereby resurrecting Sharpe's earlier dating argument.[20]

In the early 1980s, critical attention again shifted towards identifying the play's author. The work of Eric Sams was solely responsible for the resurfacing of the play in addition to its attendant controversies and scholarly feuds. An article of his published in the *Times Literary Supplement* (*TLS*) as well as his book *Shakespeare's Lost Play: Edmund Ironside* resurrected Everitt's old argument that Shakespeare wrote the play in addition to several other plays lacking definite authorship.[21] Sams inherited both Everitt's methodology and his argument, as evinced in his reliance on parallels to prove authorship. Sams's voluminous commentary in *Shakespeare's Lost Play* essentially relied on treating intellectual, theatrical, and literary commonplaces of the Elizabethan age as exclusively Shakespearean.[22] He then found examples of these phrases in *Ironside* and concluded that Shakespeare wrote the play as an apprentice in 1588. He buttresses this early date with mention of a law passed in 1589 that placed the Archbishop of Canterbury

---

[16] These include R. A. Law, 'Guessing about the Youthful Shakespeare', *University of Texas Studies in English*, 34 (1955), 43–50; M. P. Jackson, 'Shakespeare and *Edmund Ironside*', *Notes and Queries*, 208 (1963), 331–2; and Schoenbaum, *Internal Evidence*.

[17] Respectively, from the reviews by M. M. Reese, *Review of English Studies*, n.s., 6.23 (July 1955), 310–13, and Clifford Leech, *Modern Language Notes*, 70.3 (March 1955), 206–8.

[18] This argument is based on the appearance of seventeenth-century actors' names in the *Ironside* MS and their former connections with the Lord Admiral's Men. See I. Ribner, *The English History Play in the Age of Shakespeare* (London: Methuen, 1965), pp. 241–3.

[19] B. Spivack, *Shakespeare and the Allegory of Evil* (New York: Columbia University Press, 1958), pp. 340–5, 444–5.

[20] D. Bevington, *Tudor Drama and Politics: A Critical Approach to Topical Meaning* (Cambridge, MA: Harvard University Press, 1968), p. 291.

[21] E. Sams, '*Edmund Ironside*: A Reappraisal', *TLS*, 13 August 1982, p. 879, and *Shakespeare's Lost Play: Edmund Ironside* (New York: St Martin's Press, 1985).

[22] Sams accomplished this negatively – he simply didn't mention known playwrights or authors other than Shakespeare when building examples of parallel wording and imagery.

on a censorial board reviewing London plays. This law is significant because such a powerful censor would most probably not have approved of the verbal battle between the Archbishops of York and Canterbury in III.i of *Ironside*, a scene in which the two exchange highly charged political insults.[23] Sams's work generated a host of negative responses, starting in the *TLS* during the summer and autumn of 1982.[24] This initial flurry of short letters would soon transform into extended debates between Sams and his opponents, such as Donald Foster and M. W. A. Smith. Sams wrote an especially scathing *Notes and Queries* article directed at Smith and his use of stylometry, describing Smith's statistical-linguistic methodology as a pseudo-science akin to phrenology.[25] This contrasted oddly with the postscript to *Shakespeare's Lost Play*, where Sams made an optimistic reference to stylometric results freshly produced from the University of Akron.[26] Clearly, Sams condoned statistical analyses of style only if they supported his own argument.

In the same year that Sams's edition of the play was published, Louis Ule presented a concordance and stylometric analysis of the 'Shakespeare Apocrypha' that seemed to support the idea that Shakespeare did in fact write some of the anonymous plays of the late-Elizabethan period. However, there are problems with the study's methodology that are difficult to ignore.[27] *Ironside* is included in the book, yet the tight clusters it forms with the other plays are inconsistent, unimpressive, and confusing.

[23] However, both Greg (see n. 8) and Chambers, *William Shakespeare*, p. 111, argued that the play MS lacks evidence of a censorial hand. Along different lines, Sams overlooked the possibility of provincial performance when sticking to the early date (contingent solely upon the play's performance in London). Since it so happens that the early date supports the Sams–Everitt argument concerning Shakespeare's early career as a playwright, this piece of evidence (i.e. early dating) was highly advantageous to their specious arguments.

[24] The following letters to the editor of the *TLS* comprise the initial wave of responses to Sams's work with *Ironside*: Robert F. Fleissner (3 September 1982), Paul Xuereb (3 September 1982), MacDonald P. Jackson (10 September 1982), Richard Proudfoot (17 September 1982), Sams (24 September 1982), Proudfoot (8 October 1982), Proudfoot (22 October 1982), Sams (29 October 1982), Peter Milward (11 November 1982), Gary Taylor (1 April 1983).

[25] M. W. A. Smith, '*Edmund Ironside* and Principles of Authorship Attribution', *The Shakespeare Newsletter*, 38 (Autumn–Winter 1988), 50; M. W. A. Smith, 'Word-Links and the Authorship of *Edmund Ironside*', *Notes and Queries*, 35.4 (December 1988), 447–9; M. W. A. Smith, '*Edmund Ironside* (Attribution to William Shakespeare)', *Notes and Queries*, 40.2 (June 1993), 202–4; Eric Sams, '*Edmund Ironside* and Stylometry', *Notes and Queries*, 41.4 (December 1994), 469; M. W. A. Smith '*Edmund Ironside*: Scholarship versus Propaganda', *Notes and Queries*, 42.3 (September 1995), 294.

[26] Sams, *Shakespeare's Lost Play*, p. 367.

[27] L. Ule, ed., *William Shakespeare: A Concordance to the Shakespeare Apocrypha*, 3 vols. (Hildesheim: Georg Olms, 1987). Only certain anonymous late-sixteenth-century plays, the corpus of Marlowe, and that of Shakespeare are included in the analysis. Since comparing anonymous plays proves little about *who* actually wrote a given play, there are only two possibilities for the

The next critic to publish an edition of *Edmond Ironside*, Randall Martin, wisely chose the more conservative approach to the play by declining to assign it an author.[28] In the tradition of Boswell, Boas, and Greg, Martin provided a detailed analysis of the play's themes and sources, and the state of the MS. As the title of the book, *Edmond Ironside and Anthony Brewer's* The Love-Sick King suggests, Martin was reviving Dodds's thesis about the connection between the two plays in the seventeenth century. He extended her observation by claiming that *The Love-Sick King* was probably performed for King James at Newcastle in 1617. The 'Authorship and Date' section of the work presented some new ideas about the play while at the same time addressing the question of Shakespearean authorship recently argued by Sams. Martin acknowledged that owing to the play's lack of definite date, the dubious path of internal evidence must be taken and therefore literary influence one way or the other is difficult to prove (p. 363). Yet Martin convincingly showed that the passages in *Ironside* most similar to early Shakespeare are derivative in nature and exhibit weak imitations of his imagery and vocabulary.

Based on the idea that *Ironside* borrowed from Shakespeare, Martin posited a *terminus a quo* for dating purposes of May 1593 – a date corresponding to the entry for *Venus and Adonis* in the Stationers' Register. *Ironside* at least had to be written after 1590 since it uses the word *braggadochios*, first coined by Spenser in *The Faerie Queene*. Martin's argument for the *terminus ad quem* was less convincing, yet it gains support from other evidence concerning the conventions of the play. Owing mainly to scenic parallels between *Ironside* and the printed version of *A Knack to Know a Knave* of 1594 – a play that exhibits signs of influence from *Ironside* – Martin set the *terminus ad quem* at January of that year (p. 370). Martin agreed with others before him that the play was written for provincial performance, both in the late-sixteenth and seventeenth centuries. He concluded that because of similarities of casting demands between *Ironside* and other Strange's Men plays, the play was most probably performed by the amalgamated Strange's Men–Admiral's Men in their summer and autumn tours of 1593 (pp. 373–4). He cites the 6 May Privy Council warrant issued to Strange's Men – which granted them the ability to tour while the plague raged in London – as a free ticket for the company to tour the provinces, ultimately keeping the *Ironside* MS away from the censors (pp. 374–5).

author of these plays: Marlowe or Shakespeare. In addition, the tight clusters resulting from these analyses are rarely consistent and often produce results that external evidence easily dismisses.

[28] Martin, *Edmond Ironside and* The Love-Sick King.

Since Martin's edition, critics have returned to giving the play the sparse treatment that characterized earlier studies. There has also been a marked shift away from the authorship question, perhaps out of frustration or simply because of a lack of interest in the topic. Larry S. Champion includes a chapter on *Edmond Ironside* in his study of dramaturgical practice and political ideology in Early Modern English history plays. Champion summarizes the authorship debates surrounding the play, but quickly makes it clear that his interests in the play lie in its dramaturgical features.[29] Jonathan Bate's 1995 Arden edition of *Titus Andronicus* made a brief reference in a footnote to *Ironside*'s date of composition as 'the late 1590s'. He also pointed out a few, but not all, of the parallel phrases that exist between the two plays.[30]

Eric Sams's *The Real Shakespeare*, published in the same year, continued arguments first made by Everitt and seemed to be a later incarnation of the earlier scholar's *The Young Shakespeare*.[31] Here Sams again made the argument that Shakespeare wrote a large group of anonymous Elizabethan plays.[32] A 2001 *Notes and Queries* article by Sams continued this trend as he attempted to prove, through an 'essay' consisting almost entirely of verbal parallels, that *Ironside* and the anonymous *True Chronicle History of King Leir* were written by the same author, namely Shakespeare.[33] His evidence consisted solely of shared commonplaces between the two plays, such as the use of 'Troynovant', biblical quotation, rhetorical techniques such as antithesis and alliteration, and a slew of parallels that were rarely impressive.[34] In 2000, Leah Scragg wrote an article on *Ironside* that mainly discusses elements of the play's plot and historical significance while observing the authorship debate from the sidelines.[35] In the most recent article written on the play (2003), Ramon Jiménez agreed with the arguments

[29] L. S. Champion, '*The Noise of Threatening Drum*': *Dramatic Strategy and Political Ideology in Shakespeare and the English Chronicle Plays* (Newark, DE: University of Delaware Press, 1990), pp. 59–70.

[30] J. Bate, ed., *Titus Andronicus*, Arden Shakespeare (New York: Routledge, 1995), pp. 81, 159, 185.

[31] E. Sams, *The Real Shakespeare: Retrieving the Early Years, 1564–1594* (New Haven: Yale University Press, 1995).

[32] Sams's prolonged attack on the 'Shakespeare establishment' runs throughout the book, lending the work a tone reminiscent of conspiracy theories. In his review, Michael Bristol states: 'The problem is that his arguments are bound up with a specious narrative of cover-up and conspiracy in which Eric Sams stands alone against the Shakespeare establishment' (*Renaissance Quarterly*, 50.2 (Summer 1997), 607–9).

[33] E. Sams, '*King Lear* and *Edmond Ironside*', *Notes and Queries*, 48.3 (September 2001), 266–70.

[34] For instance, 'Troynovant' is found in both *Locrine* and *Friar Bacon and Friar Bungay*, the latter of which was extremely popular.

[35] L. Scragg, 'Saxons versus Danes: The Anonymous *Edmond Ironside*', in *Literary Appropriations of the Anglo-Saxons from the Thirteenth to the Twentieth Century*, ed. D. Scragg and C. Weinberg (New York: Cambridge University Press, 2000), pp. 93–106.

of Sams and Everitt but then proceeded to make an Oxfordian argument for the authorship of Shakespeare's plays.[36] The Oxfordian argument notwithstanding, Jiménez's citation of Everitt and Sams as infallible sources on the authorship of *Ironside* was particularly troubling. As the critical history of this play proves, scholars have either approached *Ironside* with extreme caution in an attempt to introduce the obscure play to a wider readership, or with bold ideas of using the play to prove larger arguments concerning Shakespeare. One could say that an honest attempt at authorship attribution divorced from ulterior motives has yet to be attempted with *Ironside*.

Affinities between passages in *Ironside* and early Shakespeare works such as *Titus Andronicus*, *Richard III*, the *Henry VI* plays, and *Venus and Adonis* have led scholars either to attribute the play to Shakespeare himself or to show that the *Ironside* playwright was heavily indebted to him. Most have joined the second camp. Through methodologies of computational stylistics, we can show that *Ironside* is well separated from Shakespeare's plays on the grounds of common and uncommon vocabulary frequency – data that can quantify both unconscious style and vocabulary choice. We have submitted *Ironside* to two tests against Shakespeare's plays and eighty-five other single-author plays written by various writers of the period. The first test is a discriminant analysis using the frequency of 200 function words in 2000-word segments of all plays considered.[37] We began by making an estimate of the reliability of the test by choosing some sample plays, withdrawing one play at a time from the Shakespeare or non-Shakespeare sets, and allowing the analysis to ascribe its segments either to the Shakespeare or the non-Shakespeare group (Table 5.1).

The results are mixed. The test is wholly accurate with three plays (*Coriolanus*, *Hengist*, and *John a Kent and John a Cumber*), but fares poorly with *A Midsummer Night's Dream* and *Love's Labour's Lost* (with these plays four out of eight and three out of ten segments respectively were classified with the non-Shakespeare group). Overall the success rate was 98 out of 117, or 84 per cent. The method has some power to differentiate – it mostly gets it right – but the task of discriminating between Shakespeare and all comers at the level of 2000-word segments is clearly a difficult one, and we need to bear this in mind in considering the results for the seven *Edmond Ironside* segments. All seven of these were classified as non-Shakespeare. It looks already as if Shakespeare's authorship of the whole play is extremely

---

[36] R. Jiménez, '*Edmond Ironside, the English King*: Edward de Vere's Anglo-Saxon History Play', *The Oxfordian*, 6 (2003), 7–27.

[37] For a discussion of this method, see Chapter 7, below.

Table 5.1. *2000-word segments of 6 test plays by Shakespeare and 6 test plays by others classified as Shakespeare or non-Shakespeare by discriminant analysis.*

		Segments correctly classified	Segments mis-classified
Shakespeare	*Coriolanus*	13	0
Shakespeare	*1 Henry IV*	10	2
Shakespeare	*King John*	8	2
Shakespeare	*Love's Labour's Lost*	7	3
Shakespeare	*A Midsummer Night's Dream*	4	4
Shakespeare	*Twelfth Night*	8	1
SHAKESPEARE TOTAL		50	12
		81%	19%
Day	*Isle of Gulls*	8	2
Dekker	*If It Be Not Good*	9	2
Heywood	*Woman Killed with Kindness*	6	2
Middleton	*Hengist*	10	0
Middleton	*Phoenix*	9	1
Munday	*John a Kent and John a Cumber*	6	0
NON-SHAKESPEARE TOTAL		48	7
		87%	13%
GRAND TOTAL		98	19
		84%	16%

Variables are frequencies of 200 function words. The training sets are segments of 27 Shakespeare plays and 85 plays by other playwrights dated 1580–1619. The test plays are chosen at random from the Shakespeare and non-Shakespeare sets.

unlikely, given that none of the seven segments were ascribed to him in this test. There is nothing here to support his authorship of any one section of the play either, though, given the results presented in Table 5.1, we could not rule out the possibility on the basis of this one test that he had a hand in some part of it. The test focuses on occurrences of function words: stylistic features that exist more covertly within a text than the appearance of rare words and phrases; the results reflect the more unconscious style of Shakespeare, the other playwrights, and the writer of *Ironside*.

The second test focuses on lexical words highly characteristic or non-characteristic of Shakespeare's vocabulary selection throughout his works. A group of 500 words commonly found in Shakespeare and 500 not usually found in Shakespeare form the basis for this test, pitting *Ironside* against Shakespeare's plays and those by others. On the graph shown in

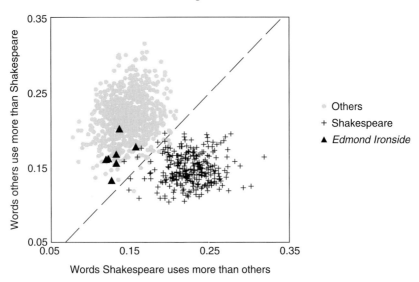

Figure 5.1 Lexical-words test: 2000-word segments of 27 Shakespeare plays versus 2000-word segments from 85 plays by others dated 1580–1619, with segments of *Edmond Ironside*.

Figure 5.1, the *x*-axis represents the proportional count of Shakespearean marker words while the *y*-axis denotes the proportional count of non-Shakespearean marker words. The two training sets of segments overlap each other, reflecting once again the difficulties of finding a neat discrimination between all the Shakespeare segments and all the rest. (Segments that have not played a part in the selection of marker words would probably be more confused still.) Nevertheless, there are clear tendencies here. In the graph the dashed line is the perpendicular bisector of a line between the two centroids, forming a boundary between the area where we can broadly expect Shakespeare segments to appear and the area where we can expect to find segments by others. All the *Ironside* segments are once again classified as non-Shakespeare.

The combined results tell us that it is most unlikely that Shakespeare wrote any substantial part of *Edmond Ironside*. There is nothing here to link the play with Shakespeare, and indeed strong evidence that its language patterns are so different from his as to rule him out as its author. Clearly the search must now focus on candidates beyond Shakespeare.

Since stylistic tests have confirmed the notion that Shakespeare didn't write *Ironside*, we need to look elsewhere for a putative author. We can

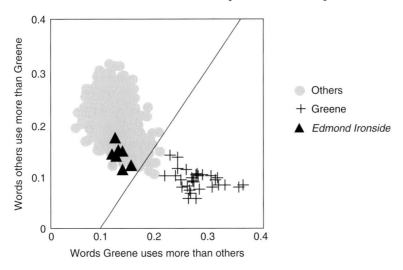

Figure 5.2 Lexical-words test: 2000-word segments of 4 Greene plays versus 2000-word segments from 108 plays by others dated 1580–1619, with segments of *Edmond Ironside.*

start with the ten playwrights apart from Shakespeare in Sams's 'identity parade' of suspects for authorship of the play.[38] Of these, four – Greene, Lyly, Marlowe, and Peele – are represented by four or more plays in our archive, and so provide a reasonably broad basis for comparison with other authors. They can be compared with *Ironside* in the manner of the second test against Shakespearean plays – that is, on the basis of the frequency of authorial 'marker words'. As one can see from the graphs in Figures 5.2 to 5.5, the 2000-word segments of *Ironside* as a group do not show any marked affinity with any of these writers' vocabularies. It is true that one segment of the play is on the Marlowe side of the bisector line in Figure 5.4, but in that case the two clusters (Marlowe segments, marked by crosses, and segments by others, marked by grey discs) overlap considerably, so that the placement of this *Edmond Ironside* segment is truly only on the fringes of a Marlowe vocabulary style.

To continue the quest for an author beyond the four already tested we can try a 'fishing expedition', starting with the vocabulary of *Edmond Ironside* this time, and seeking resemblances with various playwrights' work, even if they are represented by a single play. This is less reliable than starting with well-established authorial patterns, and then measuring the

---

[38] Sams, *Shakespeare's Lost Play,* p. 5.

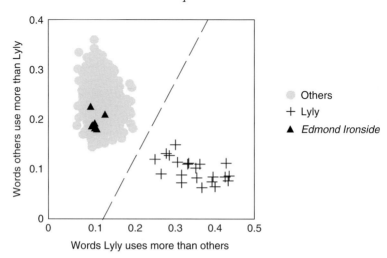

Figure 5.3 Lexical-words test: 2000-word segments of 4 Lyly plays versus 2000-word segments from 108 plays by others dated 1580–1619, with segments of *Edmond Ironside*.

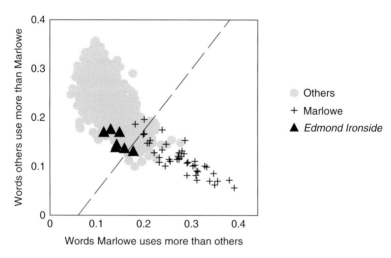

Figure 5.4 Lexical-words test: 2000-word segments of 6 Marlowe plays versus 2000-word segments from 106 plays by others dated 1580–1619, with segments of *Edmond Ironside*.

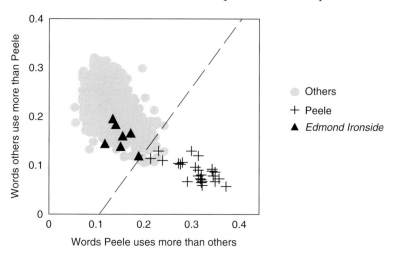

Figure 5.5 Lexical-words test: 2000-word segments of 4 Peele plays versus 2000-word segments from 108 plays by others dated 1580–1619, with segments of *Edmond Ironside*.

likeness or otherwise of the target play, but it might point to a new candidate whom we could then pursue more systematically. In this case we compare the overlap of individual plays with the total vocabulary of *Edmond Ironside*.[39] We discard the most common words and proper names, and then find how many of the words in the play occur in each of a set of plays by the eleven playwrights in Sams's list. This means we include four playwrights with just one play in the set (Chettle, Lodge, Munday, and Nashe), one with two (Kyd), one with three (Chapman), three with four (Greene, Lyly, and Peele), and one with six (Marlowe), as well as Shakespeare with twenty-seven. We then have a list of all the fifty-four plays by the eleven authors included, each with a score for how many of the *Edmond Ironside* words their plays contain. We make up eleven author variables, in each of which the plays of the chosen author are given a score of 1, and the plays by others a score of zero. We then correlate the column of scores with each author variable in turn. The higher the correlation, the more the author's plays tend to overlap with the vocabulary of *Edmond Ironside* (Figure 5.6). Lyly scores highest, but the fact that his score is hardly higher than Peele's, Marlowe's, Greene's, or Munday's demonstrates that this is only a faint

---

[39] This is a simple method for finding a so-called 'intertextual distance' between plays. For a more complex version, which takes account of information from the frequencies of the words as well as from their appearance or non-appearance, see D. Labbé, 'Experiments on Authorship Attribution by Intertextual Distance in English', *Journal of Quantitative Linguistics*, 14.1 (2007), 33–80.

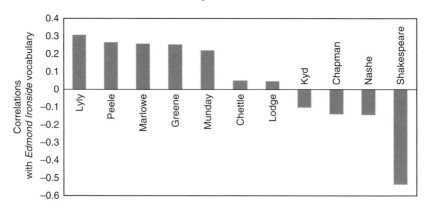

Figure 5.6 Shared vocabulary between *Edmond Ironside* and eleven authorial sets of plays.

indication of authorship. In this sort of test, after all, one of the dramatists had to score the highest. In any case, the lexical-words test of Figure 5.3 tells heavily against Lyly as a candidate. Four dramatists have negative correlations in Figure 5.6, indicating that they have lower than average overlaps with the *Edmond Ironside* vocabulary. Shakespeare, with the lowest correlation of all, is confirmed as a poor candidate for the authorship of the play.

We also attempted lexical marker-word tests along the lines of Figures 5.1 to 5.5 for Chapman, Heywood, Jonson, and Kyd (represented by three, five, twelve, and two plays respectively). In each case the *Edmond Ironside* segments clustered with the segments by others rather than those of the particular author targeted. Thus we were unable to find any sustained links with any of the candidate authors on Sams's list or with any of the others we chose for comparison. What we need now, to go beyond the negative conclusion that Shakespeare is not the author, are some well-supported candidates other than Shakespeare. It would also be useful to have a hypothesis that links particular scenes or groups of scenes within *Edmond Ironside* with one or other writer.

As yet, no one has presented any such hypothesis. The majority of the play appears to be written in a commonplace style that lacks a great deal of variation. The historical events dramatized in the play indicate that the author was closely following his chief source, Holinshed, throughout. However, there are a couple of unusual scenes that could hint at collaborative authorship. The 'flyting scene', III.i, between the Archbishops, has no historical precedent and its form could be based on a similar scene in *1 Henry VI* (III.i.1–52). The shying away from historical sources in the *Edmond Ironside* scene does not seem characteristic of the playwright responsible for the rest of the play. On the surface III.iii, owing to its form as a dumb show, stands out from the rest of the play. However, this is probably a sign of the playwright's imitative experimentation with stage conventions rather than proof that the scene was written by another author altogether. It is most likely that the dull homogeneous style of the play points toward single authorship.

In any case, there are doubts over the plausibility of many of the potential candidates for the play's authorship. If we accept the lower dating limit of May 1593, then Greene would have been dead at this time. Marlowe is killed at the end of the same month and Kyd arrested. Chapman may have been abroad, although he would be writing plays for Henslowe in a few years. Lyly did not write plays for any Henslowe-related company. Other writers who would become more prominent in the early seventeenth century and could have possibly written *Ironside* – albeit at a young age – include Day, Haughton, Dekker, and Heywood. However, the previous tests show that the last two of these are unlikely suspects.

At this point, computational stylistics cannot prove who wrote *Edmond Ironside*. With such a paucity of information about the play, its author may never be identified. Yet we should not view this conclusion as disappointing or unfortunate. Negative attributions are worth a good deal and we can now add even more evidence to support Shakespeare's lack of involvement with *Ironside*. The ramifications of this study also extend beyond the local concern of the play itself to broader concerns regarding the methodology and application of computational stylistics. We can learn more about the system by conducting more and more case studies such as my own. As resources permit such methodological refinement and exploration, computational stylistics will continue to ask questions about the mysteries of authorship in an effort to provide the answers that have eluded scholars for decades.

CHAPTER 6

The authorship of The Raigne of Edward the Third

Timothy Irish Watt

The Raigne of Edward the Third, printed by Thomas Scarlet for Cuthbert Burby, first appeared in the Stationers' Register on 1 December 1595. The title-page offered the following: 'As it had bin sundrie times plaied about the Citie of London'. In 1599, Burby entered a second quarto in the Register. With the exception of variant spellings, the attribution remained the same.

Since then scholars have debated the authorship of *Edward III* with arguments drawn necessarily from internal evidence. The two entries in the Register are the only evidence of performance on record, and no manuscripts of the play exist. A consensus of scholars – some insistent, some more begrudging – now grants *Edward III* a measure of Shakespearean participation; it is included in the New Cambridge Shakespeare and the second edition of the Oxford Shakespeare. For Richard Proudfoot, a general editor of Arden 3, the play is the last of Tucker Brooke's Apocrypha to be substantively argued as the work of Shakespeare's, with a right to canonization at least equal to the early collaborative histories included in the First Folio.

In the past, scholars have argued both for and against sole Shakespearean authorship, and both for and against collaboration. Given the ostensibly rigid split in the structure of the play, arguments have been proposed for a double-authorship, with one author responsible for the first half of the play, and another for the second half. In this case, astute literary intuition may be said to have achieved objective accuracy. The experiments conducted by computational stylistics affirm just such a double attribution.

Edward III contains what must have been troubling political content.[1] References to the Scots King David probably banished the script from the

---

[1] For a particularly apt example see I.ii.56–9:

KING DAVID:	Dislodge, dislodge: it is the King of England.
DOUGLAS:	Jemmy my man, saddle my bonny black.
KING:	Meanst thou to fight, Douglas? We are too weak.
DOUGLAS:	I know it well, my liege, and therefore fly.

stage to the booksellers and from the booksellers to near oblivion after the ascension of King James VI of Scotland to the English throne in 1603.[2] By the time that Heminge and Condell published the 1623 Folio, *The Raigne of Edvvard III* had effectively disappeared, unlike the early histories included in the Folio.

The play reappeared three decades later when Humphrey Moseley – established London bookseller and publisher famous for his Beaumont and Fletcher folio of 1647 – registered *Edward III* as the work of William Shakespeare in Roger and Ley's play catalogue of 1656. This is the first known association of the play with Shakespeare. It made no noticeable impact, either on the public or on the canon. *Edward III* vanished once again, this time for 100 years, until Edward Capell – former deputy inspector of plays – included his own modern-spelling edition in *Prolusions; or, select pieces of Antient Poetry, Compil'd with great Care from their several Originals, and Offer'd to the Publicke as Specimens of the Integrity that should be Found in the Editions of worthy Authors* (1760). Capell attributed the play solely to Shakespeare, but did so with a disclaimer: 'But after all ... its being his work is conjecture only, and matter of opinion; and the reader must form one of his own, guided by what is now before him, and by what he shall meet with in perusal of the piece itself.'[3] Capell's caveat served in the century following as a catalyst for critical response, much of it from Germany. Ludwig Tieck (1836), who had translated *Pericles* in 1811, and Hermann Ulrici (1839) included *Edward III* in their translated editions of the works of Shakespeare. Ernst Ortlepp followed suit in 1840, claiming that *Edward III* represented in structure and diction the work of William Shakespeare at his finest. Henry Tyrrell, in England, agreed, albeit tentatively. So too did Alfred, Lord Tennyson. But Ortlepp's fellow countryman, Nicolaus Delius, opposed the attribution when he re-edited Capell's modern-spelling version of the play and included it in *Pseudo-Shakesperesche Dramen* (1854).[4]

Max Molte, deferring to Delius and echoing Tyrell, included *Edward III* in his 1869 edition, *The Doubtful Plays of William Shakespeare*. It was in this edition that Alexander Teetgen first read *Edward III*. The experience left him indignant. Teetgen published his protest in London, in 1875, as *Shakespeare's 'King Edward the Third', absurdly called, and scandalously*

All citations from the play are taken from William Shakespeare, *King Edward III*, ed. Giorgio Melchiori, New Cambridge Shakespeare (Cambridge: Cambridge University Press, 1998).

[2] Shakespeare, *Edward III*, pp.12–13.

[3] Edward Capell, *Prolusions ... Part II. Edward the third, an historical play* (1760), p. x.

[4] This section draws on the summary in G. Melchiori (ed.), *King Edward III*, New Cambridge Shakespeare (Cambridge: Cambridge University Press, 1998), editor's introduction, pp. 1–51 (p. 1).

treated as, a 'DOUBTFUL PLAY:' An Indignation Pamphlet. Teetgen wrote:

The suppression into the Kingdoms of Darkness of this Masterpiece, *King Edward III*, for more than two centuries, is simply in its way a national scandal, blot, and reproach. I repeat, another of the Incredible Facts! one of the most ridiculous, futile, humiliating things in literary history. But, O Shakespeare! even in thy death thou teachest us lessons. What is Fame? – and Merit?[5]

A year previously, John Payne Collier, later discredited as a forger and liar, confessed his shame that he had not included the play in either of his two Shakespeare editions. He entitled his pamphlet '*King Edward III*: A Historical Play by William Shakespeare. An Essay in Vindication of Shakespeare's Authorship of the Play'.[6] Opinion was not swayed, not even in the New Shakspere Society itself, to which Collier belonged. Despite his penitent rectification and Teetgen's dedicated outrage, both built upon Capell's proposals, most critics continued to deny *Edward III* inclusion in the canon. Most notably Algernon Swinburne, also a member of the New Shakspere Society, and a source of numerous freelance polemics in the field of Shakespearean attribution, condemned the play, and Capell's foisting of *Edward III* on the 'apocryphal fatherhood of Shakespeare':

This editor was the first mortal to suggest that his newly unearthed treasure might possibly be a windfall from the topless tree of Shakespeare. Being, as I have said, a duly modest and an evidently honest man, he admits 'with candour' that there is no jot or tittle of 'external evidence' whatsoever to be alleged in support of this gratuitous attribution … and without the slightest show of any reason whatever he appends to this humble and plausible plea the unspeakably unhappy assertion that at the time of its appearance 'there was no known writer equal to such a play'.[7]

For the author of *King Edward III* (in Swinburne's words 'a second-rate follower of Marlowe') Swinburne reserved nothing but sheer poetic disgust: 'The blame of the failure, the shame of the shortcoming, cannot be laid to the account of any momentary excess or default in emotion, of passing exhaustion or excitement, of intermittent impulse and reaction;

---

[5] As quoted in Shakespeare, *Edward III*, p. 1. For the critical history of *Edward III*, the author is indebted to Melchiori's edition, and most especially to Edmund King, "Compounded of Many Simples": Image Clusters in *Edward III* and the Elizabethan Literary Commonplace', M.A. dissertation, University of Auckland, 1999. The author would like to thank Dr King for fruitful discussions held at the World Shakespeare Congress 2006, in Brisbane, and for generously making his thesis available.

[6] J. P. Collier, '*King Edward III*: A Historical Play by William Shakespeare. An Essay in Vindication of Shakespeare's Authorship of the Play' (London, 1874).

[7] Algernon Swinburne, *A Study of Shakespeare* (1879; London: Heinemann, 1920), pp. 233–4.

it is an indication of lifelong and irremediable impotence' (p. 235). More than a century later, Kenneth Muir noted both the mighty persuasiveness of Swinburne's rhetoric, *and* the scholarly limits of his attribution, one made entirely on aesthetic grounds.

When F. J. Furnivall – founder of the New Shakspere Society, but nevertheless often involved in disputes with Swinburne – compiled and edited his *Leopold Shakespeare* in 1887, he probably did not take inspiration from Swinburne's blistering notes. But despite the acrimony between the two members Furnivall agreed with Swinburne, arguing against a Shakespearean attribution, albeit by omission rather than commission.

Further concurrence came from Germany. Karl Warnke and Ludwig Proescholdt included *Edward III* in their *Pseudo-Shakespearian Plays* (1886), but the editors recognized the play's particularly Shakespearean dramatic merit, for which they cited a number of verbal parallels between the play and those included in the canon. However, the editors dismissed any suggestion of resonance between the play and Shakespeare's sonnets (a bizarre dismissal, given the exact replication of 'Lillies that fester smell far worse then weeds', from Sonnet 94, in *Edward III*, II.i.452).

By the end of the nineteenth century, first-rate literary intuitions stood opposed, and the attribution of the play remained inconclusive. As a result, the authorship of *Edward III* sank into a state of deepening limbo.

This limbo became exile in the first decade of the twentieth century when G. F. Tucker Brooke included the play in his *Shakespeare Apocrypha* (1908), a volume of lasting influence. On first reading, Tucker Brooke sensed a Shakespearean presence in the Countess scenes. In accordance with his golden rule (the true test for a genuine Shakespeare play is a second reading)[8] he read the play again; this time he discovered emptiness of content and insincerity of characterization.[9]

In 1953, in an effort to situate the attribution of the play more objectively, Kenneth Muir published 'A Reconsideration of *Edward III*'. Muir relied heavily on Alfred Hart's statistical compilations of 1934 for both *Edward III* and the Shakespearean canon. With these he noted the substantial likenesses in noun-participle construction, participial adjectives, and frequency of compound words.[10] This alone, as Muir pointed out, would suggest sole authorship. But another of Hart's tests, that which charted the incidence of words in *Edward III* not previously employed by Shakespeare, indicated the work of a second author. In conclusion, and

---

[8] G. F. Tucker Brooke, ed., *The Shakespeare Apocrypha, Being a Collection of Fourteen Plays which Have Been Ascribed to Shakespeare* (Oxford: Oxford University Press, 1908), p. xxxii.
[9] King, 'Image Clusters', p. 6.   [10] *Ibid.*, p. 7.

based upon the play's deployment of iterative imagery, Muir proposed Shakespeare for the Countess scenes and another author for the scenes of war. This thesis he developed more fully in his *Shakespeare as Collaborator* (1960).[11]

That same year Karl Wentersdorf completed his dissertation for the University of Cincinnati, 'The Authorship of *Edward III*'. Although never published, the dissertation remains to this day the most exhaustive attribution study of the play. Utilizing the work of Caroline Spurgeon (*Shakespeare's Imagery and What It Tells Us*), and Edward Armstrong (*Shakespeare's Imagination: A Study of the Psychology of Association and Inspiration*) Wentersdorf built his case for Shakespeare's sole authorship by cataloguing every image in the play and then analysing every image-cluster.[12] It is an effort of both rigorous devotion and flawed strategy. As Edmund King has noted, 'the reliability of the image cluster as a marker of Shakespearean authorship cannot be established until it is known that similar image associations do not exist elsewhere'.[13] Wentersdorf did not compare his findings against the plays of other dramatists.

The same methodological flaw compromises Fred Lapides' critical old-spelling edition (1980). In his introduction Lapides wrote 'there is no evidence that eliminates Shakespeare as the author of Edward III; on the contrary, every examination … presented consistently eliminates every other author but Shakespeare as the author of *Edward III*'.[14]

The attribution proposed by Wentersdorf, and endorsed by Lapides, appears somewhat syllogistic in retrospect – a subjective reading performed in the guise of a nominally scientific rigour. It may be received in agreement or in dispute, depending upon one's opinion of the intuition at hand, and the formal presentation of that intuition.

For Eliot Slater, whose *The Problem of* The Raigne of King Edward III (1988) attempted a more objective attribution, the investigation required a return to Muir's incipient method of thirty years before. Like Lapides and Muir, Slater utilized Hart's statistical compilations. Particularly, Slater focused on the 940 rarest words employed in *Edward III*. He then compared these with the *Concordance*, in the belief that recurrent linkages between the two sets would indicate Shakespearean authorship. Strong

[11] K. Muir, *Shakespeare as Collaborator* (London: Methuen, 1960).
[12] C. Spurgeon, *Shakespeare's Imagery and What It Tells Us* (Cambridge: Cambridge University Press, 1935); E. Armstrong, *Shakespeare's Imagination: A Study of the Psychology of Association and Inspiration* (London: Lindsay Drummond, 1946).
[13] *Ibid.*, p. 9.
[14] William Shakespeare, The Raigne of King Edward the Third: *A Critical, Old-Spelling Edition*, ed. F. Lapides (New York: Garland, 1980), p. 31.

associations with Shakespeare's early plays occurred. From these Slater concluded that both the Countess scenes and the military scenes were written by Shakespeare. The attribution, however, depended upon a negative and unrealistic ideal – namely, that 'a non-Shakespearean *Edward III* would link randomly across the canon'. As King has written,

Links with the early part of the canon would be expected in any play of this date; Shakespeare draws his vocabulary from a communal stock available also to other writers. All are influenced by wider, sociolinguistic trends in word use operating at the time of composition.[15]

M. W. A. Smith searched for Slater's 940 rare words from *Edward III* in two non-Shakespearean plays of the period in an article published in *Notes and Queries* in 1988. The non-Shakespearean plays produced just as many links as did Shakespeare's early plays. The result, as Smith noted, delivered 'convincing evidence that [Slater's] technique is unsuitable for studies of authorship'.[16]

Over the course of the ensuing decade, the search for methodological rigour and completeness continued. The devoted work of Wentersdorf and Slater served as instruction and cautionary tale. The efforts of Muir and Tucker Brooke before them instigated further work. Before them again, the work of Furnivall, Collier, Teetgen, and especially Swinburne situated the authorship of *Edward III* in a dynamic historical context, full of the scholarly proposal and refutation essential to the task. Earlier still, the work of the German editors kept the play sufficiently alive for study. And at the beginning of the whole discussion, Edward Capell, by offering his modern-spelling edition, saved the play from certain oblivion.

What Eric Sams contributed, with the publication of *Shakespeare's Edward III: An Early Play Restored to the Canon* (1996), is either still debated or ignored. With a rhetorical style full of slights and condemnations of other scholarship, including all of the scholarship mentioned here (with the exception of Eliot Slater's work and Wentersdorf's 'The Authorship of *Edward III*', which Sams describes as magisterial, perhaps for obvious reasons), Sams argues vehemently for sole authorship. His argument begins with a stylistically systematic dissection of previous attributions (once again with the exception of Wentersdorf's and Slater's). To this procedure he subjects even those whom he identifies as 'advocates' for Shakespearean attribution. Sams writes: 'Where convictions lack

[15] King, 'Image Clusters', p. 11.
[16] M. W. A. Smith, 'Word Links and Shakespearean Authorship and Chronology', *Notes and Queries*, 233 (1988), 57–9.

authority, the authorities lack conviction. Nothing has ever moved in modern Shakespeare studies without the sworn affidavit of leading experts. But their contributions ... had the desolating effect of halting *Edward III* at the frontier of the Shakespeare canon, where it has been officially held for questioning during most of this century.'[17] As for Teetgen before, the exclusion of *Edward III* from the canon indicates for Sams a miscarriage of justice. He opposes those critics – MacDonald P. Jackson and John Kerrigan among them – suggesting collaborative authorship, and those critics arguing a double attribution. In particular, he attempts to demolish Kenneth Muir's proposal, though by rhetorical ferocity alone.

Although Sams continually reiterates the lessons of S. Schoenbaum's *Internal Evidence and Elizabethan Dramatic Authorship*, his unconditional belief in the significance of verbal parallels between *Edward III* and the Shakespearean canon belies his discipleship and exasperates even the most sympathetic understanding. Wentersdorf's insufficient method of comparison is not discussed; Smith's critical disapproval of Slater's method is ignored; and the fact that many of the parallels reflect commonplaces of the period is only faintly glossed. Taken together, these shortcomings prove insurmountable.

However Sams's unadulterated fervour for *Edward III*, his severe commitment to sole attribution, and his clean modern-spelling edition did promote the play into the well-lighted rooms of scholarly concern. Two years after the publication of Sams's *Edward III*, Gabriel Melchiori's edition for the New Cambridge Shakespeare appeared, an inclusion not synonymous with sole authorship but with substantial Shakespearean contribution. In his introduction, Melchiori proposes *Edward III* as a quintessential Renaissance collaboration, in which several playwrights of a given company each wrote to a given scenario. A company 'plotter' then arranged the contributions into a plot, and submitted the 'book' to the company's players, who in turn added, amended, and deleted from the script in response to theatrical demands, from inflection to censor. As Melchiori notes, 'Composition as well as performance were communal activities in the Elizabethan public theatre.'[18]

Melchiori's method of attribution utilizes historical context to situate the actual writing of the play, an activity distinct from publication, and more relevant than publication to authorship. For Melchiori the stratified plot cannot be ignored as a marker of multiple authorship, and of

---

[17] William Shakespeare, *Shakespeare's* Edward III: *An Early Play Restored to the Canon*, ed. E. Sams (New Haven: Yale University Press, 1996), pp. 153–4.
[18] Shakespeare, *Edward III*, pp. 14–15.

textual layers indicating vision, revision, emendation, and addition. The date of composition also suggests multiple authorship. Melchiori proposes 1592–4, a period in which he believes the Shakespearean addition to *Sir Thomas More* to have been written as well. The mutual dating of both plays provides for Melchiori an association of process. His attribution depends upon it. As he writes, 'it was expedient to entrust the task of rewriting the relevant scenes to a young playwright who had apparently some experience in the job of remaking or adding to pre-existing plays. Shakespeare's addition to *Sir Thomas More*, whether written shortly before or after this, bears witness to his skill on such occasions' (p. 37). Thus Melchiori's parallels between the Hand-D addition to *Sir Thomas More* and the Countess Scenes of *Edward III* rely upon a proximity of date of composition. But the date of composition of Hand-D cannot be assumed. Despite A. E. Pollard's declaration ('If *More* can be proved to be as late as 1599 . . . I should regard the date as an obstacle to Shakespeare's authorship of the three pages so great as to be fatal'[19]), numerous scholars – among them MacDonald P. Jackson, Gary Taylor, and Scott McMillin – have persuasively, perhaps conclusively, argued for a later dating.[20] The discrepancy disqualifies the association. If Hand-D was composed after 1600, then no proximity of composition exists to 'bear witness to [Shakespeare's] skill on such occasions'.[21]

Edward III, I.ii, II.i, and II.ii, commonly referred to as the 'Countess' scenes, present a complete episode in which King Edward attempts mightily and fails miserably to court the Countess of Salisbury. Scenes III.i to IV.iii present a second episode, Edward's campaign against the French. In this episode the Countess does not appear, and is not mentioned. The former episode furnishes the play with a rhetoric of love, the latter with a rhetoric of war. Designating *Edward III* as broken-backed may overstate its structural crudity, but there is certainly a break in continuity between the sections, which could well be the consequence of divided authorship.

The two episodes, each between 6000 and 7000 words in length, provide substantial texts with which to perform our experiments.[22] As mentioned previously, the Countess scenes have historically been attributed

[19] A. E. Pollard, Introduction, *Shakespeare's Hand in the Play of* Sir Thomas More, ed. A. E. Pollard (Cambridge: Cambridge University Press, 1923), pp. 1–40 (p. 31).

[20] For a full rehearsal of the dating of the Hand-D addition to *Sir Thomas More*, see Chapter 7 of this volume.

[21] Shakespeare, *Edward III*, p. 37.

[22] In the texts we prepared for counting, Scenes I.ii to II.ii contain 6642 words of dialogue, and scenes III.i to IV.iii contain 6401.

solely to Shakespeare; the war scenes have historically been attributed to numerous other dramatists, though without any single strong candidate for the scenes emerging. To begin our attribution, we divided the 27 plays in the Shakespeare canon authenticated as single-author works into 6000-word segments. This yielded 90 segments in all. We then divided 85 non-Shakespearean but verifiably single-author plays from the period 1580–1619 into segments of the same size, a set of 236 for comparison with the Shakespeare ones. These two sets served as the foundational material against which experiments were made, and from which conclusions were drawn.

The methodology we use aims to be progressive and multivalent, in search of the immanent pattern of usage of any given author: tests move from one set of indicators to another, and are inclusive of and dependent upon simultaneously positive and negative attributions, in which a set of words appears in both its relation to a given playwright(s) and its statistical divergence from other playwrights. Mostly we work from securely established authorial patterns toward the characteristics of the disputed texts, but occasionally we begin with the localized data offered by the target text.

With *Edward III* we started with our usual set of 200 function words, and used the *t*-test to find the words that have markedly higher means in Shakespeare, taking into account variation within the sets. Forty-nine words exceeded a threshold for genuine difference in the two groups of samples (Shakespeare and non-Shakespeare segments), i.e. they proved to be both markedly and consistently higher or lower in one of the sets. We used these word-variables for a principal component analysis (PCA). Figure 6.1 shows the scores for the texts (including the Countess scenes and the scenes from the French campaign) on the first and second components. The separation of the two clusters is obvious, but by no means complete. The Shakespeare texts fall to the left of the plot, and occupy a smaller span along the vertical axis than the non-Shakespearean segments, which range higher in this dimension. But there is considerable overlap. No doubt the influence of genre, especially, means that in these terms segments by other writers often look like Shakespeare segments, and vice versa. On the horizontal axis the Countess scenes (the black triangle) are well to the Shakespeare side, though they are beyond the northern edge of the Shakespeare cluster on the vertical axis. The group scenes from the French campaign (the black disc) fall outside the Shakespeare area. Figure 6.1 shows a large disparity between the two *Edward III* sections, at least, and an indication that one is more like Shakespeare in style than the other.

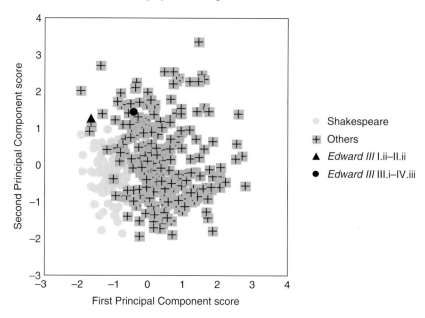

Figure 6.1 Function-words test: PCA of 6000-word segments of Shakespeare and non-Shakespeare plays dated 1580–1619, with two sections of *Edward III*. Forty-nine Shakespeare marker words are used.

To try a quite separate approach, avoiding the function words altogether, we next applied our usual variant of Burrows' Zeta method for using lexical words. We established a set of 500 words that were markedly commoner in the 6000-word Shakespeare play segments, and another set of 500 words markedly commoner in the segments by others. At the head of the list of Shakespeare markers was *spoke*, which occurred in 63, or 70 per cent, of the Shakespeare segments in the 'training' set, and in 76, or 32 per cent, of the non-Shakespeare segments. The leader among the non-Shakespeare markers was *hopes*, which appears in 68 per cent of the segments by others, and in only 32 per cent of the Shakespeare segments. Figure 6.2 shows the results of counting these two sets of 500 words in the Shakespeare and non-Shakespeare segments and in the two *Edward III* sections. The first measure, the *x*-axis, answers the question 'What proportion of the words used in this segment are from the Shakespeare set?', and the second, the *y*-axis, the complementary question 'What proportion of the words in this segment are from the non-Shakespeare set?' In the chart the Shakespeare segments are marked with discs, and the non-Shakespeare with diamond shapes. The method gives a clear separation.

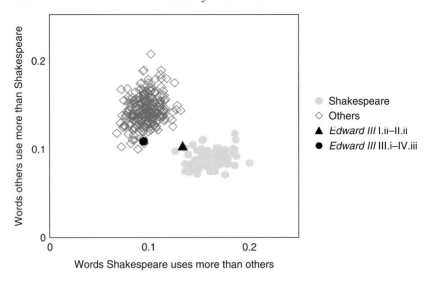

Figure 6.2 Lexical-words test: 6000-word segments of Shakespeare versus 6000-word segments of plays by others dated 1580–1619, with two sections of *Edward III*.

Each axis provides a measure of differentiation, with the bulk of the segments in distinctive ranges, and together they make a clear and complete distinction between the two groups. The two sections of *Edward III* are placed on the edges of different clusters, confirming the notion that Shakespeare wrote one but not the other.

To understand the strength or otherwise of this result we need to know how well the test works with freshly introduced segments, rather than just those that have been used to define the word lists. To test the reliability of the method with new material we re-ran the tests, leaving out the *Edward III* sections, and withdrawing one play from the set at a time and plotting its segments as if its authorship was unknown. Figures 6.3–6.8 show the results for three Shakespeare history plays (*King John*, *1 Henry IV*, and *Henry V*), and three history plays by others (Greene's *James IV*, Peele's *Edward I*, and Marlowe's *Edward II*). In each case the segments are placed correctly in one or the other cluster. Evidently the method is reliable with segments of this length, and with plays of this type, in performing a discrimination between Shakespeare and the rest.

We have established that the function-word-use and vocabulary of the Countess scenes are consistent with Shakespeare's, and that the patterns of the following part of the play are unlike his. Our comparison has been

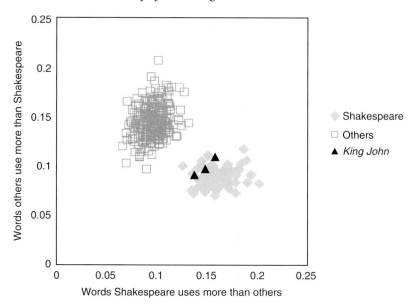

Figure 6.3 Lexical-words test: 6000-word segments of Shakespeare versus 6000-word segments of plays by others dated 1580–1619, with 6000-word segments of *King John*.

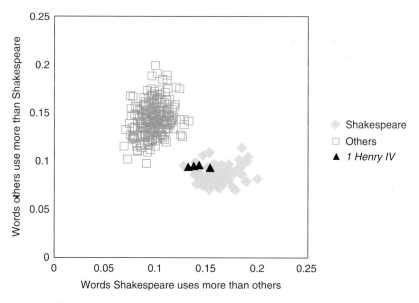

Figure 6.4 Lexical-words test: 6000-word segments of Shakespeare versus 6000-word segments of plays by others dated 1580–1619, with 6000-word segments of *1 Henry IV*.

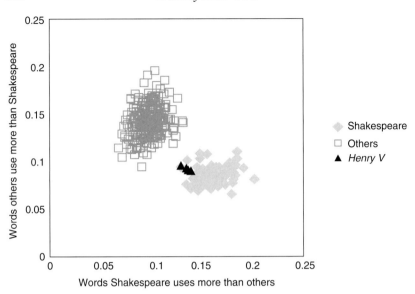

Figure 6.5 Lexical-words test: 6000-word segments of Shakespeare versus 6000-word segments of plays by others dated 1580–1619, with 6000-word segments of *Henry V*.

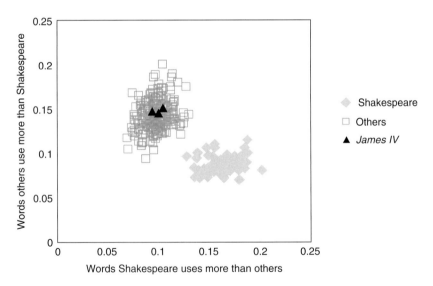

Figure 6.6 Lexical-words test: 6000-word segments of Shakespeare versus 6000-word segments of plays by others dated 1580–1619, with 6000-word segments of *James IV*.

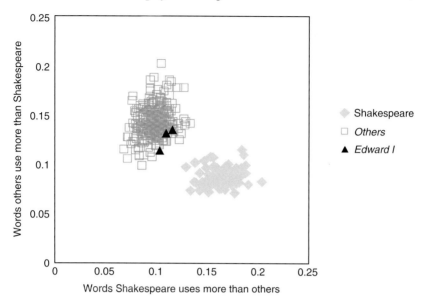

Figure 6.7 Lexical-words test: 6000-word segments of Shakespeare versus 6000-word segments of plays by others dated 1580–1619, with 6000-word segments of *Edward I.*

with the full range of Shakespeare's career and with a large mixed sample of his peers, over the four decades in which he was active. It may be wise, however, to cross-check our results using a shorter time-span. A number of scholars regard 1600 as an important watershed in the language of the drama.[23] It is possible that Shakespeare's and other writers' styles changed so much that results using texts from the 1600s and 1610s in testing a work from the 1590s might be misleading. We re-ran our tests therefore using only plays from before 1600, fifteen Shakespeare ones and thirty-five by others. Figures 6.9 and 6.10 show the results. Figure 6.9 is based on nineteen function-word variables that are Shakespeare markers for this selection from our corpus. The segments are of 6000 words as before. The Shakespeare segments, the grey discs, are less confused with the others, the crosses, than in Figure 6.1. The Countess scenes (once again marked by a black triangle) are well within the Shakespeare cluster, and the scenes dealing with the French campaign (the black disc) are well beyond it. This

---

[23] Brian Vickers collects evidence of this change from several different studies in *Shakespeare, Co-author: A Historical Study of Five Collaborative Plays* (Oxford: Oxford University Press, 2002), pp. 87–9.

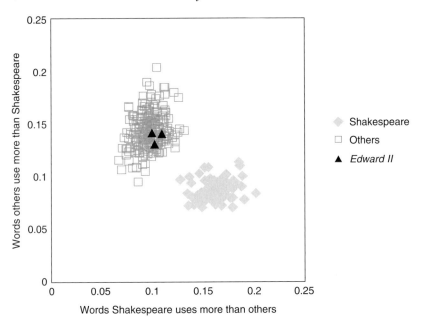

Figure 6.8 Lexical-words test: 6000-word segments of Shakespeare versus 6000-word segments of plays by others dated 1580–1619, with 6000-word segments of *Edward III*.

is a clear affirmation of the double hypotheses of collaboration in the play, and of Shakespeare's authorship of the Countess scenes.

For Figure 6.10, a lexical-words test along the lines of Figures 6.2 to 6.8, we chose two sets of lexical words for the new text groups, words that appear regularly in Shakespeare and words that do not. Counts of these words in the segments, proportional to the total number of different words in each segment, form the two axes of the graph. This time the Countess scenes fall in between the two clusters, and the later section falls into the non-Shakespearean cluster. This test would not in itself be sufficient to show Shakespeare's authorship of the Countess scenes, though it does nothing to challenge it either.

To look at the problem one last time in a different way we constructed a word list from each of the *Edward III* sections themselves, rather than using an authorial text set. We first identified the words that appear in the Countess scenes, but that do not appear in 60 per cent of the segments of plays by Shakespeare and others from 1580 to 1619. These are the relatively unusual words used in these scenes. As in the other lexical-words tests, we

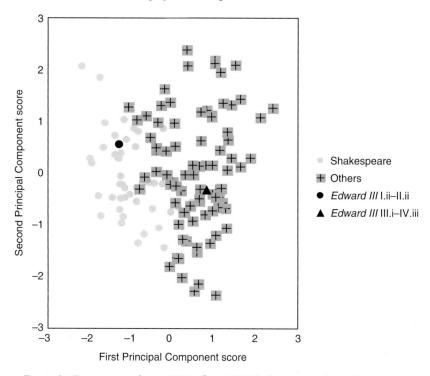

Figure 6.9 Function-words test: PCA of pre-1600 Shakespeare and non-Shakespeare 6000-word segments, with two sections of *Edward III*. Nineteen Shakespeare marker words are used.

counted appearances of each of the words in all the segments, and divided these counts by the total number of different words in a segment. If the author of these scenes is represented in the set, we would expect his texts generally to have rather more of its rare words.

For the sixteen authors with two or more plays in the corpus, we then created author variables. Each segment by the given author was assigned a value of 1 and segments by others were assigned a value of zero. Each authorial variable was correlated with the values for the word counts.[24] Large positive correlations between this variable and the counts for the rare words from the Countess scenes indicate a more than random concentration of high counts in that author, i.e. a degree of affinity between that author's vocabulary and the segment. The unusual words in the segment

---

[24] This is a point–biserial correlation. The procedure is described more fully in D. C. Howell, *Statistical Methods for Psychology* (Pacific Grove, CA: Duxbury, 2002), pp. 237–300.

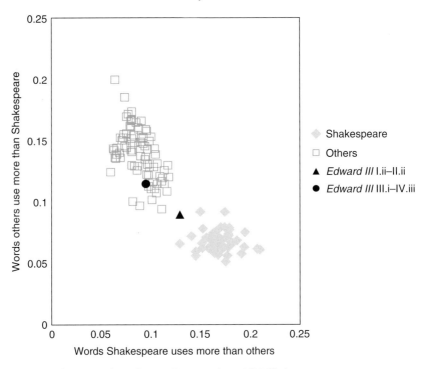

Figure 6.10 Lexical-words test: 6000-word pre-1600 Shakespeare segments versus 6000-word segments of pre-1600 plays by others, with two sections of *Edward III*.

tend to appear more often than the average in the author's œuvre overall. The results are shown in Figure 6.11. Of the sixteen dramatists, the highest correlations for I.ii to II.ii are with Shakespeare.

We then did the same for *Edward III*, III.i to IV.iii, the scenes from the French campaign (Figure 6.12). This time Shakespeare comes in the middle of the group. Marlowe, followed by Peele and Kyd, show the strongest correlations. To pursue the claims of each of these authors further, we carried out three more lexical-words tests in the manner of Figures 6.2 and 6.10, this time contrasting the segments by each author with the rest. In each case both sections of *Edward III* fell within the cluster of segments by other authors. We found nothing therefore to support the idea that Marlowe, Peele, or Kyd was the author of Scenes III.i to IV.iii of *Edward III*.

Taken together, the tests yield both attribution and anonymity. Shakespeare wrote the scenes with the Countess, a substantial

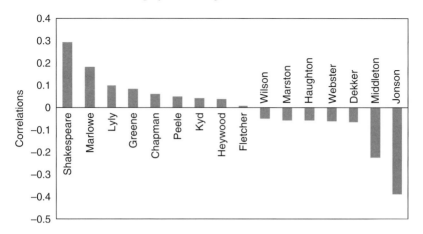

Figure 6.11 Correlations between author variables and segment scores for rare words appearing in *Edward III*, I.ii–II.ii.

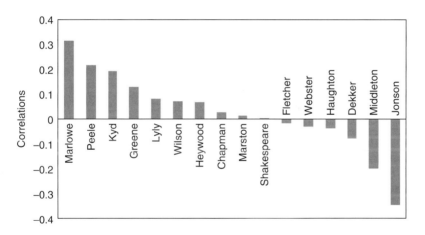

Figure 6.12 Correlations between author variables and segment scores for rare words appearing in *Edward III*, III.i–IV.iii.

contribution. The scenes describing Edward's campaign against the French are by a second writer, who remains unknown. *The Raigne of Edvvard the Third* came into being by collaboration, not by singular creation. And Shakespeare wrote the best of it, a contribution rendering *Edward III* worthy of inclusion in the canon.

CHAPTER 7

The authorship of the Hand-D Addition to The Book of Sir Thomas More

Timothy Irish Watt

Perhaps it is the duty of Shakespeareans to suffer through periodic bouts of attribution anxiety. In the case of the Addition to *The Book of Sir Thomas More* such anxiety has fostered eighty years of dispute. The reason is simple. As Arthur F. Kinney notes in his 'Text, Context, and Authorship of *The Booke of Sir Thomas More*' (in which, incidentally, he argues against Shakespeare as Hand-D): 'In all of Tudor Drama there is no more vexing text than the one ascribed on a vellum wrapper as *The Booke of Sir Thomas Moore*. There is none more important, either – since if we have any fragment of drama actually in Shakespeare's hand, this is it.'[1] These then are the stakes. To live up to them, the study of attribution requires precise methods of inquiry, which utilize but are independent of other critical approaches and their concomitant if elegantly buried hopes for a given outcome. Computational stylistics is such a method.

Computational stylistics provides a reading of text, and of authorial distinction, at a molecular level. It takes seriously the distinguishing force of both syntax (thus the importance of function words to the methodology) and vocabulary. It rouses assumptions from slumber and instantiates the possibility of deeper precision. In the case of Hand-D, computational stylistics crosses the threshold from conjecture, albeit rigorous, to probability, albeit not certain, by establishing and assuring not only a validity but a reliability unavailable to both trained literary sensibility and honed literary instinct. It is this potential crossing-of-the-threshold that offers a verifiable attribution of Hand-D, and indicates a new world for the study of Shakespeare, if not for the study of literature itself.

Our history of *More* begins on 12 October 1727, when Alexander Murray, a London book collector, lent the Oxford antiquary Thomas Hearne what Hearne later described in his diary as 'a thin folio manuscript

---

[1] A. F. Kinney, 'Text, Context, and Authorship of *The Booke of Sir Thomas Moore*', in *Pilgrimage for Love: Essays in Early Modern Literature in Honor of Josephine A. Roberts*, ed. S. King (Tempe, AZ: Arizona Center for Medieval and Renaissance Studies, 1999), pp. 133–60 (p. 133).

entitled *The Book of Sir Thomas More*'. This is, as G. Howard Metz has noted, 'the earliest surviving record of the existence of the manuscript'.[2] The manuscript passed into the possession of Edward Harley, second Earl of Oxford, and in 1753 to the British Library, where its safety was not guaranteed. Over the next 100 years the manuscript suffered the degradations of age and misuse. In 1808 *More* was bound with *The Humorous Lovers* by William Cavendish, Duke of Newcastle, in a single volume for the Harleian Catalogue. Fortunately, what one archivist brought together another put asunder. The two manuscripts were separated, and *More* bound by itself.

In 1844 the Shakespere Society issued the first printed edition of the play under the editorship of Alexander Dyce. The troubled career of *The Book of Sir Thomas More* both as play and as manuscript began in earnest. Although Dyce probably intended an accurate restoration of the play, his editorial hand was meddling and heavy. For many, his version came to represent 'neither the original nor the revised text, but a confused compromise between the two'.[3] Meanwhile air and dust continued to damage the manuscript itself. Later inept repairs left the manuscript further wracked. According to R. C. Bald, 'Holes were patched with gummed paper, and the leaves that showed signs of crumbling – six in all – were pasted over on both sides with a semi-opaque tracing paper.'[4]

Kinder fate intervened in 1911, and previous damage gave way to the judicious editorial hand of W. W. Greg, contracted by the Malone Society to produce an edition that would in no way be 'a compromise between the original and revised versions of the play'.[5] To achieve this, Greg worked closely with the manuscript itself, which he vividly describes:

The manuscript, especially the original portion, has unfortunately suffered considerably at the hand of time. The margins of many of the leaves, in particular the top and bottom edges and the outer corners, are discoloured and brittle, and one would almost suppose that they had at some time been exposed to fire, were it not for the comparatively uninjured state of some at least of the additional leaves, and for the fact that the cover, though also worn and damaged, does not exhibit the crinkling which vellum always undergoes when exposed to heat. (p. vi)

After some hesitation, Greg decided 'to print first the whole of the original text so far as it has been preserved, and then to gather together at the end

---

[2] G. H. Metz, '"Voice and credit": The Scholars and *Sir Thomas More*', in *Shakespeare and* Sir Thomas More: *Essays on the Play and Its Shakespearean Interest*, ed. T. H. Howard-Hill (Cambridge: Cambridge University Press, 1989), pp. 11–44 (p. 12).

[3] W. W. Greg, ed., *Sir Thomas More*, Malone Society Reprints (Oxford: Malone Society, 1911), p. xx.

[4] R. C. Bald, '*The Booke of Sir Thomas More* and Its Problems', *Shakespeare Survey*, 2 (1949), 44–61 (p. 44).

[5] Greg, *Sir Thomas More*, introduction, pp. v–xxix (p. xxii).

all the various attempts at revision' (p. xxii). The resulting edition remains standard (and is complemented well by Gabrieli's and Melchiori's modern-spelling edition for the Revels series). It is, as Harold Jenkins wrote in his introduction to the Malone Society Reprint, 'the necessary foundation of scholarly study for the play'.[6]

Most importantly for this study, Greg famously distinguished seven different hands in the manuscript. The first six he labelled as Hands S, A, B, C, D, and E; the seventh belongs to Edmund Tilney, Master of Revels. With regard to D, Greg notes 'these hasty pages of D's have individual qualities which mark them off sharply from the rest of the play ... So striking indeed are these qualities that more than one critic has persuaded himself that the lines in question can have come from no pen but Shakespeare's.'[7]

But if striking lines ill-fitted in a comparatively mundane play inspire scholarship, they do not indicate authorship. The prevalence of mutual and dynamic influence among the playwrights of the English Renaissance will have it no other way. In the case of *More*, the matter is further complicated by the collaborative nature of the play. Greg's critical opinion on the authorship of Hand-D is then necessarily both equivocal and distinctly suggestive:

Here possibly are three pages, one of them still legible, in the hand that so many have desired to see. The question is one of stylistic evidence, and each reader will have to judge for himself. I do not feel called upon to pronounce: but I will say this much, that it seems to me an eminently reasonable view that would assign this passage to the writer who, as I believe, foisted certain of the Jack Cade scenes into the second part of Henry VI. (p. 8)

(It is a salutary reminder of the vicissitudes of attribution that Greg evidently thought the Cade scenes were the one Shakespearean part of a play largely by others, whereas we have argued in Chapter 3 of the present volume that these scenes are among those in *1 Henry VI* least likely to be by Shakespeare.)

A. W. Pollard, in the midst of a perennial fight with unnamed anti-Stratfordians, agreed with Greg. To the cause of the 'Stratford Man', he enlisted Greg and Greg's edition, and gathered together a group of scholars of diverse techniques into what became known unofficially as 'Pollard's little company'. In 1923, with Pollard as its chief editor and guiding editorial light, the company produced *Shakespeare's Hand in the Play of* Sir Thomas

---

[6] H. Jenkins, ed., *Sir Thomas More*, Malone Society Reprints (Oxford: Malone Society, 1961), p. xxxiii.

[7] W. W. Greg, *Sir Thomas More*, p. 8.

More, the first collection dedicated exclusively to Hand-D, and to this day the most valuable. The fact that Pollard's volume was created in reaction to anti-Stratfordian arguments cannot and should not be brushed aside, for it illuminates the treacherous ground of Hand-D attribution, then and now. Desired outcome – implicit or explicit – influences technique. Subjective consciousness effects objective methodology. As Paul Werstine writes in his examination of Pollard's volume, 'Shakespeare, More or Less: A. W. Pollard and Twentieth-Century Shakespearean Editing', 'In view of the energy and labour expended by numerous prominent scholars defending Shakespearean authorship, it is not surprising to discover that this defence has influenced reception of Shakespeare's works and their editorial reproductions.'[8]

Pollard himself iterates the point with a verbal joust in his preface to *Shakespeare's Hand*, in what appears initially to be a merely *pro forma* indication of his authors' professional fair-mindedness:

They would not have their readers less critical than they have tried to be themselves, and are aware that from one quarter at least searching criticism is to be expected, since if Shakespeare wrote these three pages the discrepant theories which unite in regarding the 'Stratford Man' as a mere mask concealing the activity of some noble lord (a 17th Earl of Oxford, a 6th Earl of Derby, or a Viscount St Albans) come crashing to the ground.[9]

Apparently, the freewheeling irresponsibility of the anti-Stratfordian contingent inspired Pollard to visions of their ruin, perhaps justifiably so. Ire begat rigour and Pollard's symposium, composed of Pollard himself, Greg, E. M. Thompson, J. Dover Wilson, and R. W. Chambers. In the introduction to *Shakespeare's Hand*, Pollard declares that Greg's edition 'must always rank among the best examples of English literary and paleographical scholarship' (p. 7). At the close of the introduction, Pollard confesses: 'To me personally the alpha and the omega of the case is that in these three pages we have the tone and temper of Shakespeare and of no other Elizabethan dramatist I have read' (p. 31). In other words, Hand-D as Shakespeare makes intuitive sense to him.

Of the volume's contributors only Greg does not attribute Hand-D to Shakespeare or to anyone else. He simply recapitulates his introduction to his Malone Society edition. E. M. Thompson then presents his paleographic findings, and conclusions. He notes that the Addition is 'written entirely by one hand, in the native cursive handwriting which was still the common

---

[8] P. Werstine, 'Shakespeare, More or Less: A. W. Pollard and Twentieth-Century Shakespearean Editing', *Florilegium*, 16 (1999), 125–45.
[9] Pollard, *Shakespeare's Hand in the Play of* Sir Thomas More, p. v.

character, taught in the schools and generally used in Shakespeare's time'.[10] For his argument Thompson relies heavily, as he must, on the six known signatures. He meditates at length on the 'spurred a', found both in the signatures and in the Addition. He then develops a palaeographic comparison of a somewhat Byzantine and occasionally bewildering nature, deeply reliant upon signature six, from Shakespeare's will.[11]

Levin L. Schücking, writing from Germany two years after the publication of *Shakespeare's Hand*, challenges both the means and the conclusion of Thompson's argument.[12] In *Shake-speare: Handwriting and Spelling*, Gerald H. Rendall, an Oxfordian, offers a more colourful, and less qualified, rebuttal: 'As regards handwriting, the plain truth is that Hand-D of the "Addition" and the Shaksperean signatures are not reconcilable. To bring them into accord, Sir E. M. Thompson had first to inflict upon the penman writer's cramp, and then reduce him to the spasmodic efforts of a dying man.'[13]

Rendall's breezy dismissal of the case relies heavily on the arguments of S. A. Tannenbaum, characterized by Rendall as an 'ardent upholder of the Stratfordian tradition' (p. 11). Tannenbaum performed his own palaeographic analysis and comparison of the signatures with the Addition, after discovering the 'spurred a' in a Chapman autograph. In *Problems in*

---

[10] Sir E. Maunde Thompson, 'The Handwriting of the Three Pages Attributed to Shakespeare Compared with His Signatures', in *Shakespeare's Hand in the Play of* Sir Thomas More, ed. Pollard, pp. 57–112 (p. 68).

[11] Thompson writes: 'There can be little doubt that it [signature six] was subscribed before four and five. The first three words are written firmly and legibly; but, in attempting the surname the sick man's hand gave way. This failure to accomplish the signature successfully after beginning so well may primarily be attributed to Shakespeare's physical condition. When the will was placed before him, he was about to subscribe probably the most important signature of his life. No doubt, by a supreme effort he braced himself to the task, and, with the sense of the formality of the occasion strong upon him, he began to write, and to write fairly well, in scrivener style, with the formal words, "By me, William Shakespeare"' (Thompson, 'The Handwriting', p. 61). Giles Dawson expands upon Thompson's work, in 'Shakespeare's Handwriting', *Shakespeare Survey*, 42 (1990), 119–28. Among other findings, Dawson discovered the spurred *a* linked with the *h*, both in the Addition, in what Dawson terms a 'bulbous structure' (e.g., at lines 105, 108, and following), and in Shakespeare's signature on the deposition to the Bellot–Mountjoy case (the fourth signature).

[12] 'When Sir E. Maunde Thompson states the extraordinary similarity of the *a* in signature No. 1 to certain *a*'s in the manuscript (especially the "pointed projection or spur from the lower end of the back of the letter"), he will certainly not be contradicted, but it cannot be overlooked, on the other hand, that the two letters *h* and *s* are in all cases hopelessly and absolutely dissimilar in signatures and manuscript ... Then there are the two words of the last signature of the will; "*By me*", which contain a capital *B* which is so thoroughly unlike the capital *B*'s in the manuscript, that one is at a loss to understand how they should be written by the same hand. On the whole one gets the impression from the signatures that Shakespeare's handwriting was a good deal more angular than that of the manuscript, which is characterized by its curves'. (L. L. Schücking, 'Shakespeare and *Sir Thomas More*', *Review of English Studies*, 1 (1925), 40–1).

[13] G. H. Rendall, *Shake-speare: Handwriting and Spelling* (New York: Haskell House, 1971), p. 10.

Shakespeare's Penmanship: Including a Study of the Poet's Will,[14] Tannenbaum concludes that 'on the basis of the six unquestioned signatures the weight of the evidence is overwhelmingly against the theory that in folios 8 and 9 of *Sir Thomas More* we have a Shakspere [*sic*] holograph'.[15]

Tannenbaum also finds J. Dover Wilson's orthographic argument – the third essay in *Shakespeare's Hand* – unconvincing. Relying exclusively on the good quartos, Wilson compares the spellings of the 370 words in the Addition with those in the canonical plays of Shakespeare, with specific focus reserved for 'a leven', 'elements', 'deule', 'sealf' and 'sealues', and 'noyce'. According to Wilson,

These spellings … are, for the most part, unusual forms for writers of the period. They are old-fashioned; and it is unlikely, to say the least of it, that any two authors would be equally old-fashioned in the spelling of all these words. It is, therefore, very encouraging to find parallels in the quartos for every one of them. Our accumulation of coincidences is by this time growing into an impressive pile. Can we crown it by citing a spelling from both the Addition and the quartos which is not only old-fashioned but very old-fashioned?[16]

He answers in the affirmative, providing the famous example of 'scilens', appearing once in the Addition and eighteen times in *2 Henry IV*, and nowhere else in Elizabethan drama.[17] Wilson writes, 'When coincidences accumulate, every additional one increasing the probability of the case, it only remains to decide the point at which probability passes into certainty.'[18] The decision – into certainty – is implied.

Tannenbaum, however, compares the Addition with both the good and bad Quartos and the Folio; he uses palaeography to dispute Wilson's orthography, and provides six points of contention: five characteristics of Shakespeare's hand that can be deduced from typesetting errors in the printed texts but do not appear in Hand-D, and one spelling preference that is not shared with Hand-D.[19] In other words, to Wilson's 'Wherever we turn we discover agreement', Tannenbaum replies with a detailed no.

The final contributor to *Shakespeare's Hand*, R. W. Chambers, dedicates a close reading to *More* and presents a critical comparison of the

---

[14] S. A. Tannenbaum, *Problems in Shakespeare's Penmanship: Including a Study of the Poet's Will* (New York: Modern Language Association of America, 1927), p. 211.

[15] *Ibid.*, p. 211.

[16] J. Dover Wilson, 'Bibliographical Links between the Three Pages and the Good Quartos', in *Shakespeare's Hand in the Play of* Sir Thomas More, ed. Pollard, pp. 113–41 (p. 128).

[17] For a good overview of idiosyncratic spelling in *More*, see M. P. Jackson, 'Is Hand-D of *Sir Thomas More* Shakespeare's? Thomas Bayes and the Elliott–Valenza Authorship Tests', *Early Modern Literary Studies*, 12.3 (January 2007), 1–36.

[18] Wilson, 'Bibliographical Links', p. 131.

[19] Tannenbaum, *Shakspere and* Sir Thomas More, pp. 62–3.

Addition with the canonical plays. To begin with, Chambers notes that the Jack Cade scenes in *2 Henry VI* resemble the 147 lines of the Addition to the point of obvious kinship. (As already mentioned, this is a view we have challenged in Chapter 3, above.) Chambers continues with 'degree', both as word and as idea. In this echoing realm, it is *Richard II*, *Troilus and Cressida*, *Coriolanus*, and *Julius Caesar* to which the Addition is kin. Chambers writes:

> If the speech of Sir Thomas More be Shakespeare's, we may reasonably expect More's figures regarding government to reappear (changed to suit the speaker's circumstances) in those passages in Shakespeare's un-doubted works where this question of authority and mob-law is discussed. Such passages are the speech of Ulysses in *Troilus and Cressida* [the famous speech on degree and order], and several scenes in *Coriolanus*.[20]

Chambers also compares the repetition of 'peace' in both *Julius Caesar*,

> BRUTUS: My countrymen –
> SECOND PLEBEIAN: Peace, Silence! Brutus speaks.
> FIRST PLEBEIAN: Peace ho!
> BRUTUS: Good countrymen, let me depart alone . . . (III.ii.53–5)[21]

and in the Addition:

> SURREY: Friends, Masters, Countrymen –
> MAYOR: Peace, ho! Peace! I charge you keep the peace.
> SHREWSBURY: My master's, countrymen –
> SHERWIN: The noble earl of Shrewsbury, let's hear him. (II.iii.30–3)[22]

Chambers comments:

> What is peculiar about Shakespeare is not that he can see where the crowd goes wrong, but that he can see where it goes right: and above and beyond all, what is characteristic of him and of the author of the 147 lines is the ability to see both things together. It is not so with his contemporaries.[23]

Paul Werstine points out a fundamental flaw in Chambers' method, which indicates a flaw as well in Chambers' conclusion. Werstine writes:

> Although Chambers occludes his own interpretative role in the identification of the sequences, his method nevertheless requires him, as Shakespeareans have

---

[20] R. W. Chambers, 'The Expression of Ideas – Particularly Political Ideas – in the Three Pages and in Shakespeare', in *Shakespeare's Hand in the Play of* Sir Thomas More, ed. Pollard, pp. 142–87 (p. 157).

[21] William Shakespeare, *Julius Caesar*, in *The Riverside Shakespeare*, ed. G. B. Evans *et al.*, 2nd edn (Boston: Houghton Mifflin, 1997). All citations to Shakespeare are from this edition.

[22] V. Gabrieli and G. Melchiori, eds., Sir Thomas More: *By Anthony Munday and Others* (Manchester: Manchester University Press, 1990). All citations to the play are from this edition.

[23] Chambers, 'The Expression of Ideas', p. 182.

recently begun to appreciate, to exert so strong a hand in abstracting themes and figures from their contexts that pressing questions arise about whether evidence produced by such a method is located in the tests under examination or in the method and interests of the examiner.[24]

Schücking too is unconvinced. In his words, missing from *More* 'are the characteristic traits of Shakespeare's style' (an opinion that seems either as dubious or accurate as Chambers' own).[25]

More recently, Carol Chillington and Arthur F. Kinney have argued against Hand-D as Shakespeare. Chillington detects phrase usage in the Addition more akin to Chettle than to Shakespeare. The discrepancies accumulate: ' "upon the hip" (in *More*, the phrase figures metaphorically, suggesting verbal entrapment; Shakespeare always uses it in its primary athletic meaning); "bear down" (unexampled in Shakespeare); "ravenous fishes" (the adjective in Shakespeare is exclusively attached to wolves and tigers, but the exact image appears in *Hoffman* ...)'[26] Kinney finds the lines bereft of Shakespeare's poetry:

The poetry, in fact, is what divorces authentic Shakespearean lines from those possibly his, Addition II: the consistent power of Shakespeare's lines, the way in which iambs slip naturally into the stresses within the lines while resisting a sing-song quality, and the way in which each idea gives way to metaphor as if by natural inclination, suggest that the author of Addition II shares nothing whatever *poetically* with Shakespeare.[27]

As the critical history indicates, all those scholars arguing for a positive attribution of Hand-D to Shakespeare, and those arguing against the attribution, develop reasonable arguments from critical techniques practised by astute literary sensibilities; all of the hypotheses, however, depend finally on relative degrees of intuition. And while intuition is essential to interpretation, it is finally unreliable as a methodology for attribution. Too often what intuitively 'makes sense' has been deployed to make fact. As MacDonald P. Jackson puts it (after a discussion of a contribution to

[24] Werstine, 'Shakespeare, More or Less', p. 134.

[25] Schücking, 'Shakespeare and *Sir Thomas More*', p. 44.

[26] C. A. Chillington, 'Playwrights at Work: Henslowe's, Not Shakespeare's, *Book of Sir Thomas More*', *English Literary Renaissance*, 10 (1980), 442–3. Gary Taylor refutes Chillington's attribution in 'The Date and Auspices of the Additions to *Sir Thomas More*', in *Shakespeare and Sir Thomas More*, ed. Howard-Hill, pp. 101–29, as does Charles R. Forker in 'Webster or Shakespeare? Style, Idiom, Vocabulary, and Spelling in the Additions to *Sir Thomas More*', also in *Shakespeare and* Sir Thomas More, ed. Howard-Hill, pp. 151–70.

[27] Kinney, 'Text, Context, and Authorship', p. 153. For an invaluable and deeply influential study of Shakespeare's metre, see Marina Tarlinskaja, *Shakespeare's Verse: Iambic Pentameter and the Poet's Idiosyncrasies* (New York: Peter Lang, 1987). A metrical analysis, along Tarlinskajan lines, has not, to the author's knowledge, been performed specifically on Hand-D.

a different dispute): 'The total absence of constraints on our search for resemblances renders the calculations meaningless.'[28]

Quantitative methods, assisted in recent times by the processing power of the computer and the wide availability of electronic text, promise a way out of the impasse. They may help remedy the impotent course and re-course described by Werstine: 'So now the rhetoric of "cumulative evidence" has closed its circle: conclusive demonstration of Shakespeare's hand in *The Booke of Sir Thomas More* has been deferred from a study of handwriting to a study of spelling and from there to an examination of style and now back to handwriting and spelling.'[29] The newer methods do not necessarily lead to consensus, however. Recently, Ward E. Y. Elliott and Robert J. Valenza have argued against Hand-D as Shakespeare, utilizing what they term their 'silver bullet' method of computer-aided testing. This method deploys 'verse blocks' taken from select Shakespeare plays. These blocks are of more or less equivalent length to the verse section of Hand-D, and are used to discriminate authorship by a tally of passes or fails in a series of separate tests, and a composite measure of authorship.[30] In 'The Date and Authorship of Hand D's Contribution to *Sir Thomas More*: Evidence from "Literature Online"', MacDonald P. Jackson, who has for years been engaged in one of the most sustained attribution studies of Hand-D, rebuts Elliott's and Valenza's conclusion.[31] We return to this particular debate at the end of this chapter.

Our own venture into the empirical study of literary language begins as a series of questions directed at what might be termed the animating genome of the text. This 'genome' is created fundamentally by syntax and diction and with them it creates and sustains a constantly individuating force of distinction. The author uses grammar to create a style. Thereafter that particular use of grammar – of syntax, diction, tone, voice, point-of-view – becomes associated with that author.

But, one wonders, what of genuine divergence in a given author's body of work, or single text, or act, or scene, or series of lines? If an authorial individuality embraces such divergence, how can that individuality

---

[28] M. P. Jackson, 'Editions and Textual Studies', *Shakespeare Survey*, 40 (1988), 224–36 (p. 225).

[29] Werstine, 'Shakespeare, More or Less', p. 137.

[30] See especially W. E. Y. Elliott and R. J. Valenza, 'Two Tough Nuts to Crack: Did Shakespeare Write the "Shakespeare" Portions of *Sir Thomas More* and *Edward III*?', available at http://govt.mckenna.edu/welliott/UTConference/2ToughNuts.pdf.

[31] I would like to thank Professor Arthur F. Kinney for bringing this recent article to my attention. For Jackson's persuasive refutation of Ward and Valenza's methodological parameters, see his 'Is Hand-D of *Sir Thomas More* Shakespeare's?'. Jackson's wit-full deployment of Bayes, an eighteenth-century cleric and mathematician, and Bayes's method for detecting illness, is also one of the more mordant techniques for attribution one is likely to encounter.

possibly and positively be identified? Still further, and particularly relevant for English Renaissance drama, what actually distinguishes an authorial phrase from a circulating expression of the period? For computational stylistics the answers are found in systematic comparisons of word choice, pattern of vocabulary, and habitual syntax. The current programme of research traces with mind-numbing specificity sets of common words through 136 Early Modern plays. The frequency of a given word, or set of words, in a given play may suggest authorial signature. The frequency of a given word or set of words in a group of plays by the same author does more than suggest; it develops the possibility of authorial signature. The frequency of a given word or set of words in a group of plays by the same author, combined with the relative paucity of this word or set of words in the plays of the other selected authors, illuminates the *probability* of authorial signature.

This is the progressive methodology computational stylistics developed and follows. It is representative of the progression of a single test. But a single test, regardless of results, does not provide enough data for legitimate conclusion. Thus computational stylistics performs test after test, with variation after variation. Ultimately, test sets serve either to verify or invalidate the base set results. Together these tests reveal an immanent pattern of usage of words used distinctly over the course of an authorial career. What this usage suggests, at the level of a single word, is a certain distinction of usage over Shakespeare's career. Each additional word so suggesting contributes to an authorial pattern, and to the 'genetic' revelation of the author's lexical autograph. This autograph, it must be said, is a matter of probability, not certainty. This is true for all of computational stylistics. Great writers defeat normalization with spontaneity. And the English language permits no tyranny of absolute summation; it is flexible beyond our most flexible equations.

In application, then, computational stylistics does not certify for eternity a given work to a given author, but allows us to orient our intuitions of authorial distinctiveness more objectively, and to develop an equation between common usage and uncommon author. Among those who fashionably suppose individual authorial agency to be merely quaint, the results provided by computational stylistics may offer a different fashion – one both older and newer at once, both distinct and determined, contextualized and beyond the prescription.

Addition II (Hand-D) of *More*, together with Addition III in Hand-C (a soliloquy by More, twenty-one lines in length, and usually included in hypotheses about Shakespeare's authorship), dramatize Sir Thomas More's role in the 'Evil May Day' riot of 1517. To this day scholars debate the date of composition of the passages, while agreeing on its insouciant, if not negligent, relationship to the play of which it was to be a part. Hand-D's loose fit in *More*, described by Melchiori as 'the worst fitting in the total revision of the play',[32] suggests the method of collaboration; the dating of composition provokes and is critical to attribution, particularly those attributions that rely upon direct comparison. Alexander Dyce proposed 1590, R. Simpson 1586–7, Greg and E. M. Thompson 1594. A. W. Pollard put forth a probable composition date of 1594, with an allowance for composition as late as 1596. Beyond this he could not go. As he declared with dramatic flair in his introduction to *Shakespeare's Hand*, 'If *More* can be proved to be as late as 1599 … I should regard the date as an obstacle to Shakespeare's authorship of the three pages so great as to be fatal.'[33] E. K. Chambers, in *William Shakespeare: A Study of Facts and Problems*, professes ambivalence with regard to the date of composition, whether early, middle, or late.[34]

Critics since E. K. Chambers have been divided on the issue. MacDonald P. Jackson argues that 'if Hand-D is Shakespeare, then the linguistic evidence points to it having been composed shortly after the turn of the century'.[35] Jackson demonstrates that 'the distribution of pauses within verse lines clearly places Shakespeare's addition in the period from *Twelfth Night* to *Macbeth* (1601–1606)'.[36] Most recently, Jackson has employed *Literature Online*, searching for purposes of both dating and attribution of the Addition. Jackson's research supports many of the verbal parallels suggested earlier by R. W. Chambers and thus adds weight to the case for a post-1600 dating.[37]

Both Scott McMillin and Gary Taylor concur in *Shakespeare and Sir Thomas More* (1994), edited by T. H. Howard-Hill. For Taylor, 'the independent evidence of six metrical licences, of linguistic preferences, of vocabulary, of imagery, of exact verbal parallels, of rhetorical parallels, and of colloquialism in verse all point to the same period',[38] that is, post-1600.

[32] G. Melchiori, '*The Book of Sir Thomas More*: dramatic Unity', in *Shakespeare and* Sir Thomas More, ed. Howard-Hill, pp. 77–100 (p. 89).

[33] Pollard, *Shakespeare's Hand in the Play of* Sir Thomas More, p. 31.

[34] E. K. Chambers, *William Shakespeare: A Study of Facts and Problems*, 2 vols. (Oxford: Clarendon Press, 1930), Vol. I, p. 513.

[35] M. P. Jackson, 'Linguistic Evidence for the Date of Shakespeare's Addition to *Sir Thomas More*', *Notes and Queries*, n.s., 25 (1978), 155–6.

[36] Jackson, 'Editions and Textual Studies', p. 224.

[37] See Jackson, 'The Date and Authorship of Hand D's Contribution to *Sir Thomas More*: Evidence from *Literature Online*,' *Shakespeare Survey*, 59 (2006), 69–78 (p. 76).

[38] Taylor, 'The Date and Auspices of the additions to *Sir Thomas More*', p. 122.

Most strikingly perhaps, the Addition bears a distinct and pervasive resemblance to *Coriolanus* (1607–9), particularly to the opening scenes of potential insurrection, in which Menenius speaks to the mutinous citizens:

> I tell you, friends, most charitable care
> Have the patricians of you. For your wants,
> Your suffering in this dearth, you may as well
> Strike at the heaven with your staves as lift them
> Against the Roman state, whose course will on
> The way it takes, cracking ten thousand curbs
> Of more strong link asunder than can ever
> Appear in your impediment. For the dearth,
> The gods, not the patricians, make it, and
> Your knees to them (not arms) must help. Alack,
> You are transported by calamity
> Thither where more attends you, and you slander
> The helms o'th' state, who care for you like fathers,
> When you curse them as enemies. (I.i.65–78)

In the Addition, More proclaims to the May Day rioters:

> Look what you do offend you cry upon,
> That is the peace; not one of you here present,
> Had there such fellows lived when you were babes,
> That could have topped the peace, as now you would –
> The peace wherein you have till now grown up
> Had been ta'en from you, and the bloody times
> Could not have brought you to the state of men.
> Alas, poor things, what is it you have got,
> Although we grant you get the thing you seek? (II.iii.67–75)

George professes that it is the removal of the strangers they seek. This request launches More into the fullness of his rhetorical moment:

> Grant them removed, and grant that this your noise
> Hath chid down all the majesty of England.
> Imagine that you see the wretched strangers,
> Their babies at their backs, with their poor luggage
> Plodding to th' ports and coasts for transportation,
> And that you sit as kings in your desires,
> Authority quite silenced by your brawl,
> And you in ruff of your opinions clothed:
> What had you got? I'll tell you: you had taught
> How insolence and strong hand should prevail,
> How order should be quelled, and by this pattern
> Not one of you should live an aged man.
> For other ruffians, as their fancies wrought,

> With selfsame hand, self reasons and self right
> Would shark on you, and men like ravenous fishes
> Would feed on one another.
>   ...
> Let me set up before your thoughts, good friends,
> One supposition, which if you will mark
> You shall perceive how horrible a shape
> Your innovation bears. First, 'tis a sin
> Which oft th'apostle did forewarn us of,
> Urging obedience to authority,
> And 'twere no error if I told you all
> You were in arms 'gainst God. (II.iii.78–93, 96–103)

All interject: 'Marry, God forbid that.' More responds, in a commanding rhetoric of castigating persuasion:

> Nay certainly you are,
> For to the king God hath his office lent
> Of dread, of justice, power and command,
> Hath bid him rule, and willed you to obey;
> And to add ampler majesty to this,
> He hath not only lent the king his figure,
> His throne and sworn, but given him His own name,
> Calls him a God on earth. What do you then,
> Rising 'gainst him that God Himself installs
> But rise 'gainst God? What do you to your souls
> In doing this, O desperate as you are?
> Wash your foul minds with tears, and those same hands
> Lift up for peace, and your unreverent knees
> Make them your feet. To kneel to be forgiven
> Is safer wars than ever you can make
> Whose discipline is riot.
> In, in to your obedience: even your hurly
> Cannot proceed but by obedience ... (II.iii.105–23)

For Chambers, 'the thought which is explicit in More's speech is implicit in that of Coriolanus'.[39] Again, one may agree or disagree, or be unpersuaded by either position. Just as one may agree or disagree with the proposed date of composition, or be unpersuaded by any of the dates proposed. Is the debate, then, just a matter of polished gossip? Is it even worth critical concern anymore? Greg's remonstrance – 'though certainty may be unattainable, speculation is not therefore idle' – comes to mind. Taken a step further, where speculation is not idle, probability may be achieved.

---

[39] Chambers, 'The Expression of Ideas', p. 158.

Once edited for word-counting the Hand-D portion of *Sir Thomas More*, with Addition III in Hand-C, gives us 1214 words of dialogue as the basis for comparison with other authors. With a text of this size, we can expect some idiosyncratic variation. The longer samples are, the more local oddities are balanced out, and the more confident we can be of a definitive association with one authorial style or another. We can meet some of the difficulty with a smaller sample like these *Sir Thomas More* additions by using a variety of methods, so that the uncertainty of each individual verdict is moderated by the independent testimony of others.

As we have shown in earlier studies in this book, authors have distinct patterns in their use of lexical words: patterns that persist despite the countervailing pressures of genre, chronology, and local subject matter. Such patterns may be very pronounced – like Shakespeare's preference for *gentle*, and his neglect of *brave* – or may be more intermittent, but when used together they do serve to define a more or less exclusive territory for a given author in relation to another, or to a larger mixed group of peers. We have to remember that 'this was an age when there was a common fund of dramatic diction and everybody borrowed from everybody else', as Andrew S. Cairncross put it, casting doubts on some earlier vocabulary tests for authorship.[40] Yet we can now demonstrate beyond doubt that authors drew on this shared resource of language in their own individual fashion, using some words consistently more than their fellows, and some less. With the aid of the computer we can combine these small patterns of use as they emerge through hundreds of thousands of words of text.

Figure 7.1 presents the results of a lexical-words test incorporating the Hand-D and Addition III sections of *Sir Thomas More*. We defined two sets of plays, 27 by Shakespeare and 85 by his contemporaries, from the four decades 1580–1619, divided them into 1200-word segments to match the length of the Hand-D and Addition III sample, and identified 500 words used more in the Shakespeare segments and 500 used more in the non-Shakespeare ones. We then plotted the scores for the two sets of words divided by the total number of different words in a given sample for all the segments and the *Sir Thomas More* section. The diagonal line is the perpendicular bisector of the line joining the centroids of the two groups of samples, and marks a boundary between Shakespeare and non-Shakespeare regions of the chart. The vast majority of segments of known authorship are correctly located, but a number are on the wrong side of the line. The ratio is 1265:22, a success rate of 98 per cent. We have a powerful,

---

[40] William Shakespeare, *The First Part of King Henry VI*, ed. A. S. Cairncross, Arden Shakespeare (London: Methuen, 1962), p. xxxiii.

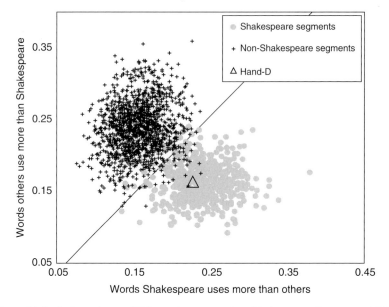

Figure 7.1 Lexical-words test: 1200-word segments from Shakespeare plays versus 1200-word segments from plays by others dated 1580–1619, with the Hand-D and Addition III portions of *Sir Thomas More*.

if not quite infallible, method for telling Shakespeare segments from the rest at the level of 1200-word samples. The Hand-D portion is placed on the Shakespeare side of the line, with scores bringing it to the heart of the Shakespeare cluster, close to the most typical Shakespeare scores.

As always with 'training' samples, we cannot expect as efficient a separation with new material. The training samples have the advantage through playing a part in the selection of marker words. Table 7.1 shows the results for the segments of six plays that we withdrew one at a time from the 'training' set and whose scores we then recalculated as if they were anonymous. These give a better guide than the patterns of Figure 7.1 to the true power of discrimination of the method. Of the 105 segments, 94 are correctly attributed: i.e. their scores fall on the right side of the line. This is a success rate of 90 per cent. There is reason to think that the odds for the correct placement of the Hand-D portion are in fact better than this, given that it falls not just to the right side of the line, but well across it. With each step away from the boundary line, error becomes less likely. In Figure 7.1 there is one non-Shakespeare 'training' segment almost as far to the Shakespeare side of the line as the Hand-D section is, but none quite as far.

Table 7.1. *Classifications of test segments from 6 plays in a lexical-words test of 1200-word segments from Shakespeare plays versus 1200-word segments from plays by others dated 1580 to 1619.*

Author	Play	Segments	Correctly classified
Dekker	*The Shoemaker's Holiday*	15	13
Heywood	*If You Know Not Me*	9	7
Jonson	*Volpone*	22	20
Middleton	*The Phoenix*	16	15
Shakespeare	*Hamlet*	24	22
Webster	*The Duchess of Malfi*	19	17
TOTAL		105	94

The lexical-words test with 1200-word segments shows that even with segments this short the distribution of the chosen words is consistent enough to separate almost all of the Shakespeare training segments from almost all of those by others. The test segments are not as well separated, as one expects, but their success rate is respectable.

We need to cross-check the result with other methods. An analysis using whole plays rather than segments to determine the marker-word lists does not show how variation operates at the 1200-word level, but it does give more clear-cut separations. The larger samples absorb local fluctuations in word use. Figure 7.2 illustrates a lexical-words test of Shakespeare plays versus non-Shakespeare plays from the period 1580 to1619. We calculated the scores for the Hand-D section for the same words sets and plotted that as well. The graph also shows the centroids for the two sets of plays. These mark the average of their scores on the two axes. If one had to choose one point to represent the group as a whole, this would be it. Instead of judging the positions of the various datapoints of the graph by eye, we can order them on a numerical basis. The Hand-D section is clearly much closer to the Shakespeare centroid than to the non-Shakespeare centroid; the distance in numerical terms is 0.019 versus 0.054. These distances are based on proportions of the same sets of marker words and are strictly comparable.

Figure 7.3 shows what happens when we carry out the same procedure with another candidate author, Thomas Dekker. We found Dekker and non-Dekker markers in the usual way, and plotted the two sets of segments and the Hand-D section, and located the group centroids. This time the distances are 0.637 from the Dekker centroid and 0.172 from the

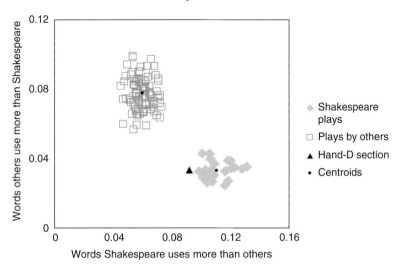

Figure 7.2 Lexical-words test: Shakespeare plays versus plays by others dated 1580–1619, with the Hand-D and Addition III portions of *Sir Thomas More*.

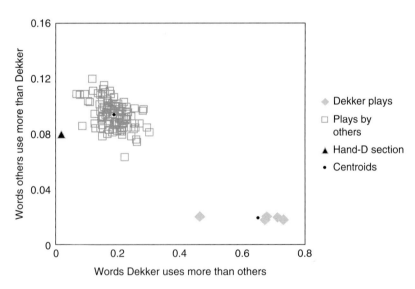

Figure 7.3 Lexical-words test: Dekker plays versus plays by others dated 1580–1619, with the Hand-D and Addition III portions of *Sir Thomas More*.

non-Dekker one. We can perform the same procedure with other authors. Table 7.2 summarizes the results for Shakespeare and Dekker, and also for Heywood, Jonson, Middleton, and Webster. Each time an author is regarded as the 'base' set and the collection of remaining plays from the 1580–1619 group is treated as the 'counter' set, following Burrows' terminology in his article setting out the Zeta principle.[41] In the case of the Jonson and Middleton sets we omitted the plays from 1620 or later. The last two columns show the distance from the Hand-D section to the base and counter centroids. The shorter distance is shaded. With the other five authors (Tests 1 to 4 and 6) the Hand-D section score is much closer to the 'counter' centroid. With Shakespeare, as already discussed in relation to Figure 7.2, it is closer to the 'base' set: in fact within the range of the Shakespeare plays (its distance is 0.019, closer than the distance of the furthest Shakespeare segment from the Shakespeare or 'base' centroid: i.e. 0.02). The contrast between the results for Shakespeare and for the other authors indicates a marked affinity for Shakespeare. The vocabulary of the Hand-D section is not marginally similar to Shakespeare's, but typical of his work.

The lexical-words data analysed through the authorial marker-words procedure thus support the attribution to Shakespeare. We wished to go a step further by moving to function-word data and a quite separate line of evidence. As already discussed, the Hand-D section is well below the optimum size for our tests. When we experimented with a principal component analysis (PCA) of the function-word set in 1200-word segments of plays of known authorship, we found that the overlap between sets was too extensive for any worthwhile classification of disputed segments. Thus we utilized a more targeted technique: linear discriminant analysis.[42] This method was pioneered by Sir Ronald Fisher in the 1930s. Like PCA, it links the variables and the observations – in our case, the word-frequencies and the text segments – by calculating a score for each observation that is the sum of the values for the chosen variables, each with a weighting. There is an important distinction here between discriminant and principal component analysis. The weightings for the first principal component in PCA are calculated so that the component accounts for the largest possible amount of the variation in the table of counts. Discriminant analysis, on the other hand, works from pre-defined groups of observations. It

---

[41] J. Burrows, 'All the Way Through: Testing for Authorship in Different Frequency Strata', *Literary and Linguistic Computing*, 22 (2007), 27–47.
[42] There is a full account in G. J. McLachlan, *Discriminant Analysis and Statistical Pattern Recognition* (New York: Wiley, 1992).

Table 7.2. *Distances between centroids and test segments, and between centroids and the Hand-D and Addition III portions of* Sir Thomas More, *in 6 authorial lexical-words tests using 1200-word segments.*

Test	Base set	Plays	Counter set	Plays	Average distance between segments and their own centroid		Maximum distance between segments and their own centroid		Distance between Hand-D and the centroids of the base and counter sets	
					Base set	Counter set	Base set	Counter set	Base set	Counter set
1	Dekker	5	Non-Dekker	107	0.075	0.038	0.186	0.12	0.637	0.172
2	Heywood	5	Non-Heywood	107	0.015	0.01	0.025	0.037	0.146	0.033
3	Jonson	12	Non-Jonson	100	0.009	0.014	0.016	0.032	0.08	0.006
4	Middleton	10	Non-Middleton	102	0.012	0.015	0.032	0.038	0.096	0.013
5	Shakespeare	27	Non-Shakespeare	85	0.009	0.011	0.02	0.023	0.019	0.054
6	Webster	3	Non-Webster	109	0.005	0.019	0.008	0.026	0.146	0.012

calculates a weighting for each variable so as to yield the greatest similarity between scores for observations within groups and the greatest difference between the groups. It is a method specifically aimed at classification, where PCA seeks factors that are latent in the data and takes no account of any prior assignation to groups.

Discriminant analysis is generally more effective therefore at separating training sets of observations. It uses information from the pre-defined groups to find the best possible classificatory vector. This is a different matter from the power to classify freshly introduced segments. The danger is that the method will be 'overtrained', i.e. so well adjusted to the particularities of the 'training' sets that it struggles with new instances from the same classes. For this reason it is especially important to test the analysis with new samples that are of known origin.

We carried out a series of discriminant analyses on data from Shakespeare segments and segments of one of five other authors at a time (Table 7.3). As test plays we used the same ones as for Table 7.1. The five authors are those tested in Figures 7.2 and 7.3, and Table 7.2.[43] In each case the analysis classified the Hand-D section of *Sir Thomas More* as Group 1, i.e. as Shakespeare. The variables included were the 100 most common from the 200 function word set. (Limiting the variables in this way minimized the danger of odd results resulting from zeros in the tables, i.e. from words in the longer list that do not appear at all in some 1200-word segments.) Among the test segments, the *Hamlet* ones were all successfully assigned to Shakespeare, but results for the non-Shakespeare plays were distinctly mixed. All nineteen *Duchess of Malfi* segments were classified as Webster, but only five of the fifteen segments from *The Shoemaker's Holiday* were ascribed to Dekker rather than to Shakespeare. (This contrasts with the results from the training segments, where eighty-two of the eighty-nine Dekker segments were correctly assigned.) We need to remember as well that we are regarding these six plays as representative of the work of the dramatist in general, but it is in fact impossible to find any truly representative test set. This would have to represent not only all the writing we know of by a given writer, but also all the writing they could possibly produce. It is also worth remembering that we have to remove a play from the training set, and thus weaken it, in order to provide a proper test. The full set, which we used to classify the Hand-D section, should be stronger, so one could argue that the test underestimates the power of the method.

---

[43] The number of plays and 1200-word segments was as follows: Dekker, 5 plays, 89 segments; Heywood, 5 plays, 71 segments; Jonson, 17 plays, 332 segments; Middleton, 12 plays, 212 segments; Shakespeare, 27 plays, 492 segments; Webster, 3 plays, 58 segments.

Table 7.3. *Five discriminant analysis tests of authorial groups, with results for test segments of known authorship, and for the Hand-D and Addition III portions of* Sir Thomas More.

Test	Group 1	Group 2	Group 1 test play	Segments	Correctly assigned	Group 2 test play	Segments	Correctly assigned	Hand-D section assigned to
1	Shakespeare	Dekker	*Hamlet*	24	24	*The Shoemaker's Holiday*	15	5	Group 1
2	Shakespeare	Heywood	*Hamlet*	24	24	*If You Know Not Me*	9	7	Group 1
3	Shakespeare	Jonson	*Hamlet*	24	24	*Volpone*	22	21	Group 1
4	Shakespeare	Middleton	*Hamlet*	24	24	*The Phoenix*	16	14	Group 1
5	Shakespeare	Webster	*Hamlet*	24	24	*The Duchess of Malfi*	19	19	Group 1

Plays used are all dated between 1580 and 1619. Variables used are the 100 most common from a list of 200 function words.

154

Taking all this into account, we can conclude that this separate func-tion-word evidence does appreciably strengthen the case for Shakespeare's authorship. The results tell us that Shakespeare is a better candidate than Dekker, Heywood, Jonson, Middleton, or Webster for authorship of the *Sir Thomas More* Addition.

As a final assay of the links between the vocabulary of the Hand-D sec-tion and our various authors we looked more closely at its unusual words, and at the otherwise common words it does not use. Here we are moving from the disputed passage out to the patterns of known authors, rather than from established authorial patterns inward. This is in principle less reliable, since we rely on what happens to be the case in one sample (what one might regard as happenstances and chance events) rather than on broad-based data from cases whose authorship is well understood. Yet it does add a third line of evidence and enables us to eke more attribution information out of our exiguous Hand-D sample.

MacDonald P. Jackson has already done something similar for phrases and collocations. He entered each phrase and collocation in the Hand-D and Addition III passages into the *Literature Online* database, and recorded all the links with five or fewer plays first performed between 1590 and 1610.[44] Fifteen plays had four or more links; of these ten were Shakespeare plays.[45] Analysing both Shakespeare and non-Shakespeare links by date showed a clear preponderance in plays dated after 1598 compared to earlier ones, leading Jackson to declare a victory for those who have proposed a date of 1603–4 for the *More* passages over those who argued for 1593–4.[46]

We began with the unusual words appearing in this scene of civil unrest and irenic intervention, rather than the unusual phrases and collocations. After discarding proper names, function words, and some other unhelpful words like imprecations and numbers, we came up with a list of 108 words that are used by Hand-D but do not appear in 60 per cent of our cor-pus of 136 single-author, well-attributed plays. They could thus be called Hand-D's rare words. We then returned to the corpus of plays dating from 1580 to 1619, and counted how often the words appear in each of them. We were looking for an overlap in unusual words between the Hand-D section and plays of known authorship. The highest number was 32, in *Othello*, as follows:

addition babes backs banish bank barbarous brawl certainly comforts discipline elem-ents fancies harbour hideous hip horrible hound infected innovation nation partly pattern procure rebels removed removing roots ruffians stillness throats trash trespass

[44] Jackson, 'The Date and Authorship of Hand D's Contribution', pp. 69–78; the results are listed on pp. 71–5.
[45] *Ibid.*, pp. 75–6.   [46] *Ibid.*, p. 78.

To take into account the size of the plays we divided the counts by the total number of different words in the play. After this adjustment *Othello* remained the highest scorer: the Hand-D rare words formed a larger proportion of its vocabulary than of the vocabulary of any other play. Moreover, Shakespeare plays accounted for seven of the ten highest proportional counts. To compare all the authors on a common basis, we created a series of author variables, one for each of our 29 authors, and gave each of the plays a value for each of these variables – 1 if the play was by the author in question, and zero if not. Thus for the 'Shakespeare' author variable his 27 plays each had a value of one, and the 85 by others had a value of zero. For the 'Dekker' variable the 5 Dekker plays had a value of one, and 108 a value of zero, and so on. We then correlated the list of play scores on the Hand-D rare words with each author variable in turn. This gave us a measure of the degree to which authors shared the Hand-D rare vocabulary across their canons. Shakespeare had the highest correlation (0.290). Fletcher was next (0.190). The lowest was Greene (–0.179).

We also identified the words that are common generally in the larger corpus, but not used in Hand-D. The rule for selection was that the word must appear in more than 60 per cent of the plays in the corpus and not in Hand-D. There were 531 of these. We carried out the same correlation exercise as with the rare words that do appear in the Hand-D section. This time we were looking for plays, and authorial groups of plays, that use many of those words that are widely used in the drama of the time but that the Hand-D writer neglects. This time the highest scorer was Lyly (0.284), followed by Middleton (0.181). The writer with the lowest correlation was Jonson (–0.379), with Shakespeare second lowest (–0.201). Here again Shakespeare conforms to the pattern we can glean from the 1200 or so words of the Hand-D section. Not only does he use the rare words appearing in Hand-D more than his peers, but he also generally eschews the common words neglected by the writer of Hand-D.

The evidence presented here is unusually consistent. The Hand-D and Addition III portions of *Sir Thomas More* are very like Shakespeare in their use of Shakespeare lexical words, non-Shakespeare lexical words, and function words. The Hand-D and Addition III portions share many rare words with Shakespeare and avoid many of the same common words. On these measures the *More* passages are not on a Shakespeare borderline but in a Shakespeare heartland. These results can be added to the many indications already in existence, from parallel passages, image clusters, rare words, idiosyncratic spellings, and indeed from handwriting: indications that led Jackson in 2007 to suggest a probability of 99.9 per cent to Shakespeare's authorship.[47]

If our methods can distinguish authors with some reliability even with a 1200-word passage, then one may wonder whether they can offer any help with its date. As already noted, scholars have disagreed sharply over the date of the *Sir Thomas More* passages. If we assume for a moment that they are by Shakespeare, then do they fit the early part of his canon better, or the later? In effect this becomes a one-on-one author comparison, this time with early Shakespeare pitted against late Shakespeare. To execute this comparison, we took the 1200-word Shakespeare segments already defined and divided them by date, one group being the segments from plays dated by the *Annals of English Drama* before 1600 and the other those from plays dated 1600 or later. We looked at the full range of lexical words used in the segments and (as before) identified a group of words that appear much more regularly in the early segments, and a second group commoner in the later segments. Plotting the scores on these two groups of words for all the segments, and the *Sir Thomas More* passages, gives us Figure 7.4. The dashed line is the perpendicular bisector of the line between the two centroids (this latter line, and the centroids, are not shown on the graph). The passages fall above the line and in the cluster of late plays (the grey discs). The verdict of this test, then, is that the *Sir Thomas More* passages, if they are by Shakespeare, were written after 1600, in line with the views of Taylor and Jackson.

Before leaving the Hand-D question it is worth addressing further the challenge to Shakespeare's claims in Ward E. Y. Elliott and Robert J. Valenza's unpublished paper, already mentioned. Elliott and Valenza report that the parts of Hand-D and Addition III in verse scored two substantial failures and one technical failure in their tests for Shakespeare authorship. Elliott and Valenza have a long history in applying quantitative measures to Shakespeare authorship. They have mounted a powerful case against the Earl of Oxford as the author of Shakespeare's works,[48] and were certainly in the right in ruling Shakespeare out as the author of *A Funerall Elegie*.[49] On the Hand-D passages their conclusion is that Shakespeare

[47] Jackson, 'Is Hand-D of *Sir Thomas More* Shakespeare's?', paragraph 26.

[48] W. E. Y. Elliott and R. J. Valenza, 'Oxford by the Numbers: What Are the Odds that the Earl of Oxford Could Have Written Shakespeare's Poems and Plays?', *Tennessee Law Review*, 71 (2004), 323–454.

[49] W. E. Y. Elliott and R. J. Valenza, 'Glass Slippers and Seven-League Boots: C-Prompted Doubts about Ascribing *A Funeral Elegy* and *A Lover's Complaint* to Shakespeare', *Shakespeare Quarterly*, 48 (1997), 177–207.

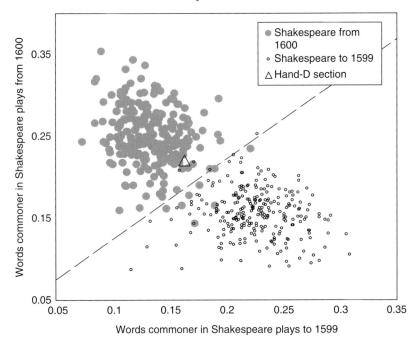

Figure 7.4 Lexical-words test: 1200-word segments from Shakespeare plays to 1599 versus 1200-word segments from Shakespeare plays from 1600, with the Hand-D and Addition III portions of *Sir Thomas More*.

authorship is 'improbable but not impossible'.[50] Their more detailed summary is that '[i]f [Hand D plus Addition III] was written in 1603, and its discrepancies are not otherwise explained away, the verse portion of it is seven to 26 times less likely to be Shakespeare than Shakespeare's farthest-outlier threshold block'.[51] The two substantial tests that Hand-D fails are Grade Level comprehension difficulty – an index combining word length and sentence length – and a count for twenty-one function words and contracted forms that distinguish *Macbeth* from Middleton's *The Witch*, which Elliott and Valenza call a 'Bundle of Badges' test. Jackson suggests that the fact that Hand-D comes to us via manuscript rather than by way of print, and is thus unusually 'ambiguous or muddled' in syntax, may well explain the failure on the Grade Level test.[52] We cannot add anything to this. The Bundle of Badges test comes closer to our methods in this book, and though we cannot replicate it fully, we can repeat part of it

[50] Elliott and Valenza, 'Two Tough Nuts', p. 1.   [51] *Ibid.*, p. 22.
[52] Jackson, 'Is "Hand D"', paragraph 30.

with different data, to help establish whether it threatens the attribution to Shakespeare or not.

For their test, Elliott and Valenza first found a set of function words commoner in *Macbeth* than in Middleton's *The Witch*, and then a second set of function words commoner in *The Witch* than in *Macbeth*. For them, function words include contractions like *I'll* and *'tis*, both of which, incidentally, they find to be markedly commoner in *The Witch*. For each of their 90 sample Shakespeare verse play segments (each around 750 words[53]), they calculate the sum of the *Macbeth* markers, deduct the sum of the *Witch* markers, and divide the result by the total of *Macbeth* and *Witch* markers. The lowest count on this measure for a Shakespeare block is 63, and the highest 712. The verse part of Hand-D comes in at 765 and thus counts as an emphatic Shakespeare rejection.[54]

Jackson has already raised some questions about this verdict. The particular subject matter, and more generally the genre, of the Hand-D passages could well explain their exceptionally high score on this measure.[55] Moreover, the ninety blocks Elliott and Valenza use as a Shakespeare template are drawn from just seven plays. Jackson argues that plays outside the sample could well give rise to much higher counts and so extend the Shakespeare range to include the Hand-D verse score.[56]

We can replicate something of the Elliott and Valenza experiments with our own data. In our texts we have expanded contractions into full forms so we cannot reassemble Elliott and Valenza's sets of markers completely. However, we can reproduce their first group of words, the *Macbeth* markers, which does not contain any contractions. We can also compute scores using the eight words proper from the *Witch* 'bundle' of ten 'flukes', omitting the contractions. From this we can calculate a variant of the Elliott and Valenza 'Bundle of Badges 5'. We can also follow the principles of the 'Bundle of Badges' method and find ten Shakespeare markers, and ten markers of non-Shakespeare plays, and combine the scores as Elliott and Valenza do.[57]

---

[53] Elliott and Valenza, 'Two Tough Nuts', p. 16.   [54] *Ibid.*, p. 17, Table 2.

[55] Jackson, 'Is "Hand D"', paragraph 33.   [56] *Ibid.*, paragraph 34.

[57] We used the *t*-test to find 2 sets of 10 words each. The first set consists of the words from our standard list of 200 function words at the top of the list of words more common in the 29 Shakespeare plays than in the 85 by other writers from the decades 1580 to 1619. The second set comprises the 10 words more common in the non-Shakespeare plays. To follow Elliott and Valenza's procedures as closely as possible for these experiments, we use a list of 29 'core Shakespeare' plays rather than our usual 27. This means adding *The Taming of the Shrew, Measure for Measure*, and a *Macbeth* '"purged"' of the Hecate passages, and excluding *Henry V* (see Elliott and Valenza, 'Two Tough Nuts', p. 36 n.). We work with percentages of total words, rather than with raw counts as Elliott and Valenza do, but it is hard to see why this would invalidate the comparison. All our segments are of similar size, so any difference will be minimal.

Table 7.4. *Tests using a selection from Elliott and Valenza's 'badges' and 'flukes', and separately calculated Shakespeare and non-Shakespeare markers, as bundles and as combinations of bundles.*

		Scores for		
		Lowest Shakespeare segment	Highest Shakespeare segment	Hand-D
1	Shakespeare 'Bundle of Badges'	6.67	21.17	18.04
2	Bundle of eight of Shakespeare 'flukes'	2.50	12.00	3.46
3	Combination of (1) and (2)	−0.11	0.79	0.68
4	Bundle of ten Shakespeare markers	2.25	7.25	3.87
5	Bundle of ten non-Shakespeare markers	0.33	3.00	2.39
6	Combination of (4) and (5)	−0.14	0.90	0.24

Scores are for 1200-word segments of 29 Shakespeare plays, and for *Sir Thomas More* Hand-D and Addition III portions. The formula for the 'combination' calculation in row 3 is (1) – (2)/(1) + (2), and similarly for row 6.

Two differences from the original in our replication worth noting are that we use the prose parts as well as the verse of Hand-D and Addition III, where Elliott and Valenza use only the verse; and we use 1200-word segments, to match the size of the complete Hand-D and Addition III portion, rather than 750-word blocks. One could argue the merits of the two approaches (selecting only verse, compared to combining verse and prose, for instance), but if the Elliott and Valenza method does detect a substantial difference between Hand-D and Shakespeare, one would expect it to emerge also in our parallel tests. The results of the latter are shown in Table 7.4. In each case we found the Hand-D score to be within the Shakespeare range. Rerunning the Elliott and Valenza experiments gives a context for their adverse finding. It is likely that if they had widened their Shakespeare baseline to include more blocks from more plays, Hand-D would have appeared less unusual for an authentic Shakespeare sample. In any case, there is no reason to expect a measure based on the differences between *Macbeth* and *The Witch* to be especially effective in telling Shakespeare and non-Shakespeare apart more broadly. When we construct a similar measure but with broader 'training' data, we find once again that Hand-D fits quite comfortably into a Shakespeare envelope. We conclude that the Elliott and Valenza 'Bundle of Badges 5' rejection does not challenge the hypothesis of Shakespeare authorship.

All of our tests, taken together, indicate that we can link the mind responsible for the Shakespearean canon with the playwright who wrote the Hand-D Addition for *Sir Thomas More*. In this matter, the threshold from conjecture to genuine probability has been crossed. This creates a presumption in favour of the second, equally vexed, question of the connection between the hand that wrote the six signatures and Hand-D. Since the nature of the manuscript indicates an author at work – correcting and amending along the way – rather than a scribe making a fair copy, this connection seems hard to resist. One recalls Kinney's description of the stakes of the attribution: 'if we have any fragment of drama actually in Shakespeare's hand, this is it'. The identification of Hand-D with Shakespeare now seems one of the better established facts about his canon, and among the surest facts of his biography.

CHAPTER 8

The 1602 Additions to The Spanish Tragedy

Hugh Craig

Thomas Kyd's *The Spanish Tragedy* is one of the most important early texts of the Elizabethan theatre, but details of its creation and early performances are sparse. It was probably written in the late 1580s. The first extant record, in Philip Henslowe's diary of theatre accounts, calls the play *Jeronymo*, after its main character, Hieronimo, and mentions a performance at the Rose Theatre in March 1592.[1] The play was printed in 1592 and again in 1594 and 1599. Kyd died in 1594. There is no mention of the author of the play in the diary or in any of the early editions. Thomas Heywood was the first to associate *The Spanish Tragedy* with Kyd in print, in his *Apology for Actors* (1612).[2]

By 1600 the copyright in the play had passed to Thomas Pavier. In 1602 he brought out an edition with some new passages. The title-page says that the play is 'Newly corrected, amended, and enlarged with new Additions of the Painters part, and others, as it hath of late been diuers times acted'. There are five Additions. There is no indication of their author.

The first new section, fifty-four lines long, is inserted just after Hieronimo has discovered the body of his son Horatio. While in the earlier version of the play Hieronimo remains sane for some time after the murder, in this added passage he loses his wits temporarily and imagines that the body is someone else's, dressed in Horatio's clothes. Shortly afterwards he returns to full consciousness of his loss ('How strangely had I lost my way to grief', he says [1.54]).[3] The second passage, ten lines in all, replaces a two-line speech by Hieronimo to Lorenzo, son of the Duke of Castile and nephew to the Spanish King. Hieronimo has come to see Bel-imperia, who is Lorenzo's sister; Lorenzo asks him if he can help with

---

[1] For bibliographic matters concerning *The Spanish Tragedy* we rely on the edition by Philip Edwards: Thomas Kyd, *The Spanish Tragedy*, ed. P. Edwards, The Revels Plays (London: Methuen, 1959).

[2] See Kyd, *The Spanish Tragedy*, ed. Edwards, p. xvii.

[3] The first numeral in references to the Additions here and below is the number of the Addition, the second the line number or numbers. Quotations here and below are from the Edwards edition.

whatever Hieronimo is seeking, since Bel-imperia is absent (in fact she has been imprisoned by Lorenzo). Hieronimo declines, mentioning the subject of his 'suit' to Bel-imperia with elaborate casualness: 'In troth, my lord, it is a thing of nothing, / The murder of a son or so: / A thing of nothing, my lord' (2.8–10).[4] The third Addition is a long speech by Hieronimo, forty-eight lines, made to two Portuguese men met by accident outside Lorenzo's house. Hieronimo muses on the drawbacks of having a son, the troubles such offspring bring, and the foolishness of a parent's love for them, but then contrasts all this with Horatio's virtues, and anticipates retribution for his murderers.

The fourth addition is the longest, at 169 lines, 1449 words in all. Hieronimo talks to servants about the night of his son's murder:

> Had the moon shone, in my boy's face there was a kind of grace,
> That I know, nay, I do know, had the murderer seen him,
> His weapon would have fall'n and cut the earth,
> Had he been fram'd of naught but blood and death. (4.48–51)

He continues in this vein to Isabella and then to a painter who is appealing to him for justice for his own murdered son. Hieronimo asks him to paint the family as they were five years ago, the scene of the murder, and his own discovery of the body by torchlight. This fourth Addition is mentioned on the title-page of the 1602 edition as 'the Painters part'. The fifth and last Addition, forty-eight lines long, incorporates a number of lines from the previous version. It comes in the final scene and expands on Hieronimo's triumphant vaunting of his revenge.

The new material is anonymous. Henslowe, however, records two payments to Ben Jonson for additions to the play. The first is dated 25 September 1601, and is for 40 shillings 'Lent vnto mr alleyn ... to lend vnto Bengemen Johnson vpon hn [probably 'his'] writting of his adicians in geronymo'.[5] Then, on 22 June 1602, there is a further payment of 10 pounds 'Lent vnto bengemy Johnsone at the A poyntment of EAlleyn & w^m birde ... in earneste of A Boocke called Richard

---

[4] John Kerrigan, 'Revision, Adaptation, and the Fool in *King Lear*', in *The Division of the Kingdoms: Shakespeare's Two Versions of* King Lear, ed. G. Taylor and M. Warren (Oxford: Clarendon Press, 1983), p. 240, suggests that these lines 'echo' *Hamlet*, presumably referring to IV.ii.27–30, Hamlet's exchange with Guildenstern over Polonius's body:

HAMLET: The body is with the King, but the King is not with the body. The King is a thing –
GUILDENSTERN: A thing, my lord?
HAMLET: Of nothing ...

[5] Philip Henslowe, *Henslowe's Diary*, ed. R. A. Foakes and R. T. Rickert (Cambridge: Cambridge University Press, 1961), p. 182.

crockbacke & for new adicyons for Jeronymo'.[6] ('Richard crockbacke' is presumably Jonson's version of *Richard III*, which was either never completed or, if it was, has since been lost.)

Chronology presents some obstacles to connecting the passages Jonson was paid for with those printed with the 1602 edition of the play. There are two parodies of the scene with the painter in the fourth Addition in John Marston's play *Antonio and Mellida*. This was printed in 1602, but is usually dated 1599, on the grounds of a character's pointed reference to that year (and evidently to Marston's age in that year) in the same scene that includes the parody.[7] This suggests that the painter scene was already being performed in 1599, some time before Henslowe was paying Jonson to revise the play. Jonson himself has a character allude to a revised version of *The Spanish Tragedy* in the Induction to *Cynthia's Revels* (first performance 1600, printed 1601): a playgoer is quoted as declaring that '*the old Hieronimo*, (as it was first acted) *was the onely best, and iudiciously pend play of Europe*'.[8] This, too, indicates a revised version of the play in performance before Henslowe was advancing money to Jonson for his 'adicians'. Henslowe had put his symbol 'ne', usually taken to imply a new play, next to a performance of *The Spanish Tragedy* in 1597;[9] it may be that the new passages printed in 1602 had been written by then, and that the anticipated revisions by Jonson were different ones, and were never completed or are now lost. It would be easy to reconcile an earlier revision to the play with the comments by the Marston and Jonson characters, and the Marston reference ties this early revision to one of the additions we have in the 1602 *Spanish Tragedy*. Jonson frequently makes reference to *The Spanish Tragedy* in later plays, returning to the idea that it is an old stage warhorse that any discerning playgoer could see was thoroughly obsolete, and giving no hint that he had been involved in revising it.[10]

---

[6] *Ibid.*, p. 203.

[7] L. Erne, *Beyond* The Spanish Tragedy: *A Study of the Works of Thomas Kyd* (Manchester: Manchester University Press, 2001), draws attention to this point (p. 122). Harry Levin, in 'An Echo from *The Spanish Tragedy*', *Modern Language Notes*, 64 (1949), 297–302; D. H. Reiman, in 'Marston, Jonson, and the *Spanish Tragedy* Additions', *Notes and Queries*, n.s., 7 (1960), 336–7; and A. Freeman, on pp. 128–30 of *Thomas Kyd: Facts and Problems* (Oxford: Oxford University Press, 1967), all conclude that the printed Additions must have been written some years before 1602.

[8] Ben Jonson, *Cynthia's Revels*, Induction, lines 209–11. Jonson's works here and below are quoted from C. H. Herford, P. Simpson, and E. Simpson, *Ben Jonson*, 11 vols. (Oxford: Clarendon Press, 1925–52).

[9] Henslowe, *Diary*, p. 55.

[10] See Ben Jonson, *Poetaster*, III.iv.215–22; *Bartholomew Fair*, Induction, lines 106–11; and *The New Inn*, II.v.82, in particular. Jonson seems himself to have taken the role of Hieronimo on a provincial tour, judging from the taunts in Dekker's play *Satiromastix* (Erne, *Beyond* The Spanish Tragedy, pp. 57 and 75 n.).

Other aspects of external evidence are more difficult to assess. Payments of 2 pounds and of a part of 10 pounds would be unusually high for the 320 lines of the added passages, though not impossibly so, as some have argued.[11] W. W. Greg deemed it improbable that passages added to the acting version would have reached print so quickly, given the June payment to Jonson and the appearance of the new edition the same year.[12] Others have disagreed.[13] All in all, the best conclusion may be that the external evidence linking Jonson to the Additions leaves the question open: it makes him only a little more likely than any other candidate to be the writer.

The other great objection to Jonson's authorship is the discrepancy of style between the Additions and Jonson's known work. This gave rise to lively debate in the nineteenth century. Charles Lamb thought Webster might be the author, finding in the passages a 'wild solemn preternatural grief' like that of *The Duchess of Malfi*.[14] Swinburne also argued for Webster as the author.[15] Coleridge was the first to suggest Shakespeare as a candidate.[16] To some the idea that Jonson could have written the Additions amounted to a sort of scandal, a violation of fundamental aesthetic polarities. Jonson was established as a touchstone of laborious and uninspired creative work, his main importance being to serve as a foil to the spontaneous fecundity of Shakespeare. For one anonymous reviewer, accepting the idea that Jonson could have changed enough from himself to write the Additions would mean that there was no certainty anywhere in literary judgment. The Additions would be 'the one effort of his dramatic imagination (supposing them to be his) which had the power of speaking to the human heart'.[17] This writer puts the question of the authorship of the Additions at the centre of his remarks on Jonson and calls it 'the greatest riddle in dramatic criticism'.[18]

---

[11] Freeman, *Thomas Kyd*, p. 129 n., and A. Barton, *Ben Jonson, Dramatist* (Cambridge: Cambridge University Press, 1984), p. 14.

[12] Thomas Kyd, The Spanish Tragedy *with Additions 1602*, ed. W. W. Greg (Oxford: Malone Society Reprints, 1925), pp. xviii–xix.

[13] Barton, *Ben Jonson*, p. 14.

[14] C. Lamb, *Specimens of English Dramatic Poets who Lived about the Time of Shakespeare* (1808; London: Bell, 1901), p. 11.

[15] Swinburne's view is quoted in the anonymous review of his *A Study of Ben Jonson*, in *The Athenaeum*, 8 March 1890, 315–18; and 22 March 1890, 379–81 (p. 317). This suggestion is not supported by the Webster editor F. L. Lucas: see his 'Appendix III: The Additions to *The Spanish Tragedy*', in John Webster, *The Complete Works of John Webster*, ed. F. L. Lucas, 4 vols., Vol. IV (London: Chatto and Windus, 1927), pp. 248–9.

[16] Samuel Taylor Coleridge, *The Collected Works of Samuel Taylor Coleridge*, 16 vols., Vol. XIV, Part I: *Table Talk I*, ed. C. Woodring (Princeton: Princeton University Press, 1990), p. 355.

[17] Anon., review of *A Study*, p. 380.   [18] *Ibid.*, p. 317.

Twentieth-century editions of *The Spanish Tragedy* have also generally taken the style of the Additions to be a block against any firm attribution to Jonson, as Herford, Simpson, and Simpson do in their Jonson edition.[19] In the 1930s and 1940s H. W. Crundell and R. G. Howarth saw parallels with the style of Thomas Dekker.[20] In 1968 Warren Stevenson made a full-dress case for Shakespeare, based on rare words and phrases in the Additions that also occur in Shakespeare's work.[21]

It was difficult with the means available to Stevenson to show that words or expressions really were rare. The *Oxford English Dictionary* (*OED*) was the only scholarly aid for surveying the wider corpus of Elizabethan and Jacobean drama. In these circumstances attribution by unusual words or phrases was chancy. Words or phrases that appeared in the disputed texts and in an author's canonical works might in fact be found in others' as well if the scholar looked hard enough. There had been notorious abuses of the method, entertainingly ridiculed by S. Schoenbaum.[22] The late 1960s, when Stevenson was writing, were, indeed, a low point in faith in internal evidence for attribution purposes.[23]

The arrival of large full-text databases of English Renaissance drama offers an escape from this difficulty, and gives us the opportunity to take Stevenson's work further. MacDonald P. Jackson shows the way in his studies of collaborative plays from the period.[24] Now, where Stevenson describes close resemblances in vocabulary or phrasing, they can be checked with a machine-readable archive of writing from the time to determine if they really are rare. On the other hand, one cannot be completely systematic in examining the evidence: it would be difficult to agree on a complete list of the 'phrases' contained in the five Additions, for instance, so that one could claim to have tested them all for links to

---

[19] Kyd, *The Spanish Tragedy*, ed. Edwards, pp. lxi–lxvi; [The Spanish Comedy; *or*,] The First Part of Hieronimo *and* The Spanish Tragedy [*or*, Hieronimo is Mad Again], ed. A. S. Cairncross (London: Arnold, 1967), pp. xxi–xxiv; *The Spanish Tragedy*, ed. T. W. Ross (Edinburgh: Oliver and Boyd, 1968), p. 5 n.; *The Spanish Tragedy*, ed. J. R. Mulryne (London: Benn, 1970), p. xxxi; and Herford, Simpson, and Simpson, *Ben Jonson*, Vol. II, pp. 240–5.

[20] H. W. Crundell, 'The 1602 Additions to *The Spanish Tragedy*', *Notes and Queries*, 164 (1933), 147–9; 'The 1602 Additions to *The Spanish Tragedy*', *Notes and Queries*, 167 (1934), 88; and 'The Authorship of *The Spanish Tragedy* Additions', *Notes and Queries*, 180 (1941), 8–9. R. G. Howarth, 'The 1602 Additions to *The Spanish Tragedy*', *Notes and Queries*, 166 (1941), 246.

[21] W. Stevenson, 'Shakespeare's Hand in *The Spanish Tragedy* 1602', *Studies in English Literature*, 8 (1968), 307–21.

[22] S. Schoenbaum, *Internal Evidence and Elizabethan Dramatic Authorship: An Essay in Literary History and Method* (London: Arnold, 1966).

[23] H. Love, *Attributing Authorship: An Introduction* (Cambridge: Cambridge University Press, 2002), p. 54.

[24] M. P. Jackson, 'Determining Authorship: A New Technique', *Research Opportunities in Renaissance Drama*, 41 (2002), 1–14.

authorial canons; and no single, hard-and-fast principle can establish the degree of closeness or the rarity of a so-called parallel. The collocations we quote below, however, are all defined by the presence of two or more vocabulary items, if with varying accidence, i.e. with forms varied according to tense or number. We have checked each in the *English Verse Drama* corpus, taking into account variations in spelling.[25]

Some of Stevenson's parallels prove to be too common to be satisfactory as authorship markers. *English Verse Drama* helps find so many instances of the phrases 'breeds teeth', 'hang'd up' and 'inestimable jewels' in other dramatists that their presence both in the Additions and in Shakespeare's work slips from being decisive (as they are in Stevenson's account[26]) to being merely corroborative of authorship. Nevertheless a number of Stevenson's parallels do prove to be genuinely exclusive, some really are rare, and there are others he overlooked.

There are some borrowings in the Additions that are so obvious that they may well have been intended as allusions, or even as parodies. Some of these have already been noticed independently of Stevenson. In *2 Henry VI*, Gloucester asks the Mayor of St Albans and his aldermen 'have you not / Beadles in your town, and things call'd whips?' (II.i.133–4). This is echoed in the third Addition, where, musing on revenge, Hieronimo says 'there is Nemesis and Furies, / And things call'd whips, / And they sometimes do meet with murderers' (3.41–3).[27] Not surprisingly, there are no other passages in *English Verse Drama* with these three elements together – 'things', 'called', and 'whips'. The sense that this is a knowing allusion rather than a surreptitious or unconscious borrowing is strengthened by the fact that the three elements occur again in Marston's *Antonio's Revenge* (1600),[28] a sequel to *Antonio and Mellida*: 'There is a thing cald scourging *Nemesis*.' Further, in Robert Armin, *Nest of Ninnies* (1608), there is the comment 'Ther are, as Hamlet saies, things called whips in store.'[29] (Hamlet says no such thing, in the surviving texts of the Shakespeare play at any rate. Stevenson suggests that Armin's confusion about the speakers comes about because Burbage played both Hamlet and Hieronimo,

[25] *English Verse Drama*, Version 2, CD-ROM (Cambridge: Chadwyck-Healey, 1995). The search engine was set to find all matches in five 'periods': 'Tudor', 'Elizabethan', 'Jacobean and Caroline', 'Moralities', and 'University Plays'. These groupings together include 745 plays, masques, and entertainments.

[26] Stevenson, 'Shakespeare's Hand', pp. 313–14.

[27] Edwards records the *2 Henry VI* parallel in his note (Kyd, *The Spanish Tragedy*, p. 126 n.).

[28] The dates given for non-Shakespearean plays here and below are those in A. C. Harbage and S. Schoenbaum, *Annals of English Drama* (Philadelphia: University of Philadelphia Press, 1964).

[29] Marston and Armin are quoted from Kyd, *The Spanish Tragedy*, ed. Edwards, pp.145 and 126 n.

and Armin knew that Shakespeare had written the Additions as well as *Hamlet*.[30])

Aaron in *Titus Andronicus* says 'I pried me through the crevice of a wall' (V.i.114); the Hieronimo of the fourth Addition says 'I pry through every crevice of each wall' (4.17).[31] Once again there are the same three lexical items in the same order, and the phrase cannot be matched elsewhere in *English Verse Drama*. Faustus in Marlowe's *Doctor Faustus* declares 'Had I as many soules, as there be Starres, / I'de give them all for *Mephostopholis*' (lines 330–1).[32] The writer of the Additions, surely expecting the allusion to be recognized, has Hieronimo say

> Had I as many lives as there be stars,
> As many heavens to go to as those lives,
> I'd give them all, ay, and my soul to boot,
> But I would see thee ride in this red pool. (5.12–15)

Erne cites two of these borrowings (those from *Titus Andronicus* and *Doctor Faustus*) and suggests that they may best be explained as interpolations by actors reconstructing the Additions from memory and filling gaps with snippets from other plays.[33] Edwards, however, had already argued convincingly that the overall condition of the text of the Additions does not support the idea of reconstruction from memory, the fourth Addition being for instance 'quite free from the muddle, weakness, and repetitions to be expected from a memorial report'.[34] It may be that the intertextual elements are playful allusions rather than signs of memorial reconstruction. Commentators have often noticed the aptness of the final lines of the fifth Addition,[35] which deftly ends with '*Nunc iners cadat manus* [Now let my hand fall idle!] / Now to express the rupture of my part …' (5.47–8).[36] The hypothesis would be that in revising Kyd's play Shakespeare, if he is responsible, offered a compendium of allusions to popular tragedies and

---

[30] Stevenson, 'Shakespeare's Hand', pp. 311–12.

[31] Kyd, *The Spanish Tragedy*, ed. Edwards, 4.17. This is from a section of *Titus Andronicus* generally apportioned to Shakespeare (see Table 2.1, above, p. 29).

[32] Christopher Marlowe, *The Complete Works of Christopher Marlowe*, ed. Fredson Bowers, 2 vols. (Cambridge: Cambridge University Press, 1973).

[33] Erne, *Beyond* The Spanish Tragedy, p. 123. In the introduction to his edition of *2 Henry VI* (Oxford: Oxford University Press, 2002), Roger Warren cites borrowings from the *Tamburlaine* plays and *Doctor Faustus* in the Quarto version of the play as evidence that the latter is a reported text (pp. 82–3). The idea is that actors when recalling speeches reverted to other similar passages from other plays (p. 82). Naturally, the Additions might still be by Shakespeare even if the 1602 text derived partly or wholly from the reports of actors.

[34] Kyd, *The Spanish Tragedy*, ed. Edwards, p. lxiii.

[35] Stevenson, 'Shakespeare's Hand', p. 320; Erne, *Beyond* The Spanish Tragedy, p. 123.

[36] Kyd, *The Spanish Tragedy*, ed. Edwards, 5.47–8 (the translation is also from Edwards).

histories (including ones by himself) for the *cognoscenti* in the audience. This would be a variation on Pistol's fragments of scraps of old tragedies in *2 Henry IV* [37] and the casual quotation from *The Spanish Tragedy* in *Much Ado about Nothing* (I.i.261).[38]

There are three other shared phrasings among those collected by Stevenson that cannot be matched anywhere else in *English Verse Drama*. These are unmistakably direct links with Shakespeare texts but are so transposed as to be more like recurrences to an unconscious authorial pattern than allusions. Hieronimo asks querulously why the moon did not shine on the night of Horatio's murder: 'She should have shone: search thou the book' (4.47). Richard III, in very similar fashion, asks for a 'calendar' to check if the sun should be up, and after consulting it concludes that 'he disdains to shine, for by the book / He should have brav'd the east an hour ago' (*Richard III*, V.iii.276–9). This combination of words in this sense – a heavenly body 'shining' with a calendar 'book' – is found nowhere else in *English Verse Drama*.[39] Hieronimo wants himself and Horatio painted with 'my hand leaning upon his head' (4.124). In *The Rape of Lucrece* there is a painting with a scene in which 'one man's hand lean'd on another's head' (line 1415). A search of *English Verse Drama* turns up no other comparable combination of 'hand', 'leaning', and 'head'. A further instruction to the painter concerns the depiction of the murderers: Hieronimo says 'let their eyebrows jutty over' (4.137–8). The combination of brows and the verb 'jutty' (i.e. jut out) occurs also in *Henry V*, and nowhere else in *English Verse Drama*. Henry bids his troops 'lend the eye a terrible aspect', and

> ... let the brow o'erwhelm it
> As fearfully as doth a galled rock
> O'erhang and jutty his confounded base,
> Swill'd with the wild and wasteful ocean. (III.i.11–14)[40]

Two others of Stevenson's parallels prove to be indeed rare, though not unique. The word 'unsquared' in the phrase 'unsquar'd, unbevell'd',

---

[37] *2 Henry IV*, II.iv.163–7, for instance, is a garbled version of lines from Marlowe's *Tamburlaine, Part 2*: see the note to this passage in *The Riverside Shakespeare*, ed. G. B. Evans *et al.*, 2nd edn (Boston: Houghton Mifflin, 1997).

[38] See the note to this passage in the *Riverside* edition.

[39] Readers will recall also that the mechanicals in *A Midsummer Night's Dream* check in an 'almanac' or a 'calendar' to see if the moon will be shining on the night of their performance at the court (III.i.51–5). The play is in prose as well as verse, so is not included in *English Verse Drama*, which is our benchmark corpus to establish the rarity or otherwise of collocations shared between Shakespeare and the Additions.

[40] Edwards refers to this passage in his note on the use of the word 'jutty' in the Additions (Kyd, *The Spanish Tragedy*, p. 132 n.). The word is used as a noun in *Macbeth*: 'no jutty, frieze, / Buttress, nor coign of vantage, but this bird / Hath made his pendant bed and procreant cradle' (I.vi.6–8).

which Hieronimo uses of a putative son (3.22) is also used figuratively in *Troilus and Cressida* (I.iii.159) and not again in *English Verse Drama*, though the *OED* records an instance in John Marston's *What You Will* (1607).[41] Hieronimo's phrase 'minutes jarring' (4.150), meaning 'minutes ticking', recalls the wording of *Richard II*: 'My thoughts are minutes, and with sighs they jar' (V.v.51). Elsewhere in *English Verse Drama* 'minutes' occur with 'jarring' in the period only in James Shirley, *Changes; or, Love in a Maze* (1632)[42] and Lewis Sharpe, *The Noble Stranger* (1639).

To these can be added other links to Shakespeare texts not noticed by Stevenson. A search of one portion of the fourth Addition, from the entry of the painter to the exit of Isabella, Pedro, and Jaques (4.79–106), yields two phrases in common with Shakespeare texts that do not appear elsewhere in *English Verse Drama* in the period. The formulation 'as massy as' in Hieronimo's simile '[a]s massy as the earth'[43] is also found in *Much Ado about Nothing*, in the phrase 'as massy as his club' (III.iii.137–8), and only there. Hieronimo says 'all the undelved mines cannot buy / An ounce of justice' (4.86). 'Delved', whether in positive or negative form, occurs with 'mines' again only in *Hamlet*: 'I will delve one yard below their mines' (III.iv.208).[44] For some comparison, we looked in Jonson plays for rare phrases shared with this passage from the fourth Addition; we found none. Slightly less rare, and from an earlier passage in the fourth Addition, is the phrase 'our grandam earth' (4.19), which also occurs in *1 Henry IV* (III.i.33), and otherwise in *English Verse Drama* in the period only in Ralph Knevet, *Rhodon and Iris* (1631).

The Additions, then, have some intimate connections with the drama of their day. Some of these may well be allusions to passages and phrases the audience could be expected to know well. Others are equally direct but so adapted to the communicative purposes of the moment that they seem (as best one can tell) better explained by the same mind reverting to idiosyncratic habits in the process of composition. This sort of evidence, as already mentioned, requires the exercise of judgment, and so is not altogether objective, but it is clear that there are some strong links between the vocabulary and phrasing of the Additions and canonical Shakespeare

---

[41] S.v. *unsquared, fig. What You Will* is mainly in prose, so is not included in *English Verse Drama*.

[42] Shirley's play quotes from *The Spanish Tragedy*, as Emma Smith points out in her edition of *The Spanish Tragedie* (London: Penguin, 1998), p. 151, so his use of 'minutes' with 'jarring' may well derive from the Additions.

[43] Kyd, *The Spanish Tragedy*, ed. Edwards, 4.96.

[44] *English Verse Drama* uses the First Folio text of the play, which omits this passage. There is one close analogue outside Shakespeare, 'Heere doe the *Miners* and *Pioners* delue / Into the Earths entrailes', in Anthony Munday's entertainment *Chruso-Thriambos* (1611); see *English Verse Drama*.

in particular. It is difficult to go further and make a conclusive case with this kind of evidence. At the very least a researcher would have to look as hard for parallels in other authors as in Shakespeare, and adjust for the fact that Shakespeare's canon is so large and so well supplied with concordances and other tools for searching. In any case, as we argued in Chapter 3 of the present volume, methods founded on the peculiarities of a disputed text, like Stevenson's, are inherently less reliable than methods founded on the regularities of well-established authorial canons.

As best one can tell Stevenson's work was not adopted, and not disputed either. Perhaps it fell foul of the prevailing general suspicion of the validity of parallel-passages methods of attribution, exemplified in S. Schoenbaum's book *Internal Evidence and Elizabethan Dramatic Authorship*.[45] Philip Edwards' 1959 edition of the play pre-dates Stevenson, but his conclusion on the Additions problem probably captured received opinion for the next couple of decades: 'It cannot be disproved that the Additions of *1602* are the relics of those for which Jonson was paid, but one is not at all happy in accepting them as such. If a really convincing case had been made out for another dramatist, and an earlier date, one would readily accept it.'[46] In 1976 Norman Rabkin expressed a similar frustration with the dissonance created by including the Additions in the Jonson canon. 'No one, to my knowledge', Rabkin says, 'has ever managed to find in them the unique Ben Jonson of everything to which he signed his name'. Jonson's 'invisibility' in the *Spanish Tragedy* passages, Rabkin feels, is part of 'the great Elizabethan disappearing act', a testament to the 'decorum according to which the collaborator serves not himself but a joint project'.[47]

In her book *Ben Jonson, Dramatist* (1984), however, Anne Barton makes a strong argument for an unequivocal incorporation of the Additions into Jonson's canon. She considers that the objections to the attribution based on Henslowe's entry can all be met, and finds that the material in the passages can be accommodated to Jonson's known work, and indeed helps to see the range and motivations of his writing in a new light. She notes that he had always responded with unusual intensity to the deaths of children, and to the father–son relationship in general. She suggests that the play he was called upon to revise, based on a father's revenge for the murder of his son, 'activated feelings and responses that were deeply buried in his

[45] S. Schoenbaum, *Internal Evidence and Elizabethan Dramatic Authorship* (London: Edward Arnold, 1966).
[46] Kyd, *The Spanish Tragedy*, ed. Edwards, p. lxvi.
[47] N. Rabkin, 'Problems in the Study of Collaboration', *Research Opportunities in Renaissance Drama*, 19 (1976), 7–13 (p. 12).

innermost self'.[48] Parallels in idea and sensibility (if not in style) can be found with Jonson's well-attributed work, so that parts of the Additions seem 'characteristic' of Jonson, 'recognizably akin' in imagination to conceits from Jonson's *œuvre*.[49] In a biography of Jonson, published in 1989, David Riggs accepted these arguments. He notes that all the added passages 'focus on the allied themes of premature death and parental bereavement, and these were subjects close to Jonson's heart'.[50] We have already mentioned Hieronimo's speech in the third Addition, where he talks of a hypothetical unwanted son in parallel to his lost son Horatio. Riggs notes that in 1601–2 Jonson had two sons, Ben (aged five) and Joseph (aged two). 'Hieronimo's plight', comments Riggs, 'suddenly takes on an uncanny resemblance to Jonson's personal situation'.[51]

In a 1992 study, the author applied some of the new techniques of computational stylistics to the Additions problem. A principal component analysis placed the Additions with Shakespeare rather than with Jonson plays. The database was the frequencies of fifty very common words in a total of eighteen plays by these two authors.[52] In the most recent book on Kyd, Lukas Erne takes Barton and Riggs to task for underestimating the external evidence against accepting that the additions Henslowe paid for are the ones that were printed in 1602.[53] Erne says that the attribution to Shakespeare is 'groundless', but notes that *Titus Andronicus* III.ii, which looks like a Shakespearean addition (it first appears in the Folio text of the play), focuses attention on the play's hero, his bereavement, and consequent madness, much in the manner of the *Spanish Tragedy* Additions.[54]

We now present results from a further computational-stylistics study of the Additions, using a much larger and more diverse corpus and set of variables than the 1992 one. Our corpus stands at 136 plays, dated between 1576 and 1642, all with reasonably secure attributions to one of 35 authors. For this analysis the plays were all divided into 2500-word blocks to match the 2663 words of the Additions (with left-over words added to the last segment). The total is 1021 segments from the plays of known authorship. This set of text samples each attached to an author is our test bed for this attribution problem.

We first ran a discriminant analysis using the frequencies of 200 common function words as variables. This is a standard procedure, available in

[48] Barton, *Ben Jonson*, p. 16.　　[49] *Ibid.*, p. 23.

[50] D. Riggs, *Ben Jonson: A Life*, (Cambridge, MA: Harvard University Press, 1989), p. 87.

[51] *Ibid.*, p. 89.

[52] D. H. Craig, 'Authorial Styles and the Frequencies of Very Common Words: Jonson, Shakespeare, and the Additions to *The Spanish Tragedy*', *Style*, 26 (1992), 199–220.

[53] Erne, *Beyond* The Spanish Tragedy, pp. 120–2.　　[54] *Ibid.*, pp. 122, 142 n.

most statistics packages for the computer (see the description in Chapter 7, above). It allows us to seek out the best match among the various authors in our archive. Each author's segments are assigned to a group and the procedure seeks to weight the variables, in this case the frequencies of the words, so as to produce the best discrimination between the pre-defined groups of observations. Of the 1021 segments, 1010 – 98.9 per cent – were assigned to the correct author, a remarkable feat given that there are 35 authors represented. Evidently, even with a large number of groups, discriminant analysis using function words is able to find weightings of the word-variables that serve to classify almost all of the 'training' sets according to pre-determined groups. On the basis of this function we then asked the procedure to assign the Additions (which had been left out of the analysis to that point) to one of the authorial sets. The Additions were judged to belong to the Shakespeare group.

To test the reliability of the procedure we examined how well it works with test segments where we in fact know the author. We chose a subset of the plays and then withdrew one of them at a time from the 'training' set, and asked the procedure to assign its segments to one of the thirty-five authorial groups, as if the segments' provenance was unknown. We tested five plays by Shakespeare in this way, and ten plays by others, concentrating on the years 1587 to 1605, but making an exception for *The Duchess of Malfi* (dated by Harbage and Schoenbaum to 1614), given that Webster is a candidate for authorship of the Additions. The results are shown in Table 8.1. The five Shakespeare plays made up 46 segments. The analysis assigned 43 of these, 93 per cent, correctly. The three failures are all in one play, *Richard III*, a reminder that overall percentages may disguise some much poorer local results. The other 10 plays made up 69 segments. The main interest in these, given that the analysis assigned the Additions to Shakespeare, is how many would be assigned to Shakespeare in error. If this figure was high, then we would regard the procedure as biased toward Shakespeare and thus the ascription of the Additions would lose credibility. In the end the tally of false ascriptions to Shakespeare was 10 out of 69, or 14 per cent. By the same token 86 per cent of the test segments by other authors were correctly labelled non-Shakespeare. Thus, treating groups of segments in exactly the same way as we did the Additions – with the system completely blind to their authorship, and not guided by having any other segments from the same play in the training set – the procedure is right 9 out of 10 times in labelling a segment by Shakespeare as Shakespeare, and right between 8 and 9 times out of 10 in labelling a non-Shakespeare segment as non-Shakespeare.

Table 8.1. *Test segments in a discriminant analysis of 2500-word
segments from plays from 1580 to 1619, in 35 authorial groups, using
200 function words.*

Author	Play	Segments	Correctly assigned (Shakespeare or not)
Shakespeare	*Hamlet*	11	11
Shakespeare	*Julius Caesar*	7	7
Shakespeare	*King Lear*	9	9
Shakespeare	*Richard III*	10	7
Shakespeare	*Romeo and Juliet*	9	9
TOTAL		46	43
Chapman	*Bussy d'Ambois*	7	6
Chettle	*Hoffman*	7	5
Dekker	*The Shoemaker's Holiday*	7	5
Heywood	*A Woman Killed with Kindness*	6	5
Jonson	*The Case is Altered*	7	3
Jonson	*Sejanus*	10	10
Marston	*Antonio's Revenge*	5	4
Middleton	*A Trick to Catch the Old One*	7	7
Peele	*The Battle of Alcazar*	4	4
Webster	*The Duchess of Malfi*	9	9
TOTAL		69	58
GRAND TOTAL		115	101

The method is thus effective, if far from infallible. It gives us a good first indication that Shakespeare is the most likely author out of the thirty-five tested. We used a second method to cross-check the result from discriminant analysis. Burrows' Zeta has shown a way to use lexical words for authorship study.[55] As in previous chapters, we use a variant of Zeta, identifying words that keep occurring in one author and are sparsely used by another. We then count appearances of the same words in the disputed text to see which of the two authors' patterns of use it resembles. This sort of one-on-one contest is more likely to yield a more definite result than establishing an author's claims against many others simultaneously.

As already mentioned, four authors have been put forward as candidates for the Additions through its critical history: Jonson, Shakespeare, Dekker, and Webster. We began with the Shakespeare–Jonson contrast in

[55] J. F. Burrows, 'All the Way Through: Testing for Authorship in Different Frequency Strata', *Literary and Linguistic Computing*, 22 (2007), 27–47.

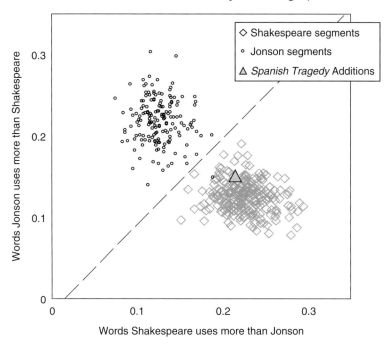

Figure 8.1 Lexical-words test: 2500-word Shakespeare segments versus 2500-word Jonson segments, with the 1602 Additions to *The Spanish Tragedy*.

lexical words. Following our usual practice, we found 500 lexical words that appear more regularly in Shakespeare segments than in Jonson ones, and 500 more common in the Jonson segments. These can be called Shakespeare and Jonson markers respectively. We counted the number of Shakespeare markers that appear in each segment, and then the number of Jonson markers, and divided each count by the number of different words in that segment. We thus obtained two scores for each segment. We did the same for the Additions, and then plotted all the segments and the Additions in a graph, using the two sets of scores as coordinates (Figure 8.1). To find a line to mark the boundary between Shakespeare and Jonson territories, we found the average values for each group on the two measures: the 'centroids' of the clusters. We then drew a line joining the two centroids (not shown in the figure), and finally a line bisecting this line at right angles, the dashed line in the graph. All 234 Shakespeare segments are on the Shakespeare side, and 163 of the 164 Jonson segments are on the Jonson side (the exception is the sixth of seven segments from

Table 8.2. *Test segments in a lexical-words analysis of 2500-word Shakespeare segments versus 2500-word Jonson segments.*

Author	Play	Segments	Correctly assigned
Shakespeare	*Hamlet*	11	11
Shakespeare	*Henry V*	10	10
Shakespeare	*King Lear*	9	9
Shakespeare	*Troilus and Cressida*	10	10
Shakespeare	*Twelfth Night*	7	7
Jonson	*The Case is Altered*	7	2
Jonson	*Cynthia's Revels*	9	7
Jonson	*Every Man in His Humour*	10	10
Jonson	*Poetaster*	10	8
Jonson	*Sejanus*	10	10
TOTAL		93	84

The Case is Altered). The Additions entries score well within the range of known Shakespeare segments both for Shakespeare and Jonson marker words.

We cannot assume that this success rate (1 failure in 398) applies to segments from plays outside the analysis like the Additions. To estimate a success rate for freshly introduced segments we need, as before, to remove one play at a time from the analysis and test that. In each case we drew a line like the one in Figure 8.1 and used that to determine if the analysis assigned a given segment to Shakespeare or to Jonson. We did this with ten plays (Table 8.2). *The Case is Altered* was a notable failure, with 5 of the 7 segments attributed to Shakespeare, but the procedure produced good results with the other plays. Overall the success rate was 84 out of 93, or 90 per cent.

We can now return to test further authors against Shakespeare. Figure 8.2 is based on presences of 500 lexical words that mark Shakespeare as against Dekker, and 500 that do the reverse. The results for the Additions place it below the bisector line, and with the Shakespeare segments rather than the Dekker ones. In Figure 8.2 the triangle marking the Additions is on the Shakespeare side of the bisector line, but while its score is well within the Shakespeare range for Shakespeare marker words (the horizontal axis), it is higher than any Shakespeare segment for non-Shakespeare markers (the vertical axis). It looks much more like Shakespeare than like Dekker, but by no means like a regular Shakespeare segment. There are some sensible possible explanations for this. Firstly, any new sample is at a disadvantage

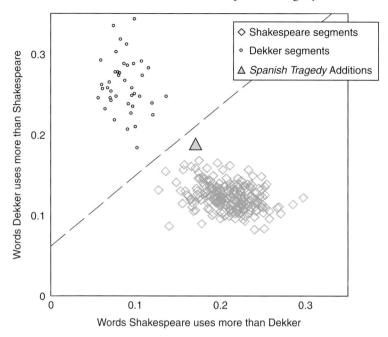

Figure 8.2 Lexical-words test: 2500-word Shakespeare segments versus 2500-word Dekker segments, with the 1602 Additions to *The Spanish Tragedy*.

compared to the 'training' segments whose vocabulary has itself been used to compile the word lists. Then the Additions are an agglomeration of discrete passages, rather than the continuous ones we are comparing it with; and the author of the Additions was performing a specialized play-doctoring task, and might be expected to have been conscious of a need to write in a way that conformed to the existing parts of *The Spanish Tragedy*. Obviously, dramatic continuity would be damaged if the actor playing the part of Hieronimo changed abruptly to sound like someone else for each of the added passages, and then back again. Moody E. Prior thought that the writer of the Additions had followed Kyd's practice to a marked degree in the handling of verse rhythms, in imagery, and in allusions to the supernatural.[56] Burrows has done some related work on *Shamela*, Fielding's parody of Richardson's novel *Pamela*. This shows that at the level of the fifty commonest words Fielding's parody of Richardson remained closer to his own style than to Richardson's, though in Burrows' graph the *Shamela*

[56] M. E. Prior, *The Language of Tragedy* (Gloucester, MA: Smith, 1964), pp. 383–4 n.

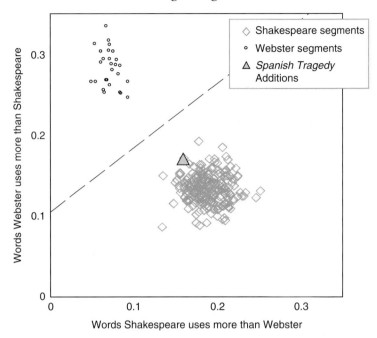

Figure 8.3 Lexical-words test: 2500-word Shakespeare segments versus 2500-word
Webster segments, with the 1602 Additions to *The Spanish Tragedy*.

segments are placed on the Richardson side of the Fielding group, suggesting a considerable movement toward the other writer's style.[57]

We ran the same analyis for the fourth candidate, John Webster (see
Figure 8.3). The Additions were again placed below the bisector line and
thus in the Shakespeare region. We carried out the same Zeta test for all
the authors with four or more plays in our corpus from 1602 or earlier –
Lyly, Marlowe, Greene, and Peele – and then on Heywood, Fletcher, and
Middleton also. In each case the Additions were placed with Shakespeare
rather than with the other author.

At this point we are reaching the limits of the methods at their present
stage of development. It would be useful to test individual parts of the
Additions, but only one is large enough for satisfactory experiments. We
tried the Zeta method using 1500-word samples and the 1449-word fourth
Addition on its own. The test placed this scene firmly with Shakespeare

---

[57] J. Burrows, "'I lisp'd in numbers": Fielding, Richardson, and the Appraisal of Statistical
Evidence', *Scriblerian*, 23 (1991), 234–41.

rather than with Jonson, but with many more failures in test segments than with the 2500-word segments.

It would be valuable, also, to be able to pose the question of 'Shakespeare, or not' with more finality than is possible when working one by one with rival candidates. This puts another sort of strain on the methods, this time the sheer range of sources of variation. In a broad-based Shakespeare-versus-non-Shakespeare lexical-words analysis for all plays, regardless of date, the Additions were placed in non-Shakespeare territory. In a modified version of this approach, on the other hand, using only plays dated 1602 (the date of publication of the Additions) or earlier, the Additions were in Shakespeare territory.

Thus on these measures the Additions are like Shakespeare, but not to the point that all doubt is removed. As the Shakespeare-versus-all-others experiment shows, whatever resemblances there are between the Additions and Shakespeare plays, they are not always strong enough to tell against other forces when we seek patterns that discriminate between Shakespeare plays and plays by all other authors and from all other periods.

The circumstances of the putative revision of *The Spanish Tragedy* by Shakespeare must remain conjectural, of course, but a eulogy for Richard Burbage includes Hieronimo among the parts he played,[58] and E. K. Chambers suggested long ago that the Chamberlain's Men, Burbage's and Shakespeare's company, might have performed *The Spanish Tragedy* in revised form around 1602.[59]

Among other candidates, Jonson seems very unlikely. The tests unearthed no affinities between his work and the Additions, either in function-word use or in wider vocabulary or, indeed, in matching phrases. If the Additions are the work of another writer,[60] this unknown must have been a close student of the Elizabethan drama, and one who, by sheer accident, or from being steeped in Shakespeare's plays and poems, mimicked them by a kind of sympathetic re-creation. The credibility of this last hypothesis is weakened if the 1599 date is accepted for the completion of the Additions as a whole, since they would pre-date the first performances of *Hamlet* and *Troilus and Cressida*, in 1601 and 1602 respectively.

[58] To add to this is the scene in the second *Return from Parnassus* play in which Burbage is made to demonstrate his acting of Hieronimo to a student. Edwards discusses both these references, and concludes that the authors were mistaken in associating Burbage with the playing of Hieronimo (p. 146).

[59] E. K. Chambers, *William Shakespeare: A Study of Facts and Problems*, 2 vols. (Oxford: Clarendon Press, 1930), Vol. I, p. 148. Cf. Freeman, *Thomas Kyd*, pp. 121–5.

[60] A further complication would be the presence of more than one writer in the Additions. Freeman argues that the 1602 edition includes elements from a number of revisions to the play by different companies (*Thomas Kyd*, pp. 129–30).

Certainly this other writer's knowledge of *Doctor Faustus*, *Troilus and Cressida*, and *Julius Caesar* did not come from printed editions, since these plays were all published after 1602.[61]

To recapitulate: of the authors tested, Shakespeare is the closest in style to the Additions on function-words measures, and closer in quite separate lexical-words tests than each of ten authors in turn, including the three candidates supported by the commentators. A re-examination of the parallels presented by Stevenson between the Additions and canonical Shakespeare shows that the claims of a number of them to be unique, or nearly so, stand up to the scrutiny possible with a large collection of searchable texts from the period. The readiest explanation for these parallels, and for the resemblance in function-word- and lexical-word-use between Shakespeare and the Additions, is that Shakespeare wrote them. If so, then there is a good explanation for the fact that they contain 'as good a scene of madness as anything in Elizabethan drama outside *Hamlet* or *King Lear*',[62] and a problem (which some have found disturbing) is removed from the Ben Jonson canon. One can certainly say with new confidence that these passages are Shakespearean in style. The evidence from word-patterns means that the attribution to Shakespeare can no longer be called 'groundless'. Indeed, taking everything into account, there is good reason to revive the claims by Coleridge and Stevenson that Shakespeare is the likeliest author of the 1602 Additions to Kyd's play.

---

[61] In their Jonson edition Herford, Simpson, and Simpson note that the scene with the painter in the fourth Addition 'recalls yet unwritten work of Shakespeare at more than one point' (Vol. II, p. 243).

[62] Kyd, *The Spanish Tragedy*, ed. Edwards, p. lxi.

CHAPTER 9

Transforming King Lear

Arthur F. Kinney

Did Shakespeare or some other person revise the text of *King Lear*? Did that person or persons have second thoughts about the work published in Quarto (Q) in 1607–8, dropping or adding scenes, changing characterizations, and reshaping the play to transform the text posthumously published in the Folio (F) of 1623? Or was Shakespeare more concerned with the plays he was writing subsequently, no longer concerned about making revisions to earlier work, leaving that to other playwrights or to changes that evolved in performances? Anxious to preserve as Shakespeare's great work what has come down to us, editors of his plays through the centuries have fabricated yet a third text, conflating all the lines in both Q and F to avoid losing anything he may have written. But others have argued that such a union of texts is a bastard version of the play that does not represent authorial intention or accomplishment at any point of time. Questions about the text of *Lear* that remain, then, which computational stylistics can address, are these: (1) did one person (or more, as in performances over time) revise the play, and (2) was Shakespeare involved?

In 1930, E. K. Chambers listed the relevant texts beginning with the entry for the play in the Stationers' Register.

[S.R. 1607] 26 Novembris. Nathaniel Butter John Busby. Entred for their Copie under thandes of Sir George Buck knight and Thwardens A booke called. Master William Shakespeare his historye of Kinge Lear, as yt was played before the Kinges maiestie at Whitehall vppon Sainct Stephens night at Christmas last, by his maiestics scrvaintes playinge vsually at the Globe on the Banksyde vj^d (Arber, iii, 366).

[Q1. 1608.] M. William Shak-speare: His True Chronicle Historie of the life and death of King Lear and his three Daughters. With the vnfortunate life of Edgar, sonne and heire to the Earl of Gloster, and his sullen and assumed humor of Tom of Bedlam: As it was played before the Kings Maiestie at Whitehall vpon S. Stephans night in Christmas Hollidayes. By his Maiesties seruants playing vsually at the Gloabe on the Bancke-side. [George and Lionel Snowden's or Nicholas Okes's device (McKerrow 316)] London, Printed for Nathaniel Butter, and are to be sold at his shop in Pauls Church-yard at the signe of the Pide Bull neere S^r. Austins Gate. 1608 [*Head-title*] M William Shak-speare His Historie, of King Lear. [*Running-title*] The Historie of King Lear.

[Sheets D, E, F, G, K are found in corrected and uncorrected forms ... There is a note on the variants by W. W. Greg in *R. E. S.* i. 469.]

[F1. 1623.][*Catalogue*] King Lear. [*Tragedies*, pp. 283–309, sign. qq 2–ss 3^r. *Head- and Running titles*] The Tragedie of King Lear.

[acts and scc. marked]^1

Extant copies of Q1 are in a tangled condition because most sheets are in both uncorrected and corrected states, sheet C exists in three states, and they are indiscriminately bound. 'Some of the corrections suggest further reference to copy', Chambers writes, 'others are clearly due to erroneous conjecture; and it is possible that in carrying them out some further blunders were made by the compositor' (pp. 464–5). Q2, essentially the same work, nevertheless compounds the problematic status of the text. The copy-text for Q2 appeared to be Q1, employing corrected sheets; uncorrected sheets for signatures D, G, and H; and some further conjectural corrections and emendations. While F seemed to be derived from an independent manuscript or prompt-book – and hence to be a possible authorial revision – it also has what Chambers calls 'a general orthographic resemblance' to Q1 (p. 465). More importantly, Q omits about 100 lines found in F, and F about 300 lines – and part of III.vi – found in Q1. F also omits many notes for properties and action in Q while adding a few new ones of its own. At least 1000 isolated words are changed between Q and F, the punctuation in the two texts is 'radically different', according to Steven Urkowitz,^{2} and verse in F is printed as prose in Q. Of the large number of variants, Chambers writes:

where one is clearly wrong, the better reading, except for a dozen or score of cases, is in F. Mislineation is a constant feature in Q. The verse is often put wrong by an initial error, and runs from central pause to central pause, until another error of the end of a speech recovers it. Occasionally it is altogether unmetrical. Prose is printed as verse. Still more often is verse printed as prose. Moreover, Q has practically no punctuation except commas, even in places where both logic and enunciation require heavier stops and these are supplied by F. (p. 564)

---

^{1} E. K. Chambers, *William Shakespeare: A Study of the Facts and Problems*, 2 vols. (Oxford: Clarendon Press, 1966), Vol. I, pp. 463–4. All citations are from Vol. I. References in round brackets and interpolations in square brackets are Chambers' own. 'Arber' is E. Arber, ed., *Transcript of the Registers of the Company of Stationers, 1554–1640*, 5 vols. (London: privately printed, 1875–94); 'McKerrow' is R. B. McKerrow, *Printers' and Publishers' Devices, 1455–1640* (London: Bibliographical Society, 1913); '*R. E. S.*' is W. W. Greg, review of Leon Kellner, *Restoring Shakespeare: A Critical Analysis of the Misreadings of Shakespeare's Works, with Facsimiles and Numerous Plates, Review of English Studies*, 1 (1925), 463–78.

^{2} S. Urkowitz, *Shakespeare's Revision of King Lear* (Princeton: Princeton University Press, 1980), p. 4.

Such factors have supplied sufficient grounds, for some critics, to argue that Q, Shakespeare's work, grew through accretions or improvements in performance, and that F is primarily an abridgment of the enlarged Q text that gives to the play sharper focus and greater clarity. As such, it needs no authorial intervention. Yet this seems denied by the addition of Merlin's prophecy by the Fool (III.ii.79–95) not in Q, something Chambers dismisses, along with others, as 'an incongruous theatrical interpolation' (p. 466). W. W. Greg agreed in essence with Chambers. In 'The Function of Bibliography in Literary Criticism' (1933) the idea of authorial revision did not occur to him; F was set from Q showing 'continual errors' in need of correction in the earlier text.[3]

Throughout the next two decades, up until the 1950s in fact, 'most critics subscribed to the theory that the Quarto text was printed from a shorthand report made in the theater by an unauthorized "pirate"', Urkowitz tells us (p. 7). That idea was first advanced in 1733 by the Shakespearean editor Lewis Theobald; elaborated over the years, it allowed Alexander Schmidt to write in 1880 that:

It could not have been difficult, where neither pains nor cost were spared, to procure by copyists in the Theatre a passable, nay, even a complete and correct printer's copy. If it proved too much for one shorthand writer, two or three could accomplish it, by relieving each other; and if it could not be finished at the first performance, it could certainly be done at the second or third.[4]

Such explanations continued to support only one authorial *Lear*; the 'shorthand-report theory', notes Urkowitz, allowed scholars, critics, and editors

to ascribe many of its variant readings to what they propose were the 'errors' made by the actors in performance, by the acting company during the preparation of the author's text for the stage, by a scribe copying out the actors' parts or the promptbook, by the shorthand reporter when he was in the theater or when he was transcribing his notes, and by the compositor in the printing house. (p. 7)

But as Urkowitz further notes, this unquestioned and uncomplicated sense of *King Lear* in which a single version was corrupted by the theatre and the printing house and not by the intervention of other writers or the same author with later thoughts, was subsequently called into question.

---

[3] W. W. Greg, 'The Function of Bibliography in Literary Criticism: Illustrated in a Study of the Text of *King Lear*', *Neophilologus*, 18 (1933), 241–62 (p. 256).

[4] L. Theobald, 'Introduction', in *The Works of Shakespeare: In Seven Volumes* (London, 1733), 7 vols., Vol. I, pp. xxxvii–xxxviii; Alexander Schmidt, *Zur Textkritik des* King Lear (1879), translated and summarized by H. H. Furness, in William Shakespeare, *King Lear*, ed. H. H. Furness (1880; New York: Dover, 1963), pp. 368–9; Urkowitz, *Shakespeare's Revision*, p. 153 n. 7.

First, after decades of debate, it has been conclusively proven and universally accepted that no technique of stenography known in England in 1608 was capable of transcribing anything as difficult as a play. Second, textual critics have realized that the exigencies of producing a large and constantly changing repertory of plays would make revisions of the type found between the Quarto and Folio of *King Lear* highly impractical once either version had been brought to the stage. (pp. 7–8)[5]

A new theory was needed. Gary Taylor and Stanley Wells have provided one in their *Textual Companion* to the works of William Shakespeare (1987).[6] In tracing the probable setting of F, they are clear that the F text represents a revision of earlier versions of the play.

The compositors' Q2 copy must have been annotated by reference to an independent manuscript. Yet this manuscript itself apparently derived from Q1: F repeats press-variant errors present in Q1 but not Q2 (I.iv.329/826, I.iv. 322/828, V.iii.45/2685). It thus seems probable that the revision began initially on a copy of Q1, and this conclusion is compatible with the evidence of sources, style, vocabulary, act divisions, and topical allusions (including possible censorship), which all suggest that the revision took place several years after the original composition.[7] The revision several years later was, essentially, a revision of Q1 and Q2 into F.

But this was not a new theory. In 1930 Chambers raised the spectre of a Shakespeare revision:

We know that cutting was a theatrical practice, since authors themselves have told us so. [Here Chambers cites Richard Brome in his prologue to *The Antipodes* (1640).] That Shakespeare's plays were not immune is shown both by the condition of the bad Quartos and by some of the omissions in parallel-text plays, for which cuts are the most plausible explanation. The latter are not extensive; they do not amount to the replacement of a three-hour play by a two-hour play. Two or three hundred lines go, to prevent normal limits from being exceeded, or merely to prevent particular scenes or speeches from dragging ... One hopes that he remained unperturbed when some of his best lines were sacrificed. (p. 229)

Furthermore,

There are textual duplications also, where one may agree with [John Dover Wilson] in thinking that corrected and uncorrected versions have been left standing together, through the absence or disregard of deletion marks. This indicates revision, no doubt, in a sense, but by no means necessarily the wholesale revision

[5] Cf. G. I. Duthie, *Elizabethan Shorthand and the First Quarto of* King Lear (Oxford: Clarendon Press, 1949).
[6] S. Wells and G. Taylor, *William Shakespeare: A Textual Companion*, with J. Jowett and W. Montgomery (Oxford: Oxford University Press, 1989).
[7] *Ibid.*, p. 529.

of the play. The alterations may be mere afterthoughts at the time of the original composition. We cannot, on this hypothesis, take quite literally the statement of Heminges and Condell [in the F] that they had scarce received a blot in Shakespeare's papers. (pp. 231–2)

Madeleine Doran was more forthcoming in an essay in *Studies in Philology* in 1933, amplifying her remarks in *The Text of* King Lear in 1931. She argued that misaligned verse in Q resulted from later matter written in the margins of pages or on slips pasted into the text and even on leaves written in the margins of pages of the original manuscript – that is, revisions such as have been found in other extant manuscripts of Elizabethan plays. She saw the play as a developing script undergoing continual revisions, and argued that the Quartos caught early stages of the creative process, while F caught the final stage. There was no single lost original version of the play. Later, however, Doran recanted. She came to disbelieve that Shakespeare could have written the chaotic text of Q, writing to Urkowitz on 9 November 1976:

the quarto looked like an author's draft in bad shape which gave the compositors a bad time … But there is a reason for doubt, and it is there whether the passages are regarded as revision or as first composition. They [the misaligned passages] imply that Shakespeare wrote out his verse as if it were prose, and at the same time did not worry about whether it would scan. Even if these passages *are* an overlay of revisions, they still mean that Shakespeare was content to compose his verse in this rough way … I can't believe such a process in Shakespeare.[8]

Thus Doran came around to the view of Greg, who finally denied the possibility of revision, finding it difficult to believe that 'at the height of his powers, [Shakespeare] could ever have written the clumsy and fumbling lines we find in Q, or that these could in general represent a stage in the development of F'.[9] Other editors followed suit. In 'The Copy for *King Lear*, 1608 and 1625', G. I. Duthie applied Chambers' words about *Richard III* to the *Lear* revision, remarking that from his perspective it was impossible that Shakespeare could have made so many substitutions in the course of rewriting *Lear* 'without any incorporation of new structures or new ideas'.[10] As for Kenneth Muir, editor of the New Arden edition of *King Lear* (Arden 2), the conflated text was so superior to either Q or F that the shorter F text must have been conceived by Shakespeare's playing

---

[8] Urkowitz, *Shakespeare's Revision*, p. 164 n. 14. These accounts of Doran, Greg, Duthie, and Muir are drawn from *ibid.*, p. 143.

[9] W. W. Greg, *The Shakespeare First Folio: Its Bibliographical and Textual History* (Oxford: Clarendon Press, 1955), p. 379; cf. Greg, 'The Function of Bibliography in Literary Criticism'.

[10] William Shakespeare, *King Lear*, ed. G. I. Duthie and J. Dover Wilson, New Cambridge Shakespeare (Cambridge: Cambridge University Press), pp. 122–39 (pp. 124–5).

company after the playwright's death.[11] For these editors, revision was simply inconceivable.

Revision of plays in Shakespeare's time was, however, commonplace. Robert B. Hornback notes that:

In his financial records Henslowe, for instance, referred to revision as providing 'new adicyones' or 'altrynge'. Such 'altrying' was not undertaken because plays were deemed unsatisfactory (since only initially successful plays were frequently revived and worth the expense of revising), but rather, as Eric Rasmussen argues, to 'keep pace with current theatrical trends'. Moreover, Roslyn Knutson finds that the dynamics of company repertory often operated according to the 'principle of duplication by way of sequels, serials, and spin-offs' to capitalize on theatrical successes.[12]

Scholars have advanced the possibility that other Shakespeare plays in F – *2 Henry IV, Richard III, Troilus and Cressida, Hamlet,* and *Othello* – are also revisions. Such revisions may be caused by cultural changes, a desire to renew appeal, a change of venue (such as moving from the Globe to Blackfriars), or (as likely in the case of *Lear*), a reconception. We know Shakespeare revised to meet the talents of the new members of his company: Falstaff does not appear as promised in *Henry V* because Will Kemp, the clown who played him, had left the company; indeed, Shakespeare shifted his very sense of clowning when Kemp, who had played a character such as Dogberry in *Much Ado about Nothing*, was replaced by the more acerbic Robert Armin, who would play the Fool in *King Lear*. The playwright John Marston also wrote specifically for Armin, adding the part of Passarello for him when revising *The Malcontent* for the King's Men in 1604.[13] George Chapman's *Bussy d'Ambois* (1607) was reprinted in a Second Quarto edition in 1641 'much corrected and amended by the Author', according to the title-page. Stanley Wells senses such a shift in Shakespeare when he observes that the Q of *King Lear* is designated a 'true chronicle history' on the title-page while the F text calls *King Lear* a 'tragedy'.[14]

---

[11] K. Muir, *Shakespeare's Sources*, 2nd edn (London: Methuen, 1961), pp. 165–6.

[12] R. B. Hornback, 'The Fool in Quarto and Folio *King Lear*', *English Literary Renaissance*, 34 (2004), 306–338 (p. 311). He is citing E. Rasmussen, 'The Revision of Scripts', in *A New History of Early English Drama*, ed. J. D. Cox and D. S. Kastan (New York: Columbia University Press, 1997), pp. 441–60, and R. L. Knutson, 'The Repertory', in Cox and Kastan, *A New History of Early English Drama*, p. 471.

[13] These examples are in Hornback, 'The Fool', p. 313.

[14] S. Wells, 'The Once and Future *King Lear*', in *The Division of the Kingdoms: Shakespeare's Two Versions of* King Lear, ed. G. Taylor and M. Warren (Oxford: Clarendon Press, 1983), pp. 1–22 (p. 6).

The present interest in F *Lear* as a deliberate revision by Shakespeare begins with Michael Warren's paper 'Quarto and Folio *King Lear* and the Interpretation of Albany and Edgar'. Warren addresses

a situation where statements about textual status are never more than hypotheses based on the current models of thought about textual recession. It is not demonstrably erroneous to work with the possibility (a) that there may be no single 'ideal play' of *King Lear* (all of 'what Shakespeare wrote'), that there may have never been one, and that what we create by conflating both texts is merely an invention of editors and scholars; (b) that for all its problems Q is an authoritative version of the play of *King Lear*; and (c) that F may indeed be a revised version of the play, that its additions and omissions may constitute Shakespeare's considered modification of the earlier text, and that we cannot know that they are not.[15]

Four years later, Steven Urkowitz made a more detailed case for revision in *Shakespeare's Revision of* King Lear, in which he claimed that the major variants between Q and F were the careful reworking of the author as theatrical artist: complex changes in characterization; newly arranged scenes, entrances, and exits; and even changes in dialogue and rhythm, all of them changes that only a playwright – but not a copyist or compositor – could make. With few exceptions, he argued, such variants could be seen as intentional (pp. 16–17).

In point of fact, Warren and Urkowitz had been anticipated by E. A. J. Honigmann in 1965 and Fredson Bowers in 1966. In *The Stability of Shakespeare's Text*, Honigmann provided abundant evidence in support of a case that MacDonald P. Jackson sums up thus: 'where we have two texts of a poem or play, variants produced by authorial revision in one may closely resemble variants produced by corruption in the other'.[16] This leads Jackson to a fundamental proposition:

The wellnigh universal tendency of revising authors to vary phrases that are exactly repeated in an early version of their work, to shift words, phrases, lines, and longer passages from one part of their poem, story, or play, to another, to emphasize by repetition certain key words and images, to work their utterance into more tidy metrical and rhetorical shape, to cut, paraphrase, enrich, and expand, and at times to tamper out of mere caprice, inevitably creates apparent evidence in the original text of anticipation, recollection, transposition, synonym substitution ('vulgarization'), omission, interpolation, and even metrical breakdown – the traditional stigmata of a memorial report. (p. 331)[17]

---

[15] Quoted in Wells, 'The Once and Future *King Lear*', p. 14.
[16] E. A. J. Honigmann, *The Stability of Shakespeare's Text* (Lincoln, NE: University of Nebraska Press, 1965).
[17] M. P. Jackson, 'Fluctuating Variation: Author, Annotator, or Actor?' in Taylor and Warren, *The Division of the Kingdoms*, pp. 313–49.

To illustrate his point, Jackson looks at several changes from Q in I.i. For instance, where Q reads:

> The map there, know we haue diuided
> In three, our kingdome; and tis our first intent,
> To shake all cares and business of our state,
> Confirming them on yonger yeares … (sig. Blv; I.i.37–40)

F reads:

> Giue me the Map there. Know, that we haue diuided
> In three our Kingdome: and 'tis our fast intent,
> To shake all Cares and Buisnesse from our Age,
> Conferring them on yonger strengths, while we
> Vnburthen'd crawle toward death. Our son of *Cornwal*,
> And you our no lesse louing Sonne of *Albany*,
> We haue this houre a constant will to publish
> Our daughters seuerall Dowers, that future strife
> May be preuented now. (through-line numbering [TLN] 42–59; I.i.37–45)

Jackson argues not merely the superiority of the F version but the rethinking that goes into what he claims to be the revision of the earlier Q passage. To show the kind of reasoning that supports authorial revision, it is worth quoting Jackson at some length.

'Shake off' meaning 'discard, rid oneself of' is common in Shakespeare, according to Schmidt's *Lexicon*, but *OED* cites no instance of 'shake' meaning 'discard' when not followed by 'off' or 'from'. So I interpret Q's 'of' in 'of our state' as primarily 'off', which gives a neat opposition with 'on' in the next line. In seventeenth-century English 'of' and 'off' were less clearly differentiated than they are today, and 'of' as a spelling of 'off' turns up in several Shakespearian good quartos. Q's 'state' compresses several relevant meanings, including the political and the personal – not just Lear's kingdom, rule, and status, but his physical condition. F unfolds the implications in 'state', partly by developing the hint in Q's 'Confirming'. F makes the latent content of 'Confirming' explicit by altering the semi-redundant 'yeares' to 'strengths', this change prompting the addition of 'while we/Vnburthen'd crawle toward death', which elaborates the personal motive to the point where Lear presents his abdication as almost a renunciation of the world, as he resigns himself to the second childhood ('crawle') of Jacques' last Age of Man. And of course F's 'Age' has already made explicit what in Q was conveyed in the antithesis between 'younger yeares' and one sense of 'our state'. Having made manifest the latent content of 'Confirming', F can replace it with the more idiomatic 'Conferring', which stresses the act of donation, instead of suggesting (as does Q's verb) the ceremonial ratifications of a decision already announced. (pp. 333–4)

Lear's political aims are further underlined in the F addition that follows, in which Lear does not merely assert political competition and dynastic marriage, but offers a dowry as well as a legacy. To return to Jackson's first example, Q's 'to shake all cares and business of our state' rephrased as '(Since now we will diuest vs both of Rule, / Interest of Territory, Cares of State)' in F (TLN 54–5; I.i.49–50) combines both abdication and divestiture as complementary and joined while his tragedy will begin when he splits the two, giving up rule and keeping the regalia, and, as Jackson himself comments, 'also introduces, in "diuest", the play's imagery of clothing and nakedness' (p. 336). In F, divestiture becomes both imagery and theme.

The year following Honigmann, Fredson Bowers was coming, if more slowly and less comprehensively, to something like the same conclusion, arguing that authors are unlikely to resist revising their work when copying it.[18] As for cuts in F, Urkowitz writes that 'It is quite conceivable that he wrote material which he later decided was excessive, and then he cut it himself' (p. 145). But the problem proved more difficult with a whole scene, such as IV.vi, the mock trial on the heath where Lear establishes an imaginary courtroom in which to arraign his wayward daughters before a naked beggar, a fool, and a servant: a moment in Q that, although omitted entirely from F, is one that in conflation no modern editor has wished to surrender. This omission has been a particular concern of Robert Warren:

> The total effect of this scene is that Lear's attempt to express his obsession with the injustice of his daughters by establishing the processes of a trial is sabotaged by the 'judges', who lapse from their 'judicial' roles to the other roles which they habitually play – Edgar to the bedlam beggar obsessed by devils, the Fool to his songs and jibes which bring everything down to earth.
>
> It could be argued that this very state of confusion is in itself an appropriate image of Lear's view of injustice, a *tour de force* of technical dexterity which combines various elements from the preceding scenes – Lear's madness, the Fool's professional folly, Edgar's mock-possession – in an elaborate climax. I think that such a climax may well have been Shakespeare's aim in writing the scene, but that in rehearsal or performance it became clear that the focus of the scene shifted from Lear's mock-justice to eccentric individual detail ... what Edgar calls 'Reason in Madness' (TLN 2617; 14; IV.vi.175).[19]

In the mad maelstrom, Warren contends, no audience member will pay much heed to the maddened Lear; he is lost in the crowd and his tragic condition is much diminished.

[18] F. Bowers, *On Editing Shakespeare* (Charlottesville, VA: University Press of Virginia, 1966), pp. 19, 107.
[19] R. Warren, 'The Folio Omission of the Mock Trial: Motives and Consequences', in Taylor and Warren, *The Division of the Kingdoms*, pp. 45–57 (pp. 46–7).

Lear's final lines differ markedly, too, and affect his characterization. In F, he is conscious of the possible loss of his daughter Cordelia:

> And my poore Foole is hang'd: no, no, no life?
> Why should a Dog, a Horse, a Rat haue life,
> And thou no breath at all? Thou'lt come no more,
> Neuer, neuer, neuer, neuer, neuer.
> Pray you vndo this Button. Thanke you Sir,
> Do you see this? Looke on her? Looke her lips,
> Looke there, looke there. (V.iii.306–12)

His concern with his own condition – asking that his button be undone – is surrounded by observations concerning his daughter. He dies in apparent joy at the mistaken understanding that she lives. The Q text is decidedly different:

And my poor fool is hanged: no, no life; why should a dog, a horse, a rat have life and thou no breath at all. O thou wilt come no more, never, never, never: pray thou undo this button, thank you sir. O, O, O, O! (V.iii.299–303)

Here he does not return his attention to Cordelia and clearly thinks she is dead. There is no hope in this darker version. But in Q, he has one final speech after an interjection by Edgar: 'Break heart, I prithee, break'. Here there is no willed delusion. With Cordelia dead, he has no desire to live.

If the mock trial is omitted, however, as it is in F, then the play moves quickly to a more striking and brutal madness in the next scene (III.vii), in which Cornwall and Regan blind Gloucester and thrust him into the cold to smell his way to Dover. In Q, Edgar's soliloquy ends III.vi, but F omits that, too, to give greater emphasis to Edgar meeting his maimed father before III.vi when the mad Lear and the sightless Gloucester meet, one maimed in the mind, the other in the body, and find solace in one another. This is not a set of variants for Warren but deliberate rewriting. This later scene of IV.vi, he argues,

brings together the mad Lear and the blinded Gloucester for the first time since the crises of their [individual] sufferings, which themselves were brought closer together by the extensive cutting of 3.6; and it is a decisive factor in the success of 4.6 that Lear's verbal arraignment of women and justice arises out of the details of their dramatic relationship, rather than through the elaborate creation of an imaginary courtroom. The reunion of Lear and Gloucester in 4.6 is a much simpler, more human scene than 3.6 – a major reason, I think, for its greater impact in performance. (p. 50)

For Jackson, it is axiomatic that 'Any attempt to determine the relationship between two or more texts must focus on the *nature* of the variants, but their *distribution* may also be revealing' (p. 313). Cutting the mock trial scene in III.vi reverberates all the way to changes in IV.vi. Another major reason advanced in favour of revision is the changed character-ization of Albany – first revealed by Michael Warren – which stretches across even more of the two texts. In Q, Albany gives the play's concluding speech as the highest-ranking nobleman and the one who will conveni-ently take over the state, but F gives the same speech to Edgar. Reasons are given: Albany has abdicated his role in the kingdom and Kent is pre-paring to leave the world altogether. But there are other reasons in F why Albany is an unsuitable person to end the play. Urkowitz notes that in F not only are many of Albany's own speeches altered, but also other char-acters refer to him differently, and there are changes in 'passages that deal with themes or issues repeatedly involving Albany, particularly the con-flicting themes of the need to fulfill social and familial obligations and the need to maintain civil order'. For Urkowitz the additions in the early part of the play, in particular, 'create for the audience an image of a man who might be sympathetic to Lear in other circumstances, but who is caught up by and succumbs to the stresses of conflicting loyalties and conflicting values' (p. 86).

In Q, Albany is clearly a moral norm and the play advances by his slow but sure separation from Goneril. But in F, writes Urkowitz, 'Albany pos-sesses a unique moral ambiguity, visible already in the first act of the play. The variants found in the Folio compound this ambiguity' (p. 86). Thus his forceful speech that sets a moral spine to work in the Q –

> Wisedome and goodnes, to the vild seeme vild,
> Filths savor but themselves, what have you done?
> Tigers, not daughters, what have you perform'd? ...
> Humanity must perforce pray on itself like monsters of the deepe
>   (IV.ii.38–40, 50; sigs. H3v–H4)

is stripped from F. Whereas Albany's forthright values are stoutly pro-claimed in Q by V.i, in F he bewilders even Edmund and Regan.

> BAST. Know of the Duke by his last purpose hold,
> Or whether since he is advis'd by ought
> To change the course, he's full of alteration,
> And selfereproving, bring his constant pleasure.
> REG. Our Sisters man is certainly miscarried.
>   (TLN 2847–52; V.i.1–5).

As for Albany's position at the close of the play, in V.iii Urkowitz finds that

when Albany himself finally articulates the moral principles which will govern his treatment of Lear and Cordelia the audience hears no word of mercy ...

Albany certainly does not espouse the Machiavellian principles shared by Goneril and Edmund, but he clearly does not intend, like Cordelia, to 'forget, and forgive'. He simply does not use such words. He will judge 'their merites, and our safety'. (p. 106)

In F, it is Albany who proposes trial by combat between Edmund and Edgar – not Edmund (as in Q) – and calls for the trumpet to herald it. Such questionable ethics make him, in the end, unsuitable to relate the woes of Lear's tattered kingdom and disqualify him from leading it. Q Albany is displaced by F Edgar, whose morality and loyalty have never been in question. The cuts in Albany's speeches 'do not essentially resemble those in the extant promptbooks', Urkowitz sums, in concert with Michael and Roger Warren; instead, they 'reflect artistic revision' (p. 145). Other characters conform to the rearranged, reconceptualized F text. The 'diminution of Kent', as Michael Warren phrases it, is caused in part by the new emphasis on Edgar in the later acts of F;[20] Randall McLeod notes that, from Act III onward, Goneril 'is ever more self-possessed than her Quarto counterpart, [and] her comparable perversity is paradoxically both more chilling and theatrically attractive – as is Edmund's – by virtue of wit'.[21]

As a final argument for revision, there is the Fool. In discussing the sharp distinction between the characterizations of the Fool in Q and F, Hornback calls on Enid Welsford's distinction, 'so often made in Elizabethan times',[22] between the artificial fool and the natural fool. Q *Lear* presents a wise, artificial, accusatory, even bitter Fool, whose intelligence matched the talents of the clown in the company of the King's Men, Robert Armin. For instance, the famous exchange between the Fool and Lear in I.iv is erased entirely from F. Likewise, it is the Fool in Q, but not in F, who mocks the mock trial in III.vi. By contrast, the natural fool, what Hornback terms 'a sweetly pathetic figure' (p. 315), is the characterization of F. This is the Fool who, instead of making satirical jibes, provides instead Merlin's prophecy (F only, TLN 1739–49; III.ii.84–96). Rather than pointed sarcasm, these lines slide into what Hornback calls 'impossibilities and enigma' (p. 328). It is this more dependent Fool to whom Lear remarks, again in F only, 'In boy, go first. You houseless poverty. / Nay, get thee in. I'll pray and then I'll sleep' (TLN 1807–8; III.iv.26–7). His invitation to the Fool, 'we'll go to supper i' the morning' (Q, III.vi.78; F, III vi.40) is responded to – only in F – by an agreeable dependency:

---

[20] M. Warren, 'The Diminution of Kent', in Taylor and Warren, *The Division of the Kingdoms*, pp. 59–73.

[21] R. McLeod, 'No More, the Text is Foolish', in Taylor and Warren, pp. 153–93 (p. 185).

[22] E. Welsford, *The Fool: His Social and Literary History* (London: Faber and Faber, 1935), p. 119.

'And I'll go to bed at noon' (TLN 2043; III.vi.41). The gentle, passive Fool of F is clearly unlike the acerbic Fool of Q.

Hornback speculates that 'the F revision to the Fool's part may … have been undertaken for Armin's apparent successor, the actor John Shank (or Shanke), who is thought to have joined the company and taken over the comic roles sometime 'between January 11, 1613, when he is [still] named in the license to the Palsgrave's troupe, and March 27, 1619, when his name occurs in the patent to the King's Men' (p. 336).[23] In *A Dish of Lenten Stuff* (1613), William Turner remarks that Shank was known for singing rhymes and authoring at least one song: this may have prompted the prophecy from Merlin.[24] But the identification also raises problems. 'If the revision was made for Shank', Hornback contends,

it becomes increasingly possible that the reviser was not Shakespeare at all, since Shank was still with Palsgrave's troupe in January of 1613 (the New Year in the Renaissance calendar began on March 25) and there was no clown available to play Will Somers in Shakespeare's *Henry VIII* in the same year, suggesting that the King's Men went without a clown for some time. In this scenario, with the Fool's part subsequently revised for Shank (perhaps as late as after 1619, three years after Shakespeare's death, when Shank first begins to appear in company records), it is most likely that Fletcher, who would then have been the King's Men's chief playwright, undertook the revision alone. (p. 337)

If this is the case, then the F revisions were the work not of Shakespeare, but of someone else. F can very well be a rewriting of Q in this narrative but, rather than by Shakespeare, by someone else, like John Fletcher.[25]

Computational stylistics can help us ascertain whether F, like Q, is the work of Shakespeare or possibly the work of another writer. An initial investigation of this problem has already been undertaken by Gary Taylor. Taylor finds that the evidence from rare words points to Shakespeare as the author of Q and F; and, furthermore, that there is a lexical relationship with *Cymbeline*.[26] In addition, 'On strong linguistic evidence Massinger, Fletcher, Middleton, Jonson, Chapman, Field, and Webster – the only candidates of any plausibility, on historical grounds – can each be ruled out as the author of the Folio alterations; the same evidence exactly accords with the hypothesis of late Shakespearian

[23] Hornback is quoting from E. Nungezer, *A Dictionary of Actors and Other Persons Associated with the Public Representation of Plays in England Before 1642* (New York: Columbia University Press, 1968), p. 317.

[24] Hornback, 'The Fool', p. 336.

[25] *Shakespeare in Shorthand* by Adele Davidson (Newark: University of Delaware Press, 2009) appeared after this chapter was written. Her Chapter 7, on the relationship of Q and F Lear, notes, "Q and F emerge from the shorthand hypothesis more fragile and interdependent than is generally recognized" (p. 228).

[26] G. Taylor, 'The Date and Authorship of the Folio Version', in Taylor and Warren, *The Division of the Kingdoms*, pp. 351–468 (p. 429).

revision.' He adds that 'The Folio text shows no signs of having suffered from incompetence or abnormal interference in the printing-house, or (with two exceptions) from censorship, or from the attentions of a high-handed scribe; allegations that Shakespeare's company altered the text without his knowledge or against his will prove, on examination, not only unsubstantiated but historically implausible as well' (p. 429). He appends to his essay as documentation two lists of rare words, one of the words shared between Q *Lear* and the unique F passages, and the other of words shared between unique Q *Lear* passages and passages common to Q and F (pp. 465–6).

We began our own investigations with the premise that Q (1608) and F (1623) represent different versions of *King Lear*: while there are passages peculiar to each text and many small differences in passages they share, bibliographic evidence demonstrates that F was set from a manuscript influenced by Q and therefore was subsequent to it. The first question we asked, then, was whether F represents a *coherent* alternative version of Q or is, in fact, a haphazard assemblage of materials from Q or from a source common to Q and F that would suggest several changes over time, as in revisions by many authors or through many performances. That is, coherency would argue against corruption. We found a consistency in the distribution of some common function words in the two versions that show a single person or a single team of persons was responsible for each text. Repeatedly, for instance, and quite evenly through the various different sections of the play, the person(s) responsible for F uses *which* where Q has *that*,[27] *doth* where Q has *does*,[28] *these* where Q has *this* or *those*,[29] and *thine*

---

[27] Fifty-five instances of *which* as a relative are common to the two versions. Q has nine not in F, all of them in sections of the text that are not in F; Q's total is thus sixty-four. Though shorter, F has fifteen instances not in Q for a total of seventy instances. In ten cases, F has *which* where Q has *that*: three are in sections not in Q, in one case F has *which* where Q has *who*, and in another, F has *which* where there is no relative in Q. This pattern, consistent in all five acts, implies one author preferred *that*, *who*, or a relative deletion to *which* as a relative, and a second author, or the first author at a different time of composition, preferred *which*.

[28] In Shakespeare's time, *does* and *doth* were acceptable alternatives: 'he does' and 'he doth' were both correct and meant the same thing. Q and F share nine instances of *does* and twelve of *doth*. Q has one instance of *does* in a section not in F, so ten in all. Q has five instances of *doth* not in F, two of them in unique passages, and three where F has *does*, seventeen in all. F has two instances of *does* in unique passages, three instances where Q has *doth* and three where Q has *doest* or *do*, so seventeen in all. F has one instance of *doth* in a passage not shared with Q, so thirteen in all. Direct changes come in one direction only. Q never has *does* where F has *doth*, and vice versa. Overall, Q has ten instances of *does* to seventeen of *doth* while F has seventeen to thirteen. If we posit a single author behind each text, one author prefers *doth* and the other *does*.

[29] There are thirty instances of *these* common to Q and F. In addition, Q has two instances not in F, so Q has thirty-two instances in all. Both such instances not in F are in sections that do not appear in F. There are six instances in F not in Q, so F has thirty-six instances in all. Of the instances not shared with Q, one is in a section not in Q, three have *these* where Q has *this*, and two have *these* where Q has *those*.

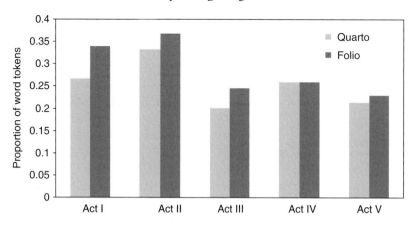

Figure 9.1 Proportional counts of *which* as a relative in acts of *King Lear* Q and F.

where Q has *thy*.[30] This clearly argues against corruption. We set our data out in bar graphs to make this observation clear, since subsequent reasoning will be based on it (Figures 9.1–9.4). These four graphs display good evidence from common words that changes in F are not random, but that F is a careful and thorough revision of Q. The changes from Q to F, then, whoever made them, are not haphazard but the work of a single person.

But can we identify this reviser of *Lear*? We felt the most coherent body of evidence to determine this would be the passages in F that do not appear in Q. These make a composite text of 902 words after our usual modifications to expand contractions and so on.[31] Gary Taylor has already established the possible candidates for the authorship of F and we used his list in our analysis, with the exception of Field, who is not in our current database. We can test the others, although since F is a revision and not an original composition there is less material to work with than in any other case dealt with in this book. Because of this, we compared pairs of authors rather than one author against all the rest.

---

[30] Q and F share fourteen instances of *thine*. Q has sixteen in all: in two cases it has *thine* where F has *thy*, in the same, or almost the same, context. F has ten instances of *thine* not in Q, or twenty-four instances in all. One is in a section not in Q; one is in a section arranged differently from Q; and eight appear where Q has *thy*. *Thine* is thus much more frequent in F proportionally, especially since F has the shorter text. The percentage of *thine* is the same in the two versions of Act 2, but greater in F in the other four acts.

[31] We included fifty-two passages from F that do not appear in Q, as follows: I.i.40–5, 49–50, 64–5, 83–5, 88–9, 163; I.ii.109–14, 137, 166–71; I.iv.261, 274, 313, 322–33; II.iv.6, 21, 46–55, 98–9, 103–4, 121, 140–5, 296–7; III.i.22–9; III.ii.79–93; III.iv.17–18, 26–7, 37–8, 58–9; III.vi.12–14, 85; IV.i.6–9; IV.ii.26; IV.vi.91–2, 96, 165–70, 185, 203, 226; IV.vii.60, 69; V.i.46; V.ii.11, 76, 89, 107, 117, 130, 145, 156, 223, 225, 283, 311. Lineation is from *The Riverside Shakespeare*, ed. G. B. Evans *et al.*, 2nd edn (Boston: Houghton Mifflin, 1997).

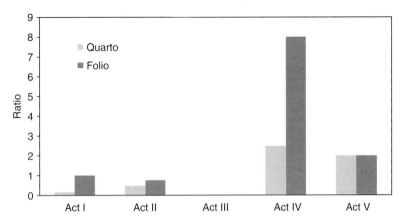

Figure 9.2 Ratio of *does* to *doth* in acts of *King Lear* Q and F.

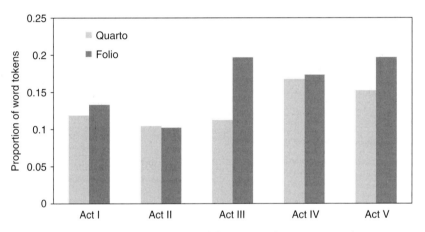

Figure 9.3 Proportional counts of *these* in acts of *King Lear* Q and F.

We began our comparisons with Shakespeare – the primary candidate for F – and Fletcher, given his collaborations with Shakespeare on *Henry VIII* and *The Two Noble Kinsmen*. We worked first with function words, along the lines of the tests of collaborative plays in Chapter 2. We omitted the Quarto *King Lear* from our usual set of Shakespeare control texts, then divided the Shakespeare and Fletcher plays into segments of 900 words each to be comparable with the total word-length of passages we located in F but that are not in Q. We then found the word-variables that differed most in frequency of use between the Shakespeare and Fletcher

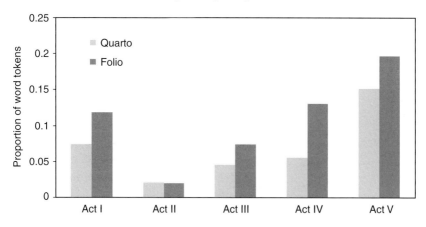

Figure 9.4 Proportional counts of *thine* in acts of *King Lear* Q and F.

sets of segments, and carried out a principal component analysis (PCA) using these words (Figure 9.5).[32] The two sets of segments – 630 from Shakespeare plays, 167 from Fletcher plays – separate sufficiently well on the two axes to make a basis for classifying a new text sample like the unique F passages, marked by the black triangle. The centroids of the clusters are marked by black dots. The F passages have scores on the two axes that put them close to the Shakespeare centroid, and far away from the Fletcher one (the distances are in fact 0.801 and 2.4 in terms of the units deriving from the principal components). Evidently the writer responsible for these passages uses the chosen function words in a way that is compatible with Shakespeare's authorship as against Fletcher's.

We then ran a test on the same set of authorial segments, but this time finding marker words from among the much larger set of lexical words, compiling one score for words Shakespeare favours more than Fletcher, and a second for words Fletcher favours more than Shakespeare (Figure 9.6). As with our other lexical-words tests in this book, we used *word-forms* (not the head words in the dictionary) that are in F but not in Q – that is, distinguishing *wench* from *wenches*, or *grace* from *graced*. This method depends on the demonstrable fact that authors tend to draw on the same set of words in their various works. Whatever vast range of words they may know, or recognize, when they write, they write within a narrower lexicon, a lexicon that comes naturally in composition. While an

---

[32] We used the frequencies of 64 function words with *t*-test probabilities of less than 0.0005 that the two groups of samples are drawn from the same parent population.

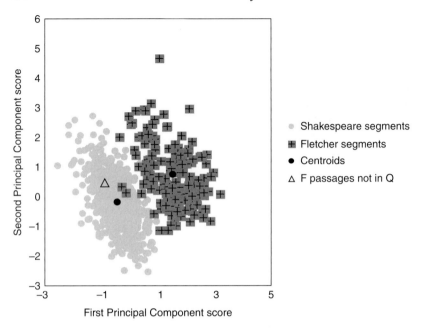

Figure 9.5 Function-words test: 900-word segments from Shakespeare and
Fletcher plays, with passages unique to *King Lear* F.

author can always extend his or her range of active words – almost every
new work introduces some new words – the strong tendency always is to
revert to familiar and customary word usage; it is these words, along with
words an author rarely or never uses, however common in the culture, that
establish a good basis for discriminating one author from another and, in
many cases, identifying an author.

The F passages, marked with a black triangle, fall within the Shakespeare
cluster, though on its edge. One Fletcher segment (from *The Faithful
Shepherdess*) is equally far from the Fletcher centroid (0.147 compared to
the F passages' 0.143). This is the cross that appears within the triangle
marking the F passages. This conjunction does not indicate any particular likeness between the two samples. They have similar scores on the two
axes, and thus use proportionately very similar numbers of Shakespeare
and Fletcher marker words, but not the same words by any means. Despite
this one incursion of a Fletcher segment into the Shakespeare cluster,
Figure 9.5 shows that the lexical-words data provide a broad general separation of Shakespeare and Fletcher segments, even with these relatively

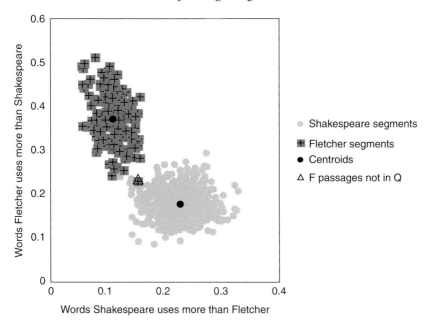

Figure 9.6 Lexical-words test: 900-word Shakespeare segments versus 900-word Fletcher segments, with passages unique to *King Lear* F.

short samples. The F passages cluster with the Shakespeare segments rather than with Fletcher's. Taking Figures 9.5 and 9.6 together, both the function-words and the lexical-words evidence, we can say that Shakespeare is a far better candidate than Fletcher as the author of the F passages. This may not clinch the case for Shakespeare, but it does rule Fletcher out.

We then proceeded to test other playwrights who are candidates in the same way: Chapman, Jonson, Massinger, Middleton, and Webster.[33] The results are similar to those for Fletcher presented in Figures 9.5 and 9.6, if not always as clear-cut: the F passages are invariably closer to the Shakespeare norms on either of the two measures. Rather than show all ten of the new tests, we have summarized the results for the full set of twelve tests (including the Fletcher ones) in Table 9.1. The first column in Table 9.1 lists the method used in a particular test (i.e. a PCA based on function words, or a Zeta variant using lexical words) and the

---

[33] The three Chapman plays in our archive yielded 66 segments of 900 words, the seven Fletcher plays (as already noted) 167, the seventeen Jonson plays 470, the two Massinger plays 39, the 12 Middleton plays 261, and the 3 Webster plays 78.

Table 9.1 King Lear F passages compared to Shakespeare and 6 other authors in turn by PCA and a lexical-words test. Summarizes Figures 9.5 and 9.6 and 10 other tests (not illustrated).

Method	Other author	Maximum distance between a Shakespeare segment and the Shakespeare centroid	(1) Distance between F passages not in Q and the Shakespeare centroid	Maximum distance between a segment by the other author and the other author's centroid	(2) Distance between F passages not in Q and the other author's centroid	Difference between (1) and (2)
PCA	Chapman	4.614	0.774	2.562	1.853	-1.079
Lexical words	Chapman	0.129	0.090	0.100	0.160	-0.070
PCA	Fletcher	3.145	0.801	3.951	2.400	-1.599
Lexical words	Fletcher	0.125	0.094	0.147	0.143	-0.050
PCA	Jonson	3.543	0.765	3.790	1.392	-0.626
Lexical words	Jonson	0.142	0.065	0.151	0.151	-0.086
PCA	Massinger	4.180	0.345	1.505	2.359	-2.013
Lexical words	Massinger	0.140	0.032	0.107	0.286	-0.254
PCA	Middleton	4.138	1.060	2.409	2.343	-1.283
Lexical words	Middleton	0.162	0.069	0.161	0.135	-0.066
PCA	Webster	3.813	0.995	2.197	2.345	-1.350
Lexical words	Webster	0.124	0.070	0.143	0.151	-0.081

All plays are divided into 900-word segments for the authorial groups. The PCA results are for the first two principal components of an analysis using the function words from a list of 200 with a t-test probability of less than 0.0005 that the two groups are from the same parent population.

second column the authorial set that is contrasted with Shakespeare's for each test. The third and fourth columns record the maximum distance of a known Shakespeare segment from the Shakespeare centroid, and the distance between the F passages and the Shakespeare centroid. In each case the F passages are closer to the Shakespeare centroid than at least one of the Shakespeare segments. Thus the F passages are always within a Shakespeare range, defined very loosely here as a circle with its centre as the Shakespeare centroid and passing through the outermost Shakespeare segment. The fifth and sixth columns give the same information for the non-Shakespeare cluster (the distance of the outermost segment of this cluster from its centroid, and the distance from this centroid of the F passages). Here we see that in half the tests the passages are also within a loosely defined non-Shakespeare range. For both Fletcher tests (the same ones that are presented in Figures 9.5 and 9.6), for both Middleton tests, and for the Chapman and Jonson PCAs, the F passages are closer to the non-Shakespeare centroid than the outermost non-Shakespeare segment. In these cases the Shakespeare and non-Shakespeare circles overlap, and the F passages are within the overlap. However, as the last column of Table 9.1 shows, the distance from the Shakespeare centroid is always less than the distance from the non-Shakespeare one. The F passages thus always fit Shakespeare's patterns better than the rival author's, even if the two clusters are not always fully distinct.

The tests all point in one direction. F is a careful, coherent, consistent revision of Q, and Shakespeare is much the most likely candidate for the changes in F *Lear* among those candidates we tested. The function-word evidence in particular is not always decisive, but it always supports the lexical-word evidence, without exception, in placing F with Shakespeare. Even though the material we had to work with – the text that is in F but not in Q – is relatively slender, the tests give strong support to the idea that F is an authorial revision. Our computational stylistics as a means of gathering evidence, based on identifiable authorial habits, thus confirms what other scholars have thought based on more impressionistic responses and should put to rest any question of whether or not Shakespeare revised his work as well as collaborated with others.

Conclusion

Arthur F. Kinney

'For the last three centuries, Shakespearean scholars have emphatically argued that the transmission of an English early modern play-text was linear: that is, from an author to acting company to theatre audience to printer to literary audience', Grace Ioppolo writes. But this is not so. 'Significant evidence', she continues, 'from dramatic manuscripts, including the handwriting of company scribes, book-keepers and censors alongside that of authors, suggests instead that this transmission is ... circular and that neither authors nor theatre personnel dissociated authors from their texts. In fact authors returned to their texts, or texts were returned to their authors, at any or all stages after composition.'[1] Drawing on the Henslowe and Alleyn archive in detail – and on contracts, financial accounts, correspondence, depositions, and commentaries – she finds abundant evidence that the author might revisit his play script 'after the scribe had copied it; after a censor had licensed it; after the book-keeper had prepared the company book; after its rehearsal and performance; before one or more later revivals; and after it was printed' (p. 99). Philip Henslowe, for instance, records that he paid 20 shillings for authorial revision on 15 May 1602: 'harey chattel for the mendynge of the fyrste parte of carnowlle wollsey', a work he had initially commissioned from Chettle one year earlier.[2] On other occasions, play scripts could be printed directly from authorial fair copy as the Folio text of Shakespeare's *Coriolanus* seems to have been since, as G. B. Evans noticed, it preserves some of the playwright's odd and identifiable spellings: *one* for *on*, *shoot* for *shout*, and, perhaps most tellingly, the added 'c's as in *Scicinius* for *Sicinius*.[3]

The text of *Coriolanus*, then, is what is aberrant. 'What seems clear from the extant manuscripts of Shakespeare's colleagues and collaborators is

---

[1] G. Ioppolo, *Dramatists and Their Manuscripts in the Age of Shakespeare, Jonson, Middleton and Heywood: Authorship, Authority and the Playhouse* (London: Routledge, 2006), p. 1.

[2] Dulwich College MS 7, fo. 105v; Ioppolo, *Dramatists and Their Manuscripts*, p. 16.

[3] G. B. Evans *et al.*, eds., *The Riverside Shakespeare*, 2nd edn (Boston: Houghton Mifflin, 1997), p. 1485.

that dramatists saw revision as a normal part of the writing process, both before and after completion of foul papers' (p. 94). John Bale rewrote *King Johan* twenty years after his first version, redesigning it for a court performance before Queen Elizabeth. *The Honest Man's Fortune* by Nathan Field, Philip Massinger, and John Fletcher was written, licensed, and played in 1613, rewritten for a revival in 1625, and finally printed with changes in the Beaumont and Fletcher Folio of 1647.[4] Massinger made thirty-three corrections in a copy of a quarto of *The Duke of Milan* (1623) and made similar changes in published quartos of *The Bondman* (1624), *The Renegado* (1630), *The Emperor of the East* (1632), *The Roman Actor* (1629), and *The Picture*. 'Such meticulous corrections and revisions to printed editions years after their original composition and performance demonstrate that [Massinger] considered his play-texts to be fluid documents that he could [always reclaim as his own]', Ioppolo sums (p. 145). Stephen J. Lynch notes that Shakespeare 'made deliberate and intentional choices' of language but adds that all of his 'revisionary strategies were shaped and influenced by multiple forces that would bear upon a professional playwright, such as contemporary stage practices, generic decorum, audience expectations, the number and quality of available actors, state censorship, and even the geographical locus and marginal cultural status of the theater itself'.[5]

Our research has convincingly shown us that Shakespeare helped revise *Sir Thomas More* and revised the Quarto text of *King Lear* to produce the Folio text of 1623. Given the practices of playwrights at the time, neither should surprise us. In *Shakespeare at Work*, John Jones also locates extensive revisions in *Troilus and Cressida*, *Hamlet*, and *Othello*. He begins, however, with a briefer example drawn from the scene in *2 Henry IV* where Falstaff and Justice Shallow reminisce about their youthful days in London.

> SHALLOW: O, Sir John, do you remember since we lay all night in the Windmill in Saint George's Field?
> SIR JOHN: No more of that, *good* Master Shallow, *no more of that.*
> SHALLOW: Ha, 'twas a merry night! And is Jane Nightwork alive?
> SIR JOHN: She lives, Master Shallow.
>
> (III.ii.191–7)

The five italicized words are missing from the 1600 Quarto, the text of the play that was printed from Shakespeare's manuscript. They appear in the next version, the 1623 Folio, which contains alterations made by him

---

[4] John Bale, *King Johan*, in Ioppolo, *Dramatists and Their Manuscripts*, p. 94; Nathan Field, Philip Massinger, and John Fletcher, *Honest Man's Fortune*, in *ibid.*, pp. 134–5.
[5] S. J. Lynch, *Shakespearean Intertextuality: Studies in Selected Plays and Sources* (Westport, CN: Greenwood Press, 1998), p. 2.

to *2 Henry IV* after he had conceived and written it. Therefore they, the intensifying adjective 'good' and the straight repetition, are a new idea and a revision.[6]

The addition of the scene in which Hal seizes the crown of his father before the King's death is another revision. So too is the deposition scene in *Richard II*, which may have been included or excluded from previous performances. Such fluidity of texts was not unexpected by playgoers at the Globe: Hamlet has no difficulty in subsequently inserting a 'speech some dozen or sixteene lines' in the *Murder of Gonzago*, and there is no indication this was an unusual act. Shakespeare was, then, like his contemporaries, not simply a writer but a reviser of plays.

He was also, our findings demonstrate, a collaborator.[7] Indeed, as Tiffany Stern points out, collaboration was necessary given the number of different plays performed in a single month:

In January 1596, the same (Admiral's) Company played on every day except Sunday and presented fourteen different plays. Of these six were only ever given one performance. The next month their new play, Chapman's *The Blind Beggar of Alexandria*, first performed on 12 February, was followed by a play they had not performed for 140 days, Marlowe's *Dr. Faustus*. During the 140 days that intervened between one *Faustus* and the next, the Admiral's Company had played 107 performances of twenty-one other works.[8]

Brian Vickers has written that 'collaboration was a normal way of sharing the burden of composition, producing a script more quickly, and taking part in a collective enterprise',[9] following the pioneering work of Gerald Eades Bentley in *The Profession of Dramatist in Shakespeare's Time 1590–1642* (1971).[10] Greene, Marlowe, and Peele all wrote collaboratively as Shakespeare did; only Kyd and Lyly did not. Such collaboration was voluntary, according to Neil Carson, but he finds some playwrights working together consistently. He identifies a 'Chettle, Dekker, Heywood syndicate' in his study of Henslowe's *Diary*, although he disagrees with the idea that the pressure of performance schedules necessitated this. He goes on to say that 'Dramatists appear to have formed loose partnerships or

---

[6] J. Jones, *Shakespeare at Work* (Oxford: Clarendon Press, 1995), p. 1.

[7] K. Muir, *Shakespeare as Collaborator* (London: Methuen and Co. Ltd, 1960).

[8] T. Stern, *Rehearsal from Shakespeare to Sheridan* (Oxford: Clarendon Press, 2000), p. 53.

[9] B. Vickers, *Shakespeare, Co-Author: A Historical Study of Five Collaborative Plays* (Oxford: Oxford University Press, 2002), p. 27.

[10] Of all plays at the time, Bentley notes, 'as many as half ... incorporated the writing of more than one man'; in the Henslowe papers, the statistic reaches nearly two-thirds. G. E. Bentley, *The Profession of Dramatist in Shakespeare's Time 1590–1642* (Princeton: Princeton University Press, 1971), p. 199.

syndicates which worked together for short periods and then broke up and reformed into other alliances.'[11] It is not surprising, then, for Vickers to open *Shakespeare, Co-Author* by proposing that:

No issue in Shakespeare studies is more important than determining what he wrote. We cannot form any reliable impression of his work as a dramatist unless we can distinguish his authentic plays from those spuriously ascribed to him, whether by publishers in his own age or by scholars in the four centuries intervening, and unless we can identify those parts of collaborative plays that were written by him together with one or more fellow dramatists. (p. 3)

This also explains Ben Jonson's self-tribute in the Prologue to *Volpone* that he in five weeks fully penned it: 'From his own hand, without a co-adjutor, / Novice, journeyman or tutor' (lines 17–18). Ioppolo discusses a 'fairly typical' case of contemporary collaboration in the instance of *The Funeral of Richard Coeur de Lion* by Henry Chettle, Michael Drayton, Thomas Dekker, and Robert Wilson. Philip Henslowe, in his *Diary*, records payments in advance of:

5 shillings to Wilson on 13 June (1598);
5 shillings to Chettle on 14 June, and 15 shillings on 15 June;
15 shillings to Chettle, Wilson, and Munday on 17 June;
25 shillings to Chettle on 21 June;
20 shillings to Munday on 23 June; and
30 shillings to Drayton on 24 June.

Also on 24 June, he paid Chettle 10 shillings for "all his parte of boockes", probably including the fees due him for *The Funeral of Richard*, and on 26 June Henslowe paid Wilson 30 shillings, "wch is in full paymente of his parte of the boocke" of the play. In total (with the 15 shilling payment on 17 June to Chettle, Wilson, and Munday divided equally), Munday earned 25 shillings, Drayton 30 shillings, Wilson 40 shillings, and Chettle 60 shillings for writing *The Funeral of Richard*. (p. 33)

Henslowe's total cost was 170 shillings for the play, just over the traditional £18 fee.

But contemporary evidence of Shakespearean authorship is not altogether reliable. In 1595 a quarto of *Locrine* was written, according to the title-page, by W. S. This was once thought to be by Shakespeare, although now it is considered one of the Apocrypha. Not until three years later, in 1598, did Shakespeare's name appear in full on title-pages – on reprints of *Richard II* and *Richard III*. His name appeared again in the

---

[11] N. Carson, *A Companion to Henslowe's* Diary (Cambridge: Cambridge University Press, 1988), p. 57.

1598 Quarto of *Love's Labour's Lost*, in 1600 on the title-pages of four more plays, and then consistently thereafter. By then he was also a collaborator on *The Play of Sir Thomas More*, as we have seen.

Yet there are no such revealing payments to Shakespeare and his collaborators as Ioppolo has found for the Chettle syndicate – his work was done for a rival company to that of Henslowe. But as we have shown in previous chapters, Shakespeare seems to have been a collaborator throughout his career – from his earliest work on *Henry VI* and *Titus Andronicus* to his final work on *Henry VIII* and *The Two Noble Kinsmen*. To this we have been able to add *Arden of Faversham*, which he wrote in collaboration with others, and *The Spanish Tragedy* of Thomas Kyd which Shakespeare, rather than Ben Jonson, revised in 1602. When we also include *Timon of Athens*, *Measure for Measure*, *Macbeth*, and *Pericles*, which have been identified previously,[12] it is clear that Shakespeare was not an isolated genius or just the Lord Chamberlain's/King's Men resident playwright working his solitary way but, like other playwrights of his time, a coauthor and, in the case of *The Spanish Tragedy*, a play doctor. He was a man of the theatre. As Stanley Wells has recently written in *Shakespeare and Co.*,

> Shakespeare [was] not ... a lone eminence but ... a fully paid-up member of the theatrical community of his time, a working playwright with professional obligations to the theatre personnel without whose collaboration his art would have been ineffectual, and one who, like most other playwrights of the age, actively collaborated with other writers, not necessarily always as a senior partner.[13]

'Collaboration', he adds, 'may have evolved as a means of throwing plays together in a hurry, but at its best could act as an imaginative stimulus, a pooling of diverse talents conducive to a wider range of dramatic style than individual authors might have achieved on their own' (p. 27). As a consequence, Shakespeare could write scenes that would later be joined to the work of others (as in the 1602 revisions). Indeed, 'collaborators appear to have portioned off sections of the play by acts or scenes to complete alone and then found a way together or separately to join the scenes (with marginal additions of cue lines, for example)', Ioppolo's documents tell

---

[12] Harold Love addresses the problem of the attribution of *Pericles* as this 'odd, ramshackle tragicomedy' in the *Times Literary Supplement* [*TLS*], 3 August 2004, 8–9. For recent attributions of the plays of Shakespeare in part reassigned to Thomas Middleton, see G. Taylor and J. Lavagnino, eds., *The Works of Thomas Middleton* (Oxford: Oxford University Press, 2007): textual commentaries on *Timon of Athens* (pp. 467–70), *Macbeth* (pp. 1165–9), and *Measure for Measure* (pp. 1542–6).

[13] S. Wells, *Shakespeare and Co.* (London: Allen Lane, 2006), p. ix. Oddly, he says elsewhere 'the only dramatist with whom, on the basis of evidence likely to be accepted in a court of law, it can confidentally be said that Shakespeare collaborated is ... John Fletcher' (p. 194).

her, 'rather than sitting in the same room and composing the entire play together, although they outlined the play, and divided it up, in advance'. She refers to several pieces of evidence for this, one of them Thomas Dekker's testimony in a lawsuit for slander in 1623, in which he deposes that he wrote 'two sheets of paper conteyning the first Act' of *Keep the Widow Waking* as well as 'a speech in the last Scene of the last Act' (p. 32). She also writes that 'Many plays show a marked difference in style and content between collaborators' shares, as in the case of *Two Noble Kinsmen*, in which Fletcher's scenes seem less polished than Shakespeare's' (p. 33). As we have shown, Shakespeare seems to have divided his portions of collaborative works by scenes or by speeches, but never by parts – that is, by a through-line of a single character.

We can go further. Robert A. Logan writes that 'the influence of Christopher Marlowe has long been considered indisputable. However, although not readily acknowledged, attempts to pin down and define this influence have frequently resulted in inconclusiveness.'[14] James Shapiro has attempted to ground such speculations in known facts. 'Both Shakespeare's and Marlowe's plays were in repertory at the Rose Theater around 1592, and a year or so later Pembroke's Men were performing history plays written by each of them ... For all we know they might have known each other as neighbors (Marlowe lived in Northern Folgate, Shakespeare in Shoreditch) or collaborated on some lost (or even extant) plays.'[15] What our evidence repeatedly demonstrates is that we can now lay claim with some certainty that the two playwrights did know each other and worked together – at least on *Henry VI* – and that the Marlovian echoes that critics have perceived in the early Shakespeare are probably due to Marlowe's strong poetic voice. Marlowe was Shakespeare's collaborator at the start of his longer career. This general redrawing of Shakespeare as an author who revised his work, perhaps routinely, and who wrote collaboratively throughout his lifetime, has come through the application of computational stylistics to matters of authorial attribution.

Authorial attribution, moreover, has gained considerable attention in recent years. As the late Harold Love has commented,

the testing of attributions is one important means by which we come to a fuller understanding of how language was produced by [Shakespeare]. This is not a

---

[14] R. A. Logan, *Shakespeare's Marlowe: The Influence of Christopher Marlowe on Shakespeare's Artistry* (Aldershot and Burlington, VT: Ashgate, 2007), p. 1.

[15] J. Shapiro, *Rival Playwrights: Marlowe, Jonson, Shakespeare* (New York: Columbia Press, 1991), p. 77. Jonathan Bate goes farthest, claiming in *The Genius of Shakespeare* (New York: Oxford University Press, 1998), p. 105, that 'Shakespeare was the rival who killed Marlowe' (quoted in Logan, *Shakespeare's Marlowe*, p. 5).

frivolous enterprise or the effect of naïve bardolatry. Much as the capacities of human musculature are more fruitfully studied through trained gymnasts than the elderly and arthritic, so our understanding of language, our most precious cultural possession, is best advanced by examining its handling by those of our species who have used it most resourcefully.[16]

Except for three pages of Hand-D – slow, measured, leisurely, flourished – there are no extant manuscripts in whole or in part of Shakespeare's work: a contemporary story has it that Shakespeare's granddaughter – Susanna's daughter – carried them away with her from Stratford, but after that the trail goes cold.[17] Thus we have necessarily worked mainly from printed texts, always aware that some of the evidence may be the result of the printing process. The printed works we do have, though, provide us with helpful paratextual matters: the information on title-pages, entries in the Stationers' Register, and booklists; the indication of specialized knowledge (such as that of the law or contemporary rural customs); arguable lines of transmission; and even possible associations, such as interest in *Arden of Faversham* by a playwright whose mother was Mary Arden. Harold Love, in *Attributing Authorship: An Introduction*, has listed other possibilities of external evidence:

(1) Contemporary attributions contained in incipits, explicits, titles, and from documents purporting to impart information about the circumstances of composition – especially diaries, correspondence, publishers' records, and records of legal proceedings;
(2) Biographical evidence, which would include information about a putative author's allegiances, whereabouts, dates, personal ties, and political and religious affiliations;
(3) The history of earlier attributions of the work and the circumstances under which they were made.[18]

While such data has helped us fill out the total significance of authorial attribution, we have concentrated on an authorial language, on a verbal profile drawn from established language usage and leading to a kind of authorial signature – a kind of verbal DNA – which our various applications of computational stylistics have enabled us to discover. 'What attribution studies ... maintain', Love writes, 'is that language is also languages

---

[16] Love, *TLS*, p. 9.
[17] See Peter Milward, 'Some Missing Shakespeare Letters', *Shakespeare Quarterly*, 20 (1969), 84–7 (pp. 84–5).
[18] H. Love, *Attributing Authorship: An Introduction* (Cambridge: Cambridge University Press, 2002), p. 51.

and that there are as many of them as there are individuals' (p. 10). Where in the past attribution of authorship has relied heavily on impressionism, parallel passages, the counting of images and image clusters, tonality, meter, or on what Muriel St Clare Byrne has called 'tricks' – matters such as the use of the vice or Senecan conventions – we have worked through progressive distillation and refinement of an author's language habits alongside that of his contemporaries to what Timothy Watt has called the 'molecular level' (p. 134). Such exercises have confirmed the observation of the linguist Edward Sapir, who has written that 'There is always an individual method, however poorly developed, of arranging words into groups and of working these up into larger units.'[19] Repeatedly we have found that, as remarked in the chapter on Q and F *Lear*, 'whatever vast range of words [playwrights] may know, or recognize, when they write, they write within a narrower lexicon, a lexicon that comes naturally in composition' (p. 197) and that 'While an author can always extend his or her range of active words – almost every new work introduces some new words – the strong tendency always is to revert to familiar and customary word usage' (pp. 197–8). Genre does not matter. Nor does age. In later years the same basic compositional and language habits of the early years are still active, more or less fashioning the author's work.

Back in 1998, Ian Lancashire predicted what Vickers has oddly called 'self-plagiarism'. 'Word, phrase, and collocation frequencies ... can be signatures of authorship because of the way the writer's brain stores and creates speech', what in our opening chapter we ascribed to a neurological and cognitive base. Lancashire continues:

Even the author cannot imitate these features, simply because they are normally beyond recognition, unless the author has the same tools and expertise as stylometrists undertaking attribution research. Reliable markers arise from the unique, hidden clusters within the author's long-term associative memory. Frequency-based attribution methodology recognizes these and depends on a biological, not a conceptual, paradigm of authorship.[20]

Watt has elaborated on this by asking 'what actually distinguishes an authorial phrase from a circulating expression of the period?' (p. 143). The individual signature of language is not only affected by individual cognitive experience but by cultural habits of expression that are also cognitive.

---

[19] Edward Sapir, *Selected Writings in Language, Culture and Personality*, ed. D. C. Mandelbaum (Berkeley: University of California Press, 1958), p. 542; Love, *Attributing Authorship*, p. 8.

[20] I. Lancashire, 'Paradigms of Authorship', *Shakespeare Studies*, 26 (1998), 299: Love, p. 158. See also I. Lancashire, 'Empirically Determining Shakespeare's Idiolect', *Shakespeare Studies*, 25 (1997), 171–85.

Cyrus Hoy's study of playwrights' linguistic habits, for example, shows that the choice between *thou* and *ye* or *you* is based in cultural rules but nevertheless Fletcher constantly prefers *ye* over *you*, while Massinger is just the opposite; furthermore, Massinger uses *hath* far more than *has* and *them* far more than *'em*.[21] While cultural rules and expressions impinge on individual language practices, they are always subordinated to the individuating combination of experience and usage, of selective practices. Shakespeare has his own idiolect; he too uses *mought* for *might* only once, while his contemporaries make routine use of it. He uses *hath* four times as often as *has*, *doth* three times as often as *does*. And he uses *brothers* seven times as often as *brethren*.

Computational stylistics relies on such distinctive practices. By register-ing enormous amounts of data characterizing these practices, it locates subterranean habits of lexicon and grammar that the human ear does not recognize, and, working from known single-author texts as the necessary valid and reliable training texts, examines target texts to identify author-ship. Assisted by Burrows' Centre for Literary and Linguistic Computing at the University of Newcastle, Australia, we have added tests of rare words and occasionally of strings of words as correlative ways of confirming the results of our initial studies. As Timothy Irish Watt once remarked, the process is an intensification of the granularity of our vision, progressing from the obvious to the subtle to the unseen. While Love has listed the various results of attribution tests from the most secure to the least – what he terms assured, confident, or tentative, followed by plausible specula-tion, confident discrediting, or informed suspicion (p. 216) – we have combined our investigations, always beginning with known single-author texts from which we can assemble reliable individual practices. The results, as we have put forth in this book, are those with the greatest degree of cer-tainty that the known evidence will allow.

Such quantitative evidence and such scientific practices will seem inim-ical to literary scholars who are accustomed to less precise measurement of language while nevertheless attempting to locate, analyse, and appreciate the individual styles of poets and playwrights. But, in the end, we have only been able to deduce what the isolatable language practices can tell us about the identity of authors. Beyond this, we cannot go. We cannot, that is, explain the mystery of what produces one individual style *rather than* another; we cannot explain the innermost secrets of memorable poetry or the characterizing mysteries of style. We cannot account for the stunning

---

[21] C. Hoy, 'The Shares of Fletcher and His Collaborators in the Beaumont and Fletcher Canon (I)', *Studies in Bibliography*, 8 (1956), 129–46 (p. 145); Love, *Attributing Authorship*, p. 105.

beauty of Shakespeare's language nor the haunting passages of his work that have lodged themselves in individual or communal memories through the centuries. We never suspected we could – nor would we find that especially desirable. What we have been able to do is to establish the habits of one playwright's language and, doing so, we have been enabled to redefine Shakespeare's contribution to and place in the Renaissance English theatre.

Plays in the corpus

Genre and *date* are as in Alfred Harbage and S. Schoenbaum, *Annals of English Drama 975–1700* (Philadelphia: University of Philadelphia Press, 1964).

Groups: 1, single-author, well-attributed; 2, collaborative, well-attributed; 3, disputed authorship; 4, second version.

Author	Title	Genre	Date	Copy-text	Date of copy-text	Group
Beaumont, Francis	*The Knight of the Burning Pestle*	Burlesque romance	1607	STC1674	1613	1
Beaumont, Francis, and Fletcher, John	*The Maid's Tragedy*	Tragedy	1610	STC1676	1619	2
Brome, Richard	*A Jovial Crew*	Comedy	1641	Wing B4873	1652	1
Carey, Elizabeth	*Mariam*	Tragedy	1604	STC4613	1613	1
Chapman, George	*Bussy d'Ambois*	Foreign history	1604	STC4966	1607	1
	The Revenge of Bussy d'Ambois	Tragedy	1610	STC4989	1613	1
	Widow's Tears	Comedy	1605	STC4994	1612	1
Chettle, Henry	*Hoffman*	Tragedy	1602	STC5125	1631	1
Davenant, William	*The Unfortunate Lovers*	Tragedy	1638	Wing D348	1643	1
Day, John	*The Isle of Gulls*	Comedy	1606	STC6412	1606	1
Dekker, Thomas	*The Honest Whore, Part 2*	Comedy	1605	STC6506	1630	1
	If It Be Not Good, the Devil Is In It	Comedy	1611	STC6507	1612	1
	Old Fortunatus	Comedy	1599	STC6517	1600	1
	The Shoemaker's Holiday	Comedy	1599	STC6523	1600	1
	The Whore of Babylon	Allegorical history	1606	STC6532	1607	1
Fletcher, John	*Bonduca*	Tragedy	1613	Wing B1581	1647	1
	The Faithful Shepherdess	Pastoral	1608	STC11068	1610	1
	The Loyal Subject	Tragicomedy	1618	Wing B1581	1647	1
	The Mad Lover	Tragicomedy	1617	Wing B1581	1647	1
	Monsieur Thomas	Comedy	1615	Wing B1581	1647	1
	Valentinian	Tragedy	1614	Wing B1581	1647	1
	The Woman's Prize	Comedy	1611	Wing B1581	1647	1

Table (*cont.*)

Author	Title	Genre	Date	Copy-text	Date of copy-text	Group
Fletcher, John, and Massinger, Philip	*The Double Marriage*	Tragedy	1620	Wing B1581	1647	2
Ford, John	*The Broken Heart*	Tragedy	1629	STC11156	1633	1
	The Fancies Chaste and Noble	Comedy	1635	STC11159	1638	1
	The Lady's Trial	Comedy	1638	STC11161	1639	1
	The Lover's Melancholy	Tragicomedy	1628	STC11163	1629	1
	Love's Sacrifice	Tragedy	1632	STC11164	1633	1
	Perkin Warbeck	History	1633	STC11157	1634	1
	'Tis Pity She's a Whore	Tragedy	1632	STC11165	1633	1
Goffe, Thomas	*The Courageous Turk*	Tragedy	1618	STC11977	1632	1
Greene, Robert	*Alphonsus*	Heroical romance	1587	STC12233	1599	1
	Friar Bacon and Friar Bungay	Comedy	1589	STC 12267	1594	1
	James IV	History	1590	STC12308	1598	1
	Orlando Furioso	Romantic comedy	1591	STC12265	1594	1
Greville, Fulke	*Mustapha*	Tragedy	1596	STC12362	1608	1
Haughton, William	*The Devil and his Dame*	Comedy	1600	Wing G1580	1662	1
	Englishmen for My Money	Comedy	1598	STC12931	1616	1
Heywood, Thomas	*The Four Prentices of London*	Heroical romance	1600	STC13321	1615	1
	If You Know Not Me You Know Nobody	History	1604	STC13328	1605	1
	The Rape of Lucrece	Tragedy	1607	STC13363	1638	1
	The Wise Woman	Comedy	1604	STC13370	1638	1
	A Woman Killed with Kindness	Tragedy	1603	STC13371	1607	1

Author	Title	Genre		STC		
Jonson, Ben	The Alchemist	Comedy	1610	STC14755	1612	1
	Bartholomew Fair	Comedy	1614	STC14753.5	1631	1
	The Case is Altered	Comedy	1597	STC14757	1609	1
	Catiline His Conspiracy	Tragedy	1611	STC14759	1611	1
	Cynthia's Revels	Comedy	1601	STC14773	1601	1
	The Devil Is an Ass	Comedy	1616	STC14754	1640	1
	Epicene	Comedy	1609	STC14751	1616	1
	Every Man in His Humour	Comedy	1598	STC14766	1601	1
	Every Man Out of His Humour	Comedy	1599	STC14767	1600	1
	The Magnetic Lady	Comedy	1632	STC14754	1640	1
	The New Inn	Comedy	1629	STC14780	1631	1
	The Poetaster	Comedy	1601	STC14781	1602	1
	The Sad Shepherd	Comic pastoral	1637	STC14754	1640	1
	Sejanus His Fall	Tragedy	1603	STC14782	1605	1
	The Staple of News	Comedy	1626	STC14753.5	1631	1
	A Tale of a Tub	Comedy	1633	STC14754	1640	1
	Volpone	Comedy	1606	STC14783	1607	1
Kyd, Thomas	The Spanish Tragedy	Tragedy	1587	STC15086	1592	1
(trans.)	Cornelia	Tragedy	1594	STC11622	1594	1
Lodge, Thomas	The Wounds of Civil War	Classical history	1588	STC16678	1594	1
Lyly, John	Gallathea	Classical legend (Comedy)	1585	STC17080	1592	1
	Love's Metamorphosis	Pastoral	1590	STC17082	1601	1
	Sappho and Phao	Classical legend (Comedy)	1584	STC17086	1584	1
	The Woman in the Moon	Comedy	1593	STC17090	1597	1
Markham, Gervase, and Sampson, William	Herod and Antipater	Tragedy	1622	STC17401	1622	2

Table (cont.)

Author	Title	Genre	Date	Copy-text	Date of copy-text	Group
Marlowe, Christopher	Doctor Faustus A text	Tragedy	1592	STC17429	1604	1
	Doctor Faustus B text	Tragedy	1592	STC17432	1616	4
	Edward II	History	1592	STC17437	1594	1
	The Jew of Malta	Tragedy	1589	STC17412	1633	1
	Massacre at Paris	Foreign history	1593	STC17423	1594	1
	Tamburlaine the Great Part 1	Heroical romance	1587	STC17425	1590	1
	Tamburlaine the Great Part 2	Heroical romance	1588	STC17425	1590	1
Marlowe, Christopher, and Nashe, Thomas	Dido, Queen of Carthage	Classical legend (Tragedy)	1587	STC17441	1594	3
Marmion, Shakerley	The Antiquary	Comedy	1635	Wing M703	1641	1
Marston, John	Antonio's Revenge	Tragedy	1600	STC17474	1602	1
	Sophonisba	Tragedy	1605	STC17488	1606	1
Massinger, Philip	The Roman Actor	Tragedy	1626	STC17642	1629	1
	The Unnatural Combat	Tragedy	1626	STC17643	1639	1
Middleton, Thomas	A Chaste Maid in Cheapside	Comedy	1611	STC17877	1630	1
	A Game at Chess	Political satire	1624	Trinity College, Cambridge MS	1624	1
	Hengist, King of Kent	Tragedy	1618	ed. R. C. Bald	1938	1
	A Mad World, My Masters	Comedy	1606	STC17888	1608	1
	Michaelmas Term	Comedy	1606	STC17890	1607	1
	More Dissemblers besides Women	Comedy	1615	Wing M1989	1657	1

Author	Title	Genre		Reference		
	No Wit, No Help like a Woman's	Comedy	1613	Wing M1985	1657	1
	The Phoenix	Comedy	1604	STC17892	1607	1
	A Trick to Catch the Old One	Comedy	1605	STC17896	1608	1
	The Witch	Tragicomedy	1615	Malone Society Reprint	1949	1
	Women Beware Women	Tragedy	1621	Wing M1989	1657	1
	Your Five Gallants	Comedy	1605	STC17907	1608	1
Middleton, Thomas, and Rowley, William	The Changeling	Tragedy	1622	Wing M1980	1653	3
Munday, Anthony	John a Kent and John a Cumber	Pseudo-history	1589	Malone Society Reprint	1923	1
Nashe, Thomas	Summer's Last Will and Testament	Comedy	1592	STC18376	1600	1
Peele, George	The Battle of Alcazar	Foreign history	1589	STC19531	1594	1
	Edward I	History	1591	STC19535	1593	1
	King David and Fair Bethsabe	Biblical history	1587	STC19540	1599	1
	Old Wives' Tale	Romance	1590	STC19545	1595	1
Porter, Henry	The Two Angry Women of Abington Part 1	Comedy	1588	STC20121.5	1599	1
Rowley, William	All's Lost by Lust	Tragedy	1619	STC21425	1633	1
	A New Wonder, a Woman Never Vexed	Comedy	1625	STC21423	1632	1
Shakespeare, William	All's Well that Ends Well	Comedy	1602	STC22273	1623	1
	Antony and Cleopatra	Tragedy	1607	STC22273	1623	1
	As You Like It	Comedy	1599	STC22273	1623	1
	The Comedy of Errors	Comedy	1592	STC22273	1623	1
	Coriolanus	Tragedy	1608	STC22273	1623	1

Table (cont.)

Author	Title	Genre	Date	Copy-text	Date of copy-text	Group
	Cymbeline	Tragicomedy	1609	STC22273	1623	1
	Hamlet	Tragedy	1601	STC22276	1604	1
	1 Henry IV	History	1597	STC22280	1598	1
	2 Henry IV	History	1597	STC22288	1600	1
	Henry V	History	1599	STC22273	1623	1
	1 Henry VI	History	1592	STC22273	1623	3
	2 Henry VI	History	1591	STC22273	1623	3
	3 Henry VI	History	1591	STC22273	1623	3
	Julius Caesar	Tragedy	1599	STC22273	1623	1
	King John	History	1596	STC22273	1623	1
	King Lear Folio	Tragedy	1605	STC22273	1623	4
	King Lear Quarto	Tragedy	1605	STC22292	1608	1
	Love's Labour's Lost	Comedy	1595	STC22294	1598	1
	Macbeth	Tragedy	1606	STC22273	1623	3
	Measure for Measure	Comedy	1604	STC22273	1623	3
	The Merchant of Venice	Comedy	1596	STC22296	1600	1
	The Merry Wives of Windsor	Comedy	1600	STC22299	1602	1
	A Midsummer Night's Dream	Comedy	1595	STC22302	1600	1
	Much Ado about Nothing	Comedy	1598	STC22304	1600	1
	Othello	Tragedy	1604	STC22305	1622	1
	Richard II	History	1595	STC22307	1597	1
	Richard III	History	1593	STC22314	1597	1
	Romeo and Juliet	Tragedy	1595	STC22323	1599	1
	The Taming of the Shrew	Comedy	1594	STC22273	1623	3
	The Tempest	Comedy	1611	STC22273	1623	1

Author	Title	Genre	Date	STC	Date	No.
	Troilus and Cressida	Tragedy	1602	STC22331	1609	1
	Twelfth Night	Comedy	1600	STC22273	1623	1
	The Two Gentlemen of Verona	Comedy	1593	STC22273	1623	1
	The Winter's Tale	Tragicomedy	1610	STC22273	1623	1
Shakespeare, William, and Fletcher, John	Henry VIII	History	1613	STC22273	1623	3
	The Two Noble Kinsmen	Tragicomedy	1613	STC11075	1634	3
Shakespeare, William, and Middleton, Thomas	Timon of Athens	Tragedy	1607	STC22273	1623	3
Shakespeare, William, and Peele, George	Titus Andronicus	Tragedy	1594	STC22328	1594	3
Shakespeare, William, and Wilkins, George	Pericles	Tragicomedy	1608	STC22334	1609	3
Shirley, James	The Cardinal	Tragedy	1641	Wing S3461	1652	1
	Love's Cruelty	Tragedy	1631	STC22449	1640	1
	The Traitor	Tragedy	1631	STC22458	1635	1
Suckling, John	Aglaura	Tragedy	1637	STC23420	1638	1
Tourneur, Cyril	The Atheist's Tragedy	Tragedy	1609	STC24146	1611	1
Uncertain	Arden of Faversham	Realistic tragedy	1591	STC733	1592	3
	The Bloody Brother	Tragedy	1619	STC11064	1639	3
	Edmond Ironside	History	1595	Malone Society Reprint	1927	3
	Edward III	History	1590	STC7501	1596	3
	King Leir	Legendary history	1590	STC15343	1605	3
	The Revenger's Tragedy	Tragedy	1606	STC24150	1608	3

Table (*cont.*)

Author	Title	Genre	Date	Copy-text	Date of copy-text	Group
	The Second Maiden's Tragedy	Tragedy	1611	Malone Society Reprint	1909	3
	Selimus Part 1	Heroical romance	1592	STC12310a	1594	3
	Soliman and Perseda	Tragedy	1590	STC22894	1592?	3
	A Warning for Fair Women	Tragedy	1599	STC25089	1599	3
	A Yorkshire Tragedy	Tragedy	1606	STC22340	1608	3
Webster, John	*The Devil's Law Case*	Tragicomedy	1617	STC25173	1623	1
	The Duchess of Malfi	Tragedy	1614	STC25176	1623	1
	The White Devil	Tragedy	1612	STC25178	1612	1
Wilmot, Robert, *et al.*	*Tancred and Gismund*	Senecan tragedy	1591	STC25764	1591	1
Wilson, Robert	*The Cobbler's Prophecy*	Comedy	1590	STC25781	1594	1
	The Three Ladies of London	Moral	1581	STC25784	1584	1
	The Three Lords and Three Ladies of London	Moral	1588	STC25783	1590	1

A list of 200 function words

The part of speech is specified for some of the words. These are words we have tagged in our machine-readable texts to separate homographs with distinct grammatical functions.

A — C

a about above after again against all almost along although am among amongst an and another any anything are art [verb] as at back be because been before being besides beyond both but by [adverb] by [preposition] can cannot canst could

D — F

dare did didst do does done dost doth down durst each either enough ere even ever every few for [adverb] for [conjunction] for [preposition] from

G — I

had hadst hast hath have he hence her [adjective] her [personal pronoun] here him himself his how I if in [adverb] in [preposition] is it itself

J — L

least like [adverb] like [preposition] like [verb]

M — O

many may me might mine more most much must my myself neither never no [adjective] no [negative particle] none nor not nothing now O of off oft often on [adverb] on [preposition] one only or other our ourselves out over own

P — R

past perhaps quite rather round

S—U

same shall shalt she should since so [adverb of degree] so [adverb of manner and conjunction] some something somewhat still such than that [conjunction] that [demonstrative] that [relative] the thee their them themselves then there these they thine this those thou though through thus thy thyself till to [adverb] to [infinitive] to [preposition] too under unto up [adverb] upon [preposition] us

V—Z

very was we well were wert what when where which [interrogative] which [relative] while whilst who [interrogative] who [relative] whom whose why will [verb] with within without ye yet you your yours yourself yourselves

Glossary

Centroid
The centre of a cluster of datapoints. The centroid's coordinates are the average of the values for the cluster on each axis. The centroid is a convenient single reference point, so that (for example) we can compare the distance of a target text from one cluster to the distance from another. If we have a cluster on two axes and with just two points, one at (5, –2) and the other at (3, 4), then the centroid is at (4, 1).

Correlation
A relationship between two columns of values, summing up the degree to which they move up or down together in the various observations. A perfect correlation of 1.0 indicates that they move exactly in step, a perfect negative correlation (–1.0) indicates that they move in exactly opposite ways, and a zero correlation indicates that the fluctuations within one column are unrelated to the fluctuations in the other. A correlation coefficient is a useful way of making an objective estimate of the likeness of the frequencies of two variables in the same set of observations. We might collect the frequencies of *hath* and *has* in a set of plays, for instance, and correlate them. A very high correlation between the two sets of frequencies would tell us that the two words tend to be common in the same plays. A strongly negative correlation would indicate that where *hath* appears one is unlikely to find *has*, and vice versa.

Discriminant analysis
A mathematical procedure using multiple variables (word-frequencies) to classify observations (texts). It works by weighting the variables to maximize the difference between groups of observations, and to minimize the difference between scores within the groups. It is unlike principal component analysis (PCA) in that the observations used for training are assigned to a group before the process begins. 'Ungrouped' observations can then be added, either to test the power of the method to discriminate, or to assign observations of unknown or disputed origin to one or other of the known groupings. Discriminant analysis can be run with just two groups (for example Shakespeare plays and plays by others) or with multiple ones (for example plays by twenty different authors).

Dummy variable

A variable created for a specific purpose that gives some observations an arbitrary value of 1 and others an arbitrary value of 0. If we have a table of data from plays by various authors, for instance, we might create an additional dummy variable for which plays by Author A are given a value of 1 and plays by all other authors are given a value of 0, for use in correlations with the other variables.

Euclidean distance

The distance between two points, calculated using Pythagoras' theorem that the square of the hypotenuse of a right-angled triangle is the sum of the squares of the other two sides. We can regard the difference between two points on the *x*-axis as the horizontal side of the triangle, the difference on the *y*-axis as the vertical side, and the shortest distance between them as the hypotenuse of this triangle.

Function words

Words can be classified into function words and lexical words (with just a few doubtful cases). Function words have a grammatical function; examples are *the*, *and*, *she*, *before*, and *of*. There is a limited number of function words and new ones are added only rarely across the centuries. They dominate the list of the very commonest words.

Lexical words

Nouns, verbs, adjectives, and adverbs, which can be substituted for each other in a given position in a sentence. They range from those that are quite common in some texts (like *king* or *mother*) to words that may occur only once in a large corpus. In a living language new lexical words are constantly being introduced while others are becoming obsolete. They are thus an open class, where function words are a closed class.

Mean

The average value, found by taking the sum of all the values and dividing by the number of observations. The mean can be thought of as a single representative point for a group of values, or as the most likely value for any fresh sample from the same population.

Perpendicular bisector line

To find the perpendicular bisector line between two clusters of datapoints, we find the centroids of the two clusters, join the centroids with a straight line, find the half-way point along this line, and draw a line at right angles crossing at this point. This is a simple way to divide the space in which datapoints can appear into Group A territory and Group B territory (or potentially into multiple such territories). New observations that fall on the Group A side of a perpendicular bisector line between Group A and Group B we can regard as more like Group A observations than like Group B ones, and vice versa.

Point–biserial correlation

A correlation between two columns of values, one of which is graduated data (counts that can vary freely across a range, like frequencies of a given word) and the other is data that can only have one of two values (e.g. a dummy variable with values 0 or 1, which might represent texts by Author A and texts by Author B).

Principal component analysis (PCA)

A 'data reduction' technique, aiming to find a few 'latent' variables that account for most of the variation in data from a much larger collection of 'manifest' variables. It finds first the most important overall factor or component in a table of counts, then the next most important factor independent of the first, and so on. The procedure begins with a table of the correlations between the chosen variables, with the result that variations in the units of these variables do not play a role (so that the frequencies of the most common words do not dominate in an analysis of word frequencies, for instance). In the simplest case, PCA can create a single combined variable from a pair of original variables. A table of heights and weights of schoolchildren, for example, would yield a single new variable that might be called 'size', with a weighting for height, and a weighting for weight. This will explain most of the variation of the original table. Each of the children would have a score on this new variable. It would give users most of what they needed to know from the original table. In a more complicated example, with scores of variables, there might be several principal components of interest. In function-word frequency data from a mixture of plays by a single author, the first component might well weight *I*, *me*, and *you* positively, and *the*, *of*, and *they* negatively. This indicates that words from the first group tend to occur together in one set of texts, while words from the second group tend not to occur in those same texts. The reverse is true for a second set of texts. Looking at text scores on the component, we might find plays with short personal exchanges at the positive end and those with long declamatory speeches at the negative end. The second component might contrast texts with *you* and *for* as a conjunction (plays set in ancient Rome) against those with *thou* and *not* (plays set in contemporary London).

Standard deviation

A measure of dispersion about the mean, calculated as the square root of the mean of the squared deviations from the mean. A large standard deviation indicates values varying widely from the mean, and a low standard deviation indicates values clustered closely around the mean. The standard deviation is expressed in the same units as the original variable, so that if we are finding the standard deviation of the heights in centimetres of a group of individuals, the standard deviation will be expressed in centimetres: for one such group, for example, the standard deviation might equal 7 cm, and for another 12 cm. The standard deviation has the property that approximately two-thirds of the values of a normal distribution will be within a range from one standard deviation below the mean to one standard deviation above.

t-test

A mathematical procedure to determine if the difference between the means of two sets of observations indicates a real difference or is just the result of random fluctuations. The difference between the means of the two groups is divided by the standard deviation of that variable. The resulting *t* value can be compared with a published table that yields a probability that it could have come about by chance, given the number of observations. A low probability indicates that it is unlikely that the difference is a matter of chance, and thus the two groups are likely to be members of different populations.

Target text
The text that is the focus of the current experiment, typically a text of disputed authorship, date, genre, etc., and to be distinguished from the training set of texts that are of known authorship, date, or genre, and are serving to define the classes into which the target text should be placed.

Test set
Observations of a known classification that have not been used to formulate a classification method, and so can be used to estimate the power of the method to classify newly added observations.

Training set
Observations whose classification is known from the beginning, and that are used to choose or weight variables that can then be the basis for classifying observations with an unknown or disputed classification.

Word-tokens
Term used to make explicit the sense of *words* in 'twenty-five words or less' or 'segments of 2000 words each', i.e. *words* thought of as the total of instances of all vocabulary items.

Word-types
Distinct vocabulary items. 'To be or not to be' has six word-tokens but four word-types.

Zeta test
A method developed by John Burrows, and specific to computational stylistics, for classifying texts. It is based on finding words commoner in one set of texts as opposed to another. Instead of starting with a fixed set of variables, like the function-word frequencies used in computational stylistics with PCA or discriminant analysis, we select a small proportion of the available words, using a rule (or a combination of rules) based on their distribution across the text groups. In one variation of the method, we construct an index of differentiation: the proportion of texts in Group A in which the word occurs, plus the proportion of texts in Group B in which it does not occur. A perfect score on this index is 2 – the word appears in all segments of A and in none of B; the lowest possible score is 0 – the word appears in none of the segments of A and in all of the segments of B. We choose the words that have values greater than a given threshold on the index, or simply a fixed number of words starting from the highest scorers on the index. We can then find the words that are characteristic of Group B rather than Group A. We now have two lists of marker words. We then count the number of

words that occur from each list in each of the texts, and express this count as a proportion of the total number of different words in each text. Each text thus has two scores, for the markers of Group A and the markers of Group B. We can plot these on a two-dimensional scatter-plot. We might then add a target text and plot its scores also, and thus find whether its vocabulary style is more like Group A or Group B. The Zeta test is suited to data from the less common words, like lexical words, which are not dense enough in distribution for multivariate tests like PCA or discriminant analysis.

Index